ON BURNING GROUND

ON BURNING GROUND

GROUND

A Son's Memoir

MICHAEL SKAKUN

ST. MARTIN'S PRESS ☙ NEW YORK

Note to the Reader

Everything contained in this narrative is factual. The author has taken a small degree of license with such details as weather, occasional dialogue, and other minor particulars that do not detract from the veracity of this story.

ON BURNING GROUND: A SON'S MEMOIR.

Dust jacket images

Background, top: Joseph Skakun's French entry visa, 1948.

Inset photo: Joseph Skakun posing as Stefan Osmanov at Nazi police station in Germany, 1943. This photo was later affixed to the foreign passport issued to him, which confirmed his "racial status" as a Lithuanian and set the stage for his entry into the Waffen SS.

Background, bottom: Novogrudek's pre-war marketplace.

Book design by Casey Hampton

ISBN 0-312-20566-X

First U.S. Edition: June 1999

10   9   8   7   6   5   4   3   2   1

FOR MY FATHER

and in memory of

Chaim Chaikel Skakun, my grandfather,
who died during the Soviet occupation of eastern Poland in June 1940,

and

Chaja Elovich Skakun, my grandmother,
murdered together with thousands of other Navaredkers on December 8, 1941.

May their souls be bound up in the bonds of eternal life,
an everlasting blessing among us.

We are, I know not how, double in ourselves, so that we believe we disbelieve, and cannot rid ourselves of what we condemn.

—MICHEL DE MONTAIGNE

A Note on Spelling

The variant spellings of the names of Eastern European cities and towns are a product of the region's tumultuous history and frequent border changes. Two spellings are used throughout this memoir of my father's birthplace: Nowogródek (Polish), though in this text the more phonetically friendly spelling, Novogrudek; and Navaredok (Yiddish). A Russian variant is Novogrudok and the Belorussian one is Navahrudak.

In the case of Vilna, the Yiddish spelling is used throughout. A Polish city between the two wars, it was known as Wilno. In Russian it is spelled Vilnyus, and today, as the capital of Lithuania it is called Vilnius.

CONTENTS

ON BURNING
GROUND

PROLOGUE
I

~⊗⊗⊗~

Winter 1999

For as long as I can remember, I have been the confidant of a man's conscience. When I was a child, Father sat me down and recounted a story of terror that defied all logic. He conveyed it with such vivid emotional conviction that it became the substance of my life, until it achieved an immediacy as palpable as my own skin.

It was a narrative of war and bloodshed, of unspeakable cruelty and unnameable crimes, but more uniquely a story of choice and moral improvisation and of the strange amalgam of free will and bold instinct. It wove the unfettered urge for life with a conspiratorial precision threaded by desperation and cunning.

In the safety of Brooklyn, I grew to learn how it was that a onetime rabbinical student in Poland, and a *mussarnik* (an ethical pietist), was driven into subterfuge, how he adopted numerous masks to conceal his Judaism, and how he transformed himself into a Nazi recruit.

Everything about Father's wartime experience struck me as a defiance of destiny. This coddled only son (*a tsitsiterter ben-yokhid*), steeped in religious life, devised a manner of survival that strains credulity. Here was a curve of invention to outrun the most unbridled imagination. Then as now, Father's artifice astonishes me. He reconfigured a life of moral austerity into the cruel, martial world of the Waffen SS. The life of the fabled Lithuanian yeshiva boy—its high intellectualism, its spiritual aspirations, its dog-eared penitential tracts—was forced into the maw of the beast.

To me it was above all, a story of a man's invincible solitude. Ordinarily, in times of danger people huddle together. But here Father, thrown back on his own slight resources, secretly crafted a new identity out of whole cloth—created a mask so tight-fitting that it become nearly one with his life.

In an act at once deliberate and ominous, Father leapt into the unknown. It was prefigured in our surname: Skakun, in Russian, to jump, to spring, a word conveying something of the nimble horsemanship of the Cossack and the daring of the fearless equestrian. To me, at least, his war years found him bestriding two steeds at full gallop across dark woods and dizzying precipices.

It was every Friday at the Sabbath table that Father's narrative gifts flourished. For him, memory vanquished distance and time as the past was pushed into the foreground. Amid the subdued tinkle of wineglasses and the radiance of the silver candelabrum, the fugitive ghosts of war rose up to take their unquiet seat among us. On the Sabbath all of life commingled in a haunting simultaneity of time past and time present. We sat among a congregation of the dead, Father's voice and their disembodied echoes merging in one vast fretwork of sound.

Perhaps it could not have been otherwise; the act of remembrance had always been tied to the central meaning of the Sabbath. "Remember that you were a slave in the land of Egypt and the Lord your God freed you from there with a mighty hand and an outstretched arm; therefore the Lord your God commanded you to observe the Sabbath day," the Bible said. Father had been a slave in the land of Germany, and while redemption came tardily, for God had in those days turned His face away from the world, Sabbath would henceforth be always an act of reclamation.

His recounting would begin with the lyric-imbued landscape of Novogrudek, or Navaredok in Yiddish, a favorite site of both literary romantics and dreamy Jewish youth. Framed by fir trees, birch groves, and clear lakes, this borderland town was the birthplace of the Polish national poet, Adam Mickiewicz, who as a political exile had visited Goethe in Weimar, had ridden with James Fenimore Cooper through the Roman suburbs, and had introduced Paris to the work of Ralph Waldo Emerson. George Sand rather grandly declared he could stand equal to the prophets of Zion, for the moral imagination, as much as Poland, was his ideal homeland. Others professed that his mysticism, at times, had the metaphysical ambition of Kabbalah.

Indeed, Mickiewicz's epic poem *Pan Tadeusz* is a paean to Novogrudek and its paradise of woods.

Father's gaze came to rest on the town's legendary Castle Hill, or Schlossbarg, topped by the spectral ruins of a medieval fortress, a timely reminder of the vanity of earthly ambitions—"an Ecclesiastes in stone." From its scarred heights, he heard the sound of the "murmuring forests" and watched the foaming billows of grass swept by winds hurtled west to Poland. Founded in 1044, Novogrudek was a sort of geographical divide. North of it rivers flowed via the Nieman into the Baltic Sea; south of it they streamed via the mighty Dnieper into the Black Sea and homewards to the blue Mediterranean. Father recalled this luminous world with simple eloquence that grew keener with time and repetition. Rarely have I known anyone to cultivate so strong a sentiment of place.

In this town, where Jewish religious life had been presided by some of Eastern Europe's leading spiritual leaders, Rabbi Isaac Elkhanan Spektor, Rabbi Yekhiel Mikhel Epstein, and *Der Alter* Rabbi Yoizl Hurwitz, Father heard the first soundings of the Ten Commandments. Navaredok, as he described it, appeared as a bible living in brick and mortar. It was successively earth, heaven, and hell; in winter it lay in snow, in spring it became an arboreal eden. But after 1939, it turned into a latter-day Gehinnom, the site south of Jerusalem where in ancient times pagans sacrificed children. In this provincial Polish town, Father found the greatest measure of life and death.

Navaredok was, as well, a center of *mussar*, a doctrine of ascetic instruction in the ways of right conduct. It raised stringent probity to the authority of a religious commandment. *Mussar* crushed the embers of human pride by reminding its aspirants that the flea preceded man in creation's order. The young mussarniks were haunted by the finiteness of man, the infinity of God, and the redemptive capacity of thought, illuminating E. M. Forster's comment that "death destroys a man; the idea of death saves him." Their austere faith was so intense that they awaited daily the blare of the messianic trumpet marking the end of time.

In Navaredok and in its satellite centers, *mussar* often became an extreme form of psychological paring, a vivisection of motives, a cutting and hacking away of the outer layers of cant, deceit, and posturing. Its stress on moral self-examination and humility linked with spiritual exaltation created a kind of "echt Yiddish Tolstoyism" that brought Judaism to the brink of monastic self-denial. Indeed, in a last work, *A Calendar of Wisdom*, Tolstoy quotes a Talmudic passage that could not have suited the *mussarniks* better: "Some of your friends praise you, and others blame you and criticize you; be closer to those who blame you and further from those who praise you." It was, in the end, a form of Jewish ethical piety, expressed often in somber, even melancholy, sing-song, that did for rabbinical intellectuals what Hasidism had done for the lay masses, to inspirit religion with penitential fervor and to raise the roof of the soul.

But then war began, and Novogrudek became part of the perilous terrain of history. Life turned into a hieroglyphics of suffering. Father sought to explain this but to no avail—it was an agony of reason. One thing we did come to understand, however, was that only when Novogrudek was no more, when it became part of the flotsam of history, and Father had been forced elsewhere, did it become the true country of his imagination, the place he came to inhabit for all time, a place beyond the reach of death. Father came to embody a central element of Proustian time: "The only true paradise is always the paradise we have lost."

Father was strangely comforted in reciting the details of his life, and through his recitation I became a party to his grief. On wintry Sabbath afternoons in the 1960s, Father and I would gently shut the door of the synagogue behind us and return home from morning prayers. Ours was a Brooklyn *mussar* synagogue, framed in a modest brick building housing the Navaredok yeshiva, which had transplanted itself to America's shores. Father would then reverse the arc of time and recount pages from his early life. Sometimes in a steady voice, sometimes in a cry, choking with pain, he would recount a story of stark contrast and absolute paradox: how he came to save his life through the mastery of a triple identity.

PROLOGUE
II

Fall 1944

*Joseph Skakun posing as Stefan Osmanov
in a Nazi police station, 1943*

S LATE-GRAY CLOUDS DARKENED the north German sky. A gust-
ing wind lashed them into fleecy ribbons. In a cavernous building,
Nazi physicians examined candidates for recruitment into the motorized
Waffen SS division, which was readying for a last struggle against East and
West.

"Stefan Osmanov!" A tall SS military doctor summoned Father by his
assumed name.

"Jawohl, mein Herr!" he said, dissembling, stepping naked into the center
of a chalked circle. The lights around him shone surgically bright. The SS
doctor's probing eyes were fixed on Father's back, now turned in his direction.

"Turn around!" he demanded in clipped German. Father did as he was
told, his gaze stern and unblinking. He stood poised against fatality, the
architecture of his body his certificate of death.

Along the walls SS officers—a group Hitler described as "hard as Krupp
steel, as tough as shoe leather, as fast as greyhounds," men of some presumed
exalted order—stood in the slanting light of the sun. Their runic SS symbols, woven into their uniforms, served as a kind of gruesome antiquari-
anism. Father knew that he had girt more deceit into his false identity than
it could likely bear, sensing the final accounting must come soon.

It was just then that he remembered the rabbis in his Polish hometown,
Navaredok, reciting the biblical lines: "God said to Abraham . . . You shall

circumcise the flesh of your foreskin, and that shall be the sign of the covenant between me and you. And throughout the generations, every male among you shall be circumcised at the age of eight days." Circumcision, which had been a consecration to God, would now become a sacrifice to Moloch.

"Turn around!" the SS man spat with impatience. Blades of light came streaming in through the tall windows.

In the next room solid-bodied recruits were undressing. An air of suppressed menace filled the room. Father heard the thick growl of a dog. To the right, frost as fine as powder lay on the open window and a film of ice covered the streets.

The hideous images of physical torture raced through Father's mind, nearly robbing him of his sanity. His brain was so taut he could almost sense it pushing through his skull. In a moment everything would be plainly manifest. The SS would unearth his buried genealogy and the rack would be readied.

He found it increasingly hard to breathe, a palpitation at the pit of his stomach throbbing incessantly. The SS officer's stare struck with the force of a knotted club. Father wanted to hide, to sink beneath the floorboards. Nowhere more than in Nazi Germany was anatomy destiny.

"Turn left!" the SS man said with an appraising eye.

"Jawohl," Father repeated, anxiety keeping him ceremonious. Formality was now the other, more decorous, face of panic.

His mind suddenly echoed with the now incongruent circumcision blessing: "O give thanks unto the Lord; for he is good; for his loving kindness endures forever. This little child, may he become great. Even as he has entered into the covenant, so may he enter the Law, the nuptial canopy, and into good deeds."

After looking him up and down, the Nazi doctor sat down at his desk, took a silver-tipped pen, and scrawled in longhand on a fresh piece of paper. Father stared bracingly ahead.

"Step outside of the circle!" he ordered.

Father instinctively covered his nakedness.

"Stefan Osmanov!" came the command of the next SS doctor.

He stepped forward in cold composure, knowing himself to be alone in the world. All that kept him from extinction were the capricious scissors of fate. Like Damocles, he would never dance more artfully than beneath a sword hung by the frailest of threads.

⸺∞⸺

SEEMINGLY EVERY MOTION OVER the last few years had thrust this *yeshiva bokher*, a reclusive rabbinical student once incapable of deceit, into the center of a vortex; every step drew him closer to recruitment in the Waffen SS or certain death.

The Waffen SS were, of course, those "gladiators" Heinrich Heine had satirically depicted a century earlier, in 1834, destined to fight in an apocalyptic struggle. In *On the History of Religion and Philosophy in Germany*, which he had written as a reaction to the positive portrayal of the German romanticism by Madame de Staël, Heine declared with breathtaking prescience: "German thunder is of course truly German; it is not very nimble but rumbles along rather slowly. It will come, though, and if some day you hear a crash such as has never been heard before in world history, you will know the German thunder has finally reached its mark. At this commotion the eagles will drop down dead from the skies, and the lions in the farthest desert of Africa will put their tails between their legs and hide themselves in their royal lairs. A play will be performed in Germany compared with which the French Revolution might seem merely an innocent idyll." With preternatural instinct, Heine had grasped how easily the patina of culture cracks. Few could have understood as well that Germany would become an abyss.

And now Father stood amid a prophecy come cruelly alive. In this moral wilderness called Germany, he sought to make his lone encampment. Here he would scheme of self-preservation. A performing aerialist with no safety net—youth and desperation his only assets—he knew a mere stumble would fling him off the rope suspended across the abyss.

For years Father had been running and dodging, only to have arrived at this extremity of solitude and contradiction—a rabbinical student among SS recruits. What was the nature of his elaborate act of illusion, and how had he managed his collision of worlds?

My childhood years would be spent learning precisely how Father had unhooked the chain of ancestry by vandalizing a whole line of strange and foreign lineages. I discovered how he had schooled himself in cunning and stealth to arrive at a diabolic crossroad where limits and proportions were banished. In the end I came to grasp the darker meaning of what Paul Valéry meant when he said, "I believe in all sincerity that if each man were not able to live a number of other lives beside his own, he would not be able to live his own life."

CHAPTER
1

---∞∞∞---

*Death Selection in
Novogrudek*

"GUT SHABES, MAMEH!" JOSEPH said, keeping any trace of alarm from his voice.

"*Tayerer oytser!*" Dear treasure! She embraced him with tears of gratitude at seeing him unhurt.

The previous night his mother had awoken in a cold fright, having dreamed of a firestorm racing through the center of Novogrudek. Upon greeting her now at dusk, Father saw the troubled appeal in her eyes. Ever since the Germans had arrived in Novogrudek in early summer, a drumbeat of fear pervaded the town. But on this first Friday of December 1941, he sensed anew how deep her dread had become. He resolved not to mention the Nazi curfew that would shortly go into effect.

Near the curtained window they watched the season's first snow descend. Father's expression betrayed nothing of the sad news shortly to come. Grandmother's fine features quavered in the lamplight. This was the time of year when northeastern Poland, which had earned the sobriquet *kleyn Siber*—Little Siberia—was gripped by a band of Arctic ice.

For her the greatest comfort was the coming of Sabbath. She would always remind Father that an extra soul was given to the faithful each rest day. She quoted the rabbis that the joy of the Sabbath was a sixtieth of the blessing of the world to come reserved for the righteous. It was the truest "load of immortality" this side of paradise. She had longed to die on a

Friday so that, as she always said, she "could come unto Eternity on the Sabbath"—*aheym kumen far Shabes.*

"Come, Mother, it's time to light the candles," Father said.

She rose, struck a wooden match, and lit the Sabbath candles. She wove her hands over the flames and then cupped her eyes in tearful welcome of the holiest day of the week. The wavering brightness shone against the wisps of her blond hair. Her face had by then acquired a translucence that let through an otherworldly light. Father felt tinged with enjoyment as the glow of her eyes merged with the flame of the wick. For a moment the presence of the Sabbath hung in the air like a mystic truce.

His paternal aunt Rivke, with whom they lodged after the German Luftwaffe destroyed their home on Yiddisher Street and scattered death over Novogrudek five months earlier, burnished her old candelabrum to a high buff and lit her candles in turn. Every Friday she invested the coming of the Sabbath with what slender dignity remained. Father and his mother then approached the set table on which Uncle Shloimke leaned heavily, his face a furrow of strain. Rivke gazed at two empty chairs and sighed; both their children had escaped to the woods as a precautionary measure.

Shloimke thumbed through the yellowed pages of the Hebrew prayer book, its cover illegible from long use. Father and he turned in the direction of Jerusalem to recite the evening devotions. For a brief moment it was as if all nature began to sing a hymn of twilight.

They then moved in the direction of the table. Shloimke's voice, hardly more than a whisper, rose fitfully as he launched into the blessing over the loaves, which lay skinny and forlorn under the frayed white tablecloth flecked with wine spots. His voice trembled in an unsteady crescendo, all the while reading the words with a steady frown. They all stood in thought, their heads bowed.

When he finished, they sank down heavily in their chairs. Aunt Rivke ladled the thin broth with an old wooden spoon. Her motion awoke in Father a train of reflections. He was transported back to prewar Polish Sabbaths when the air was thick with the fragrance of *khale,* the aroma of yellow chicken broth cooked with marrow bones, the fried savor of *gribbenes* (cracklings), and the delicate whiteness of linen cloth. He remembered the days when his parents' grocery was stocked with candied delicacies to charm a child's heart. Jellies, glazed apples, and preserves were piled high on the counter and made his mouth water. On the far side, barrels of briny cu-

cumbers and baskets of aromatic poppy-seed rolls bulked large. Fields of rye and buckwheat lay outside, and Novogrudek slumbered in deep shade.

The dull rattling of the front gate arrested his daydreaming. Suddenly a shout tore through the quiet air. A violent motion shook the door and their heads turned in unison. A wild, chalk-faced neighbor, Avreml Kalmanov-itch, rushed in.

"Jews! Graves are being dug!"—*Yidn m'grobt griber!*—he shouted.

"What are you saying?" they demanded in a tumult of voices.

"Two hundred White Russians are digging trenches outside of town!" he cried, his voice pitched over their heads.

They rose as one and again repeated in an agony of alarm, "What are you saying?"

For a moment they stood like darkened figures in a murky space, the line between life and death appearing to fade.

Then the neighbor turned around and flew out the door.

Father looked at his watch. It was six-thirty; the curfew was set for seven. Minutes remained before the trap would shut them in, blocking their escape routes.

At first his thoughts flew in every direction. But the prospect of death concentrated his mind, forcing a mental clarity amid the chaos. The image of the Nazi Ortskommandant's bunker, which he had swept clean that very morning as part of his daily work assignment, leaped into his vision. It was small and narrow, not much larger than an oversized pipe, but big enough to shelter Grandmother and him from harm, if only they might reach it safely. Who, he thought, could imagine them finding refuge right under the noses of their tormenters, in the bunker of the local chief of the Wehr-macht?

"Mother, listen to me," he said with death rattling at the door. "I know the layout of the Ortskommandant's house."

Grandmother leaned her face against the wall. The oil lamp illuminated her grayish blond hair, throwing her face into shadow. She then turned to him and said, "Thank God your father is shielded by death."

The minutes ticked away. There was no time to vacillate. He took hold of his mother's hand and urged, "Let's flee. I know a place we can hide."

She stared straight ahead, then turned to face him. "Were you talking to me?" she asked, as if incurious about her fate.

"We must hide before they come for us," he pleaded.

"It's useless," she whispered. "Let's stay here."

"There's no use panicking," Aunt Rivke said. "We're staying. If the children return and don't find us here, they'll assume the worst." Shloimke nodded.

"You must listen to me," Father said, turning to his mother. "I have a safe haven near the Ortskommandant's house."

He kept looking at the clock on the wall. Grandmother saw the agony etched on his face, heard the desperate pitch in his voice, and relented. He bounded to the closet, tore the door open, and then grabbed her thin and only cloth coat and her knitted cap. He helped her into her coat and then flung his winter jacket on his shoulders.

Grandmother crunched her handkerchief into her palm and dabbed her eyes. She turned to Rivke and Shloimke and embraced them in round-shouldered intimacy. Father fell upon them and pressed them close. Rivke then opened the door to let them out. A cold blast rushed in and slammed the door behind them, two phantoms in the night.

They toiled uphill with the full moon hung in the sky like a silver globe, its smooth circularity mocking their fate. It was piercingly cold, and the fine frigid scent of snow rushed in on them.

As his mother walked with a stammering gait, tugging her kerchief tighter over her head, Father strode along with a firm tread.

"Please, Joseph, slow down. I can't keep up with you," she pleaded.

"Just this little hill and then it will be easier," he said in a tone of affectionate remonstrance, knowing they couldn't afford even a short respite.

Father was afraid of everything. He was afraid that her stamina would not last if he rushed her, but he feared most what would be in store for them if they were caught. He supported her arm, but it didn't much ease the strain of walking.

He knew he needed strength for them both. He guided his mother to a side alley, hoping this roundabout route would enable them to avoid passing the police station. They crept under fences, now silvered by frost, and emerged like ill-fated wanderers onto the street.

"Halt!" a shout rang out.

They froze in place.

Two hulking White Russian policemen, spotting their joint silhouettes, trained their guns on them.

"Where are you going?" they demanded.

Father drew out the Ortskommandant's water-main key from his coat pocket and handed it to them. He explained with as much tranquil audacity as he could summon that if he did not return it to the commandant's staff right away, there'd be hell to pay.

The policemen looked them up and down and then took counsel one with the other.

"Get moving!" the taller one finally barked, putting his gun back into its holster.

They turned on their heels and marched away. Grandmother and Father held their breath till the brutes disappeared from sight.

"Got tsu danken!" Grandmother heaved a sigh.

Hedged about with danger, Father and his mother returned to the side road, following its curves and bends. From afar they heard sharp explosive crackles which made them hasten their step. The wind enveloped them and raked their faces as they ducked under a succession of fences. Grandmother was puffing and out of breath, her eyes bent upon the ground. Father could hear her murmur, "Oysbrukirt mit tsores iz der veg tsum beys-hakvores"—The path to the grave is paved with troubles.

They finally came upon a wall that edged into the Ortskommandant's quarters. The cylindrical bunker—their refuge—was off to one side. The building's cellar would have been the better choice, but the trapdoor rested on rusty hinges; opening it might have alerted the occupants of the house.

It was minutes before seven when they finally slid into the bunker buried under a skin of ice. Grandmother gasped from exertion and soon began to shiver but did not complain, sitting absolutely still to conserve her fading strength. Father put his arm around her shoulder and held her close. Her hands were numb and her teeth began to chatter softly. He breathed on her hands, massaged her fingers as he fought with the cold. He trembled to think what would happen when her strength gave out.

In time their hunger pangs grew sharp, but their food ration consisted of a loaf of hard black bread Uncle Shloimke had thrust into his hands when they left. He pulled it from his pocket; it was as cold as the night itself. He broke a piece from the end and warmed it in his hands. Their teeth nearly broke as they drove into its hard crust. They softened it with their saliva and chewed on it for a hour, remembering their interrupted Sabbath meal, a repast once reserved for sanctity and delight.

The broad ends of the pipe could not be blocked, and the wind cut through them like a knife. Death skulked in the frigid air. Father remembered how he had snuggled into his blanket at home before the war and how the soft drowsiness of approaching sleep spread through him on a late Friday night. Now they huddled together on the icy floor, twisting themselves into positions of warmth; the moonlight sidling across the borders of gray cement marked the passing hours. Time became a weight as ponderous as night itself.

In this catacomb, their ears were roused to a high pitch of tension. In the silence, every noise was magnified, with periodic gunfire rattling their nerves. Unspoken thoughts hung like their breath in the air, and amidst the gloom they fought weariness, fearing sleep would spell death in the glacial night.

He thought of his dead father and of the many boyhood stories he had related to him. Like so many young Jews at the turn of the century, Grandfather had dreamed of America, the lodestar of his ambition. This was the country with a franchise on the future, of which it was said that every route might become a straight line to infinity.

When Grandfather was barely an adolescent, already rashly enterprising, he ran away from Novogrudek to Libau, the Latvian port on the Baltic Sea. Father imagined him as a young boy, scraping around the old wharves, watching the seabirds cavorting in the briny air and skimming the surface of the waves. From a great distance he would hear the foghorns sounding at sea. Then an old hulk bound for New York steamed into port and Grandfather stole his way inside. Imbibing the salt reek of the tide, he left his childhood behind, as the harbor fell away.

Aboard the ship, Grandfather recited the Jewish hymn "Nishmat," which sang of the faithful as "mouths full of song as the sea, and their tongues of exultation as the multitude of its waves, and their lips of praise as the wide-extended skies . . . their eyes shining light like the sun and the moon, and their hands spread forth like the eagles of the air. . . ." He gazed upon the expanding horizon, his mind freighted with the biblical associations of a shtetl youth.

The port of New York with its black funnels of smoke proved fearsome for so young a fellow in 1906. It was a city with a wild hunger for sensation and the promise of freedom. This was where Alexander Harkavy, the noted Yiddish lexicographer and one of Navaredok's famous sons had come. Here on the eastern seabord he transformed himself into the teacher par excellence of two generations of Jewish immigrants, and into the translator of *Don Quixote* and a revised King James English Bible into Yiddish. In one boat's journey, Grandfather entered the urban industrial world of the twentieth century.

Set ashore with little money in his pockets, Grandfather found his way to relatives, the Falks, in Borough Park, which had been recently parceled out of the estates and cow pastures of Blythebourne. But his sojourn ended disappointingly. He spent four years of sorrow and loneliness in New York, fitfully navigating the unsparing currents of the American marketplace—what he called *"Amerika ganif"*: America the thief. Sailing back to Russia, Grandfather would never return to the United States. He was unable to find "freedom's larger play" in Brooklyn, where economic failure was synonymous with moral transgression.

On his return journey, he was accosted by a ghostly aboriginal vision that rose from "the script of the waves," divulging the sea's awful secrets. While others were overcome with the nausea of seasickness, he leaned bravely against the handrail of the vessel a day into the Atlantic. To his consternation, he saw on the line of the horizon an ocean-crossing eagle land on the back of a whale gliding among the waves. The seabird's talons had become entangled in the great fish's blubber. The whale rolled in agony, trying to free itself of the bird's talons. Two monarchs of the sea, the soaring fowl and diving mammal, drifted as phantoms on the ocean's surface, bound in a terrible conjoining of life and limb.

Upon hearing this fable of destruction in the Atlantic, I was reminded during my adolescence of Melville's story of the whale and its multiple layers of emblematic meaning. My grandfather's ominous sighting recalled an apocalyptic passage in *Moby-Dick*, in which one of the *Pequod*'s gigantic sailors accidentally nails a sky hawk to the mast while the accursed whaling ship sinks: "The bird chanced to intercept its broad fluttering wing between the hammer and the wood . . . and with archangelic shrieks . . . went down with his ship, which like Satan, would not sink to hell till she dragged a living part of heaven along with her, and helmeted herself with it."

Hebrew Scripture teaches that the sea yields the darker truth of reality; but in 1941, the heart of Europe far exceeded the ocean in sheer malignity. This swath of burning ground—Eastern Europe—with no cleanly defined littoral frontiers, had suffered the worst sort of imperial conquest. Fortunate were those continents—the American in particular—whose borders were washed by the seas of the world.

But of what use could such memories of America be at that moment? Grandfather was dead, and America lay beyond the reach of Europe. How unfair were life's favors apportioned, Father thought, sinking deeper into his winter jacket while his mother leaned against the pipe's harsh interior. Morning would soon be upon them, and if they did not exit the rusty pipe before the first rays of dawn, they would be trapped for at least another twelve hours.

Grandmother awoke in a shiver of light. They had to move to the cellar—it would be warmer and would muffle the howl of the wind. But how would they open the heavy door whose rusty hinges made such a racket? Father was terrified of making the least noise because of a resident in the building above whose shrewish wife had no second thoughts about betraying Jews. If she heard anything, she could alert the Gestapo.

Father wracked his brains till the first fugitive light of day lay on the ground. They would simply have to chance it.

Taking Grandmother's hand, he emerged from the pipe and headed toward the rusty cellar door. A powerful blast of wind swirled snow around them. Father winced as he placed his hand on the door handle. Even before he made any movement, he could already hear the noise reverberating in his ear. But to his surprise, the door miraculously gave way without its customary screech.

He led Grandmother down the dark wooden stairs. They advanced slowly, groping blindly with their hands and feet amid the basement's baronial provisions. The cellar ran the entire length of the house and was partitioned into storerooms filled with ample provisions for the Germans. They reached a lit passageway and soon found a backroom lined with flour sacks, which Father arranged on the floor as makeshift bedding.

It was warmer in the cellar than in the pipe, but the Russian winter penetrated even these thick basement walls. Father wrapped his winter scarf around his mother to give her an extra layer of warmth. They held each other in the darkness. By late morning the diabolical wind subsided. But soon the tension of waiting became unbearable. Would it not be better to anticipate rather than merely react to events? he thought. Why wait till disaster loomed?

He retraced his steps to the entrance and climbed out onto the lawn. He knew one Nazi adjutant in the building who might be amenable to a special request. It was a grave risk, but he was counting on his constant need for an extra hand during the morning's chores.

Father's chest pounded as he mounted the stairway. What could he credibly say if he was confronted by a hostile Nazi official at the Ortskommandant's headquarters? But he was lucky; the building was fairly empty. He breathed more easily when he saw the adjutant racing downstairs.

"*Ach*, Joseph, good you're here. I'm shorthanded this morning."

"At your service, sir," Father said promptly.

"Go, run down and haul some water from the outdoor pump."

These words brought the world back to him. If only his duties of attendance could serve as a refuge.

FATHER WORKED DISTRACTEDLY ALL morning, cleaning milk jugs, polishing the Ortskommandant's boots, doing sundry menial tasks which absorbed some of his fear. But Grandmother's precarious safety troubled him. She was shivering in the cellar, he knew. And she ran the very real danger of being caught.

He used every excuse he could to run down to the basement and check on her. By late afternoon he was making repeated trips down the stairs when he sensed that he was being watched. He understood immediately it was the woman upstairs, who in making humble obeisance to the Nazi occupier reserved malice for the Jews. She had been prying and peering behind her closed shutters. Father's heart stopped when he saw her raise her window suddenly.

"You!" she shouted from her window. "What's going on in the cellar?"

"Just trying to keep warm," Father yelled back. "It's cold out here."

Once her suspicions were aroused, she would not yield without checking for herself. When he descended to the cellar a little later, he heard her menacing footsteps. He raced in and saw her advancing from room to room.

They came face to face. Father caught the calculating gleam in her eye.

"What are you looking for?" he asked, trying to keep his voice calm.

"I don't have to answer you!" she snapped, and continued her search amid the bins.

"If you need something, I can get it for you," he offered affably, foolishly thinking he could stir some hidden vein of benevolence.

"Don't bother!" she replied, baring her broken teeth.

Before he could stop her, she rounded a corner and discovered his mother praying in a darkened corner.

"What is *she* doing here?" she screamed.

Grandmother's face was an unmoving white spot in the dark. The local woman sensed her fright.

"Get out! You have no right to be here, you wastrel!" Her voice rose in a shrill crescendo of hate.

She then turned to Father with a triumphant smile. "So this is your mother! You thought you could fool me? But you will soon learn you can't."

"Have a heart," he voiced a vain entreaty. "It's so cold outside."

She shot him a stony look, spat a few anti-Semitic curses, and strode out. Her distant figure was a small bundle of sharp, angular gestures and choice imprecations. Father hated this witch of calamity for whom at the moment no malediction seemed adequate.

Grandmother understood that they had finally been routed from their unquiet haven. She burst into tears while Father made a great effort to seem composed.

"What a *beyzeh khaye*"—a vicious animal—he said.

Alas, all too often in those terrible days, her kind proved to be the rule rather than the exception. A leader of a German annihilation squad wrote to Berlin, "It is difficult to imagine the joy, gratitude and delight our measures awoke . . . in the local population. We had to use sharp words to cool the enthusiasm of women, children, and men who with tears in their eyes tried to kiss our hands and feet."

"Come, Joseph," his mother pleaded, "this place isn't ours. We should go."

He agreed, but they found themselves in a real fix now. They were forbidden to be outside on pain of death. Father thought for a moment and then mounted the indoor stairs leading to the office of the adjutant, whom he knew to be a fairly decent sort. He gambled on the dubious hope that the adjutant might find a way to issue him a transit permit. Under the curfew rules, Father was as good as dead if he stepped out with no protective clearance.

"Sir," he began, "is it possible for me to carry a pass giving me liberty to do all my errands for you without hindrance?"

"Well, I don't see why not. You have been doing your work steadily, so I can't imagine why that should be a problem," he answered.

He took out a pad he carried with him and wrote quickly that Father should not be harmed during his work assignments. He handed it to him with a flourish.

"Thank you, sir," Father said.

Grandmother's face was etched in sorrow as they left the Ortskommandant's headquarters and headed back to their relative's residence in Peresheka. Crows flew overhead in a dense shifting canopy. Though it was only afternoon, the day was dark around them. A great black cloud bank descended on them. Near the bombed-out center of town they were intercepted by White Russian police once again. They could not proceed and saw that around the bend in the road thousands of Jews were streaming from the direction of Peresheka toward the courthouse on the edge of town.

Father could smell danger in the air as fear gripped them in an expanding and contracting ring. The sight of people being herded like cattle from their homes and hiding places confirmed his worst fears. The interminable sky stretched in a wide, dark expanse.

Despite Joseph's pass, they were swept into a confused sea of humanity, carried down the avenue in a chaotic surge, tossed amid the stampeding crowd, now consisting of thousands of Novogrudek's Jews clutching their last possessions. The German army and SS units, armed with their pointed bayonets and rifles, were flanked by the White Russian guards, their loutish collaborators, who prodded the throng toward the two courthouse buildings on the far side of town.

Women clutched infants to their bosoms and pulled toddlers along behind. Cries and oaths mingled with desperate pleading voices: "Where are we going? What will they do with us?" But the White Russian police and Wehrmacht soldiers herded them along silently across the broken cobblestones. They had to proceed toward the district courthouse square, where a solid wall of SS men, their ruddy faces wreathed in smiles, waited for them in a diagonal line.

In the eastern regions, the German army and the Einsatzgruppen, the mobile killing units, operated so closely together they considered themselves Waffenbrüder, comrades-in-arms. The basis for their cooperation was an order by the High Command of the Wehrmacht earlier in 1941, which stated that in the area of army operations the SS had been assigned special missions pursuant to the order of the Führer.

In Novogrudek SS Officer Traube headed this special operation and served under the command of Wilhelm Kube, the Gauleiter and governor of White Russia, a graduate of the University of Berlin who had joined the Nazi party in 1928 and sat as a deputy in the Reichstag. In 1936 he was removed from all his positions by the chief of the Nazi Party court on charges of blackmail, seduction of colleagues' wives, and embezzlement, but Himmler, upon hearing that Kube had volunteered for the Waffen SS at the age of fifty-three, had him appointed master of White Russia.

Twilight's purple haze hung over the captive Jews as the Sabbath drew to a close. The five thousand were squeezed into the open yard between the two court buildings, sitting on their bundles or squatting on the cold ground.

Grandmother and Father had brought nothing with them, so they leaned against each other. The Germans kept their guns trained on them.

Rumors spread through the yard like wildfire through dry grass. Many knew graves had been dug in Skridleva but could not fully comprehend what that meant. To mask the unnameable, people spoke of the establishment of two ghettos, one for the old and the other for the young and skilled.

Finally the SS officers threw open the massive wooden courthouse doors and herded the crowd inside. "Single file!" they shouted, but the Jews were too panicked to listen. Families held hands and rushed inside in groups. Whip- and stick-wielding Nazis, attired in pressed green-and-black uniforms and looking famously jut-jawed and steely-eyed, flanked the crowd and lashed out at will. Their mien augured some dreadful business was close at hand.

The crowd moved at the behest of the cracking whips. The air was thick with shouted orders and strangled sobs as the mass streamed through the door into the corridors. Father and Grandmother were among the last to enter. Once they were all inside, the doors were pulled shut behind them.

At first it was hard for many to give reality its proper weight. Families ran from room to room in wild processionals, searching for loved ones and combing every last rumor which raced along like nimble fire. Grandmother and Father made their way to the second floor of the structure, where they spotted Aunt Rivke and Uncle Shloimke standing at the threshold of a room far too crowded to give entry.

"Look, Shloimke, there are Chaja and Joseph!" Aunt Rivke shouted. They fell into each other's arms and sobbed, as they recounted the savage roundup in Peresheka after Father and his mother had left on their ill-fated journey to the Ortskommandant's bunker.

In a few minutes Father spotted Itche, another of his uncles, seated with his wife and children in a waste of dislocation and gloom. They were in the middle of the bursting room, which made reaching them impossible. Never before had Father heard so many multiplying rumors of ghettos and graveyards, while the *Judenrat*, darting to and fro, strained to maintain calm and "negotiate" with the Nazis on the main floor.

Father and Grandmother sank to the floor against the wall in the hallway. The shadow on her face deepened. They both sat in a great glare of comprehension, knowing in some incontrovertible way that the end was near. It was now that the last floating plank of their old world sank.

Sepia-toned photographs of prewar Navaredok rose in Father's mind: the first fruits of the season, the children's singsong recitation of the aleph-beth, the baking of matzohs, for which the town was famous far and wide.

Grandmother turned her face away in prayer, in a monotone as hoarse as a sea dirge. Her entreaty no longer included supplication for herself—as if she had been released from all earthly cares—but only for her son. In spite of all she had seen, nothing could sway her from the conviction that God was the steersman of all things, and that every life was held in submission to him. The ebbing of her hope did not diminish her faith. Father turned as well to petitionary prayer, now that every earthly effort had been exhausted.

They nibbled at the stale crusts Father had buried in his pocket until their shrunken stomachs pinched. With clouded eyes, he tried to pierce the obscurity. But despair now brought with it its own clarity and certitude.

Later Grandmother experienced a sharp pain in her side. She had taken ill a year earlier with an undefined ailment and had journeyed to Lemberg to be operated on for what was feared might be cancer. She was never to regain her strength. She now inquired if there were any bathrooms, but since no one seemed to know, they moved from floor to floor. Finally a good soul shouted out, "In the basement."

Father guided his mother down steep steps into a dim cellar where the stench was overwhelming. She gave him her coat and knitted cap as she lifted her skirt and waded through a pool of urine to reach an open drain. Father could see how shrunken she had become, her attenuation now surpassing mere exhaustion. They then trudged back up the stairs, Grandmother holding her handkerchief to her mouth.

Night deepened. It was difficult to breathe. The damp air was solid with fear, and Grandmother gasped, coughing up phlegm. She had not eaten a full meal in days. Near her sat a father crooning over sick children who could not be comforted.

"Let me find you a piece of bread and some tea," Father pleaded.

"No, Joseph," she said, "it's best now to do without," waving her hand in resignation.

People were heard speaking of God and providence, of messianic birth pangs and other eschatological schemes, of Russian victories and the supreme power of public opinion, but scarcely of what was in store for them. From dusk to dawn every consolatory myth was duly regarded and each delusional prediction was carefully examined.

"Graves! For children? *Ach*, it's impossible! It cannot be," some said. "They'll divide us into ghettoes, you'll see. What is it that we say, '*Oyb Got vil ken a bezem shisn*'—if God wills it, a broom can also shoot?" Rumors and adages of varying reliability and credibility circulated widely. As the hours progressed, mercurial shifts of mood swept the courthouse.

Time stretched interminably. A nerve-peeling tension hung in the air. Grandmother said, "At least your father has been spared all this. Earth is the best shelter." That was her only consolation as night drifted into day. Toward dawn on Sunday new rumors were aflutter: death for the old and infirm; hard labor for the young and fit.

Now the race for life was on in earnest. Even devout women, ignoring their feelings of outraged modesty, opened their bundles and dug feverishly for whatever might serve as makeup kits. There was a frantic traffic in the accoutrements of acquired youth: lipstick, tweezers, eye pencils. Pious grandmothers applied rouge, darkened their eyebrows, and draped scarves around their necks. Men and women pinched their cheeks to restore color to their ashen faces. Even the most sedentary scholar with the customary bent shoulders and studious pallor tried to appear ruddy and straight-backed.

"Mordecai, what are you doing?" a wife screamed at her husband.

"What do you mean?" he said, as he continued trimming his snowy locks with a pair of rough scissors in front of a hand mirror, hoping to shear ten years off his appearance.

A teenage girl near them urged her mother with filial tenderness, "Here, take my comb and do your hair. Let it fall over your shoulders like when you dated father."

"Az okh 'n vey"—woe betide—the woman replied, "who would I be kidding?" Then she resignedly drew the comb through her thinning hair. Her daughter patted her hands with the speechless softness used to soothe a child.

Tension mounted as impending doom hung heavily.

On early Monday morning Father decided to press through the crowd in the chamber to speak to his uncle Itche before all passage became impossible.

As Father negotiated his way into the room, he suddenly heard the metallic click of heels. Two Wehrmacht soldiers rushed down the hallway, guns sagging at their hips. "Everybody inside!" they shouted.

Grandmother, Aunt Rivke, and Uncle Shloimke were crowded with others at the threshold, unable to get inside. Then a German *Feldgendarme*, fitted in a great fur-trimmed green coat, tried to force entry but failed. His face darkened. He crushed his cigarette against the wall and expelled the smoke in a long hissing sound. Drawing his pistol from his holster, he shouted, "Damn it! It's too crowded in there! I want more space made immediately!" There was a sudden violent shoving as people tried to obey his command. Somehow, Father found himself thrown against the back wall, separated even from Uncle Itche, trapped in the churning vortex.

A low murmuring Yiddish curse, *"Der malekh-hamoves"*—the angel of death—rose from the condemned crowd.

After the shoving and pushing died down, Grandmother stood beside the *Feldgendarme*. He grabbed her by the collar of her thin coat and with a cold homicidal stare shouted, *"Raus!"*—Get out!—shoving her out of the door. Fire raged in Father's brain as he saw his mother disappear. The steely glint of the Nazi's pistol pinned him to the spot.

Furious with impatience and spite, the Nazi *Feldgendarme* sprung upon

Aunt Rivke and flung her down the hallway. Uncle Shloimke, who was standing beside her, followed. Fear held Father still. Over and over came the bloody yell *"Raus!"* as scores of Jews were torn from the room. The German's shrill voice reverberated with the sound of hell. When the German cleared the area near the doorway, he began a more orderly screening.

The elderly couples near him were reciting Judgment Day prayers, normally uttered on Yom Kippur, invoking images of the Binding of Isaac (the Akedah): "And Abraham lifted his eyes, and looked, and behold, before him a ram caught in a thicket by his horns: and Abraham went and took the ram and offered him for a burnt offering in the stead of his son."

Father was pressed against the rear wall, watching as the *Feldgendarme* waved his pistol as each individual approached, announced his trade or profession, and pointed to his immediate family members. Heads of households presented work cards in hopes of appearing indispensible, but nothing softened the exterminating angel.

Uncle Itche's turn came on the selection line. He had worked for the Gebitzkommissar, the regional commissar, and tried to use this to his advantage. He presented his work papers, diligently pointed to his wife and children, and then waited expectantly as so many before him.

"Raus!" the German barked. "All of you!"

When Itche protested softly, the Wehrmacht soldier tightened his finger on the trigger. He did not need further encouragement.

An elderly couple who had lost sight of their children pleaded quietly with a fellow of twenty near Father to claim them as his parents. But their ploy failed, as so many others did; hardly anyone was given a reprieve. The selection continued until the room was practically empty.

The guard had cleared the side walls, working his way to the back. Father's turn approached. His options seemed no better than the others, but he frantically turned each of them over in his mind. He checked the note of the Ortskommandant's adjutant, granting him permission to be outdoors on errands.

Only two people separated Father from the gendarme. He could no longer put two thoughts together, as if he had been stunned by a poisoned dart. He was past all intelligent deliberation. He grew dizzy and dangerously faint, and the polished wood of the courtroom floor reeled beneath his feet.

Suddenly he stood in front of his tormentor.

"*Was machst du?*"—What do you do?—he bellowed. Father felt naked under his gaze.

"I work in the private quarters of the Ortskommandant," he answered, rallying his faltering thoughts. He then unfolded his identity paper and handed it to the *Feldgendarme*.

The German gave him a sharp appraising look and with his free hand grabbed Father by the lapels of his green coat—a color strangely similar to that of the Wehrmacht uniforms. He gripped him while with his other hand he brandished his pistol. He shuttled Father back and forth, uncertain what to do with him.

Father set his jaw and looked straight at him, trying to meet his glance with a semblance of composure. The gendarme tightened his grip and Father's collar tore a little as he was shaken to and fro. Then the man flung Father against the back wall. He nearly lost his balance, but managed to stay on his feet, much as a piece of cork cast onto the snarling crest of the sea waves: one minute sinking into the depths, the next bobbing back to the surface.

The *Feldgendarme* worked through the end of the line as a trowel through soft loam. When he finished, hundreds had been ordered out of the chamber. Only seven stood with Father against the wall. He returned his pistol to its holster, gave them a last sharp look, and strode out, slamming the door behind him.

No one dared walk to the door and open it. They stared at the blank wall, listening to the panicked pleas rising from the courtyard outside. The wailing of the small ones, writhing in pain and fear, was the most unbearable.

The room's only window had been smashed in the bombing and was covered with tin. There were no gaps or crevices to spy through. Father tried to force the metal but it would not give. He rummaged through his pockets and found a nail under his mother's knitted cap which she had given to him to keep. He began to bore it into the hard-to-pierce tin plate. He worked at it for a long time, keeping one eye on the door. He sensed that the very light by which he searched for his mother would also be the fire by which his spirit would be consumed. The screams in the courtyard intensified, turning into a solid wall of unearthly wailing.

He heard the sound of running motors, and it was then that he finally pierced the tin. A long line of black trucks drove into the compound outside, confirming the horrific truth. He squinted hard, trying to spot his mother in the crowd. He gripped the nail with all his might and he enlarged the hole to get an unobstructed view: whereupon he saw SS men and White Russian auxiliary police pushing, tossing, hauling people into the trucks, shoving them into oblivion. With obscene wantonness, the elderly and the infirm were butted with rifles, the tips of which were smeared with blood and brains. Many were lacerated, some had skulls cracked open. The trucks quickly filled.

People Father had known since childhood were visible, but not his mother. His eyes wished to close but could not cease seeing what leaped before them. As he watched the trucks leaving the now depopulated yard in a long column, the door to his chamber flew open. Uncle Itche, beaten and bleeding profusely from the head, was roughly thrown in. Pale as death, he ran straight to Father, shaking uncontrollably. Torment wracked his entire body. His cries, full-throated howls of anguish, came quick now. But after a while, he recovered his breath and said haltingly that the German officer for whom he labored had been in the courtyard and decided on the spur of the moment to pull him off the truck. "I pleaded with him to let me take my wife and children, but another soldier who heard me slammed me with his rifle," Itche said in a rush of words.

Dark rivulets of blood streamed from his wounds and he could not stem their flow. Father tore out the lining of his coat and pressed it over his uncle's cuts, feebly consoling him and wondering out loud what had kept them from being condemned as those who now rode in the trucks awaiting their final sentence.

"Don't try to understand," Uncle cried in a blistering voice of pain. *"Es iz ek velt."* It is the end of the world.

"Did you see my mother?" Father whispered, barely finding the strength to utter the question.

"Yes," he said. "She asked that we all forgive one another, for the end had come. 'The world is being called to account. Today is like Yom Kippur, the Sabbath of Sabbaths, and we are all being judged,' she said over and over again. Her prayers were only for you. She had ceased praying for herself."

They fell on each other's neck as the room reverberated with an unearthly echo of five thousand voices crying in a plangent swell of sound, *"Shema Yisrael."* Hear, O Israel: the Lord our God, the Lord is One!

I have often imagined that Grandmother Chaja, like Rabbi Akiva, who had been publicly tortured by the Romans nearly eighteen hundred years earlier, must have prolonged the final word of the Shema—*Ekhod* (One)—so as to die pronouncing God's inalterable unity in one breath.

⸺∞⸺

LATER THAT MORNING, THERE came a deafening report. The distant rattle of gunfire—deeds eternity itself could not annul—mowed down thousands for hours, as the blind majesty of the forest blotted out the sky. Shovelfuls of earth fell to the ground.

CHAPTER 2

Escape Plans

HOUR AFTER HOUR FATHER and Uncle Itche sat shrouded in darkness. They crouched in mute emptiness, their hearts cracked as desert cisterns. Trapped in the Novogrudek ghetto, they finally knew Judgment Day to be a court in perpetual session.

How lucky is the man who can count his sorrows; theirs were beyond number. Their pain exceeded the language of sense, for tragedy can only be defined within language, and this is what they now lacked. Father remembered that in *kheder* (grammar school) he had been taught that when the time came for Moses to die, the angels were reluctant to carry out the death decree and so God came to him like a loving father and took his soul away with a kiss. But Father's generation was to have it otherwise.

All that remained of his mother was her sky-blue knitted cap that he had clutched in his bare hands when they were separated during the German selection. As he now held her head covering tightly, her image swam before his eyes and he once more inhaled the breath of home. He felt a harrowing remorse for not having joined her in her final moments. He would then, as later, be haunted by recurring guilt, as well as by the image of his late father, recounting his adolescent journey to and from America.

What wouldn't he have given now to be across the Atlantic, as Grandfather once was, on the far shores of the New World! If only he had stayed in America! If only he had not turned his back on New York, with its hectic, discordant beauty! Of course, Grandfather had been too solitary, too grounded in Navaredok, to cultivate a fixed sense of place in America. Russian Poland would forever remain his home, and like so many of his fellow Jews, landless for centuries, he viewed its *shtetlakh* (small towns) with near-biblical sanctity.

As the hours lengthened in the Nazi-guarded courthouse, America lay beyond reach. Uncle Itche and Father were isolated in the courthouse with no inkling of the war's progress in the rest of Europe, let alone Asia, where three hundred Japanese planes had raced to Pearl Harbor on that very day. Little could they know as well that on the very morning that Navaredok's Jews were taken to their deaths, seven hundred Jews were gassed in the Polish village of Chelmno, a historical first and the day some historians regard as the beginning of the Final Solution—chemical extermination. Three weeks later Belzec, the annihilation camp, inaugurated the use of stationary gas chambers. Father, his uncle, and the other survivors resembled those blind historical figures who, Paul Valéry once wrote, enter the future backwards.

Later that afternoon as their eyes traveled despairingly about the room, an SS man entered and motioned for them to follow him. They were led to the courtyard where earlier thousands of their brethren had shouted heavenward *"Shema Yisrael."* In addition to this group of nine, only a few hundred of their kinsmen were left alive, and they were assembled in rows of five and then marched at gunpoint back to Peresheka, again to be ghettoized.

As they entered the grounds of their new prison, Father saw that Uncle Shloimke's home, the very one that Grandmother and he had left, still stood, framed by black-barked trees, its gray roof bordered with droplets of melting snow. A light flickered inside, and he spotted through the window two shadows fluttering on the wall. At first he was too fearful to approach. After hesitating some minutes, he neared and knocked softly on the pane. The door opened and his cousins Leyzer and Meylekh, Shloimke's and Rivke's children, stood under the wavering light. Somehow they had found their way back to the ghetto after the slaughter.

Father fell into their arms, unable to speak. For a long time his eyes were bent upon the ground, but he then recovered himself with a violent effort and told them in a stammering voice that their parents and his mother were now permanently joined in death.

They lay pell-mell on the floor that night, wrestling sleep from the darkness. His cousins' home soon became a makeshift prayer house, where Kaddish, an intercession for the souls of the dead which mentions not a word about death or even the world to come, was constantly recited. A chant of praise to God, the Kaddish was counterpointed by a recitation of a passage from Psalm 44.

> *Rouse yourself; why do you sleep, O Lord?*
> *Why do you hide Your face*
> *Ignoring our affliction and distress?*

No family was spared in Navaredok, and those who were left alive were paralyzed by grief. In the twilight gloom, many now said the mourning prayer for themselves, cognizant that their days were numbered.

Conditions in the new ghetto proved wretched. Before long they exhausted their miserable stock of provisions. More than fifty people crowded into his cousins' home, which could only accommodate a fraction of that number. They kept each other mournful company, as they held on to the small decencies. But hunger and dirt soon began to breed disease. Indeed, all of life teemed with the imminence of death. There was nowhere to wash, a situation further compounded by their severe economy of soap and water, and they had no choice but to sleep in their clothes. By then appearances had stopped counting for much anymore. They all lived with fear at the base of their brains, knowing they could be shot at any moment. Every passing day was merely a reprieve.

At night they awoke in cold and gloomy anticipation, keenly observant of every sound. The predawn hours were the most terrifying, for selections took place then: the sudden arrival of the Nazi police and their collaborators, who promptly encircled the ghetto. Then words and blood came together: shouts, curses, truncheons and whips flailing in the air. Nothing gave the Nazis more sadistic pleasure than tearing their victims from sleep, dwarfing their nightmares with ever new tortures. They sought to wear out their stamina, wreak every insult on them, and finally drive the iron of despair so deeply into their spirit that they would be dead before their bodies were destroyed.

IN JANUARY 1942, THE water pipes of the Gebitzkommisar's residence had frozen on a frigid night, and the ground around it needed to be softened. Father and a couple of others were assigned to ignite a fire and hack away at the frozen earth with shovels.

Instant compliance was demanded and given. The workers reached the spot without delay, but toward the end of their task, their German overseer suddenly appeared. He wielded a gun and with no provocation began shooting in their direction. A month earlier he had done the same, leaving three Jews dead and one badly wounded. A bullet grazed Father's shoulder, and blood spurted out of his shirt. He sank writhing to the ground. His pallor signaled that he needed help immediately, and the others, ducking and crawling, came to his aid. They dragged him to the side and bound his wound perfunctorily. When the rifle shots subsided, he dragged himself back into the ghetto. It was late, but the ghetto doctor was at his post. He set his surgical instruments and operated on Father in stealth. His deftness and skill helped stanch the blood and set him on the road to recovery.

—∞∞∞—

GIVEN THE DIRE DANGERS that existed in the ghetto, flight into the forest was the only chance at life. In the first weeks of 1942, with the first slaughter of Novogrudek's Jews at barely a month's remove, Father was determined to escape a fate that for most seemed ineluctable. Thoughts whirled through his head, and he examined every measure that would allow him to circumvent the dead end of the ghetto. He toyed with a grandiose plan of finding a pathway to the balmier haven of the Black Sea. Perhaps he could escape south to Galicia and from there cross the dust-choked borders to Romania and then somehow smuggle himself into Turkey. His mind flew, as the Poles used to say to *Wyraj*, to the warm countries where the birds migrate, to those blissful lands lying beyond the seas. He might even reach the palm trees and vineyards of the south. Here he would find the Mediterranean where a young Camus had written, "The sun taught me that history is not everything."

Father embroidered these fantasies with the fervor of late adolescence. The Middle East, in his overheated imagination, meant the scorching breath of the desert and phalanxes of plumed and fezzed soldiers. Most importantly for him, it signified the pioneer farmers of the *yishuv* in Palestine. His fervent hope was to reach the Holy Land, from which his ancestors were uprooted and exiled two thousand years ago by the Roman legions of Titus and Vespasian, commencing a tragedy which was now reaching its bloody culmination.

In the heart of the Novogrudek ghetto, Father thought of the ancient Jewish city of Beersheva, the site where the patriarch Abraham planted a citrus tree after his long journey from Ur in the Fertile Crescent and across the hill country of Canaan. Beersheva was the gateway to the south, and Father knew that the chronicle of the Jews was inextricably bound with the desert. Indeed, the Bible's opening chapters could not have been scripted anywhere but in its austere reaches. Ernest Renan, the nineteenth-century French scholar, had spoken of the desert as "the highway of monotheism," the exact geographical correlate of Jewish divinity, possessing something of the elementary, the final and the irrevocable, of the first and last things, that could not but remind the believer of the incommensurate grandness of the God of Abraham.

But unbeknownst to Father, Jewish Palestine hung then in mortal balance, and history was everything. Erwin Rommel's Afrika Corps, racing toward Egypt, seemed unstoppable. The German Desert Fox, as quick as greased lightning, assaulted Tobruk, the besieged fortress with its strategic deep-water harbor, on June 20, 1942. The next day the English surrendered, leaving the German road to Palestine open and hugely vulnerable.

His ignorance of such events allowed Father to pore over the few ragged maps left in the ghetto, tracing paths from one country to next. But he soon veered from confidence to despair. What point in dreaming of the Mediterranean's azure radiance when everything was coated by an iron gray? How could he get to Turkey, much less Palestine, if he could not get past the Novogrudek ghetto? These phantasms soon vanished like the shapes of a mirage.

⸺⸙⸺

IN MARCH FATHER JOINED a work detail that returned nightly to the ghetto. Treated as a gang of convicts, it toiled at repairing tracks crossing the forest. Yet once outside the confines of the ghetto, he thrilled to every vanished scent of freedom, sensing oddly that chance might be on his side.

At the work station, the group needed water to cleanse its hands. When

Father went to beg among the neighboring peasants, he was treated with uncharacteristic kindness. At first unaware that he was a Jew, they readily agreed to his entreaty. These chance encounters only strengthened his resolve to flee, to take any road, to get as far away from the ghetto as was possible.

Rumor had already spread in Navaredok that a large Jewish ghetto existed in Warsaw. In his naiveté, Father imagined that a semblance of civilization must still exist in the Polish capital. Warsaw, not Palestine, therefore, became his new destination, when he shelved escape plans to the south and the Mediterranean. But here too his hopes were easily daunted. He had no way of getting to Warsaw in these times. Well, perhaps by going on foot to the town of Slonim and then riding the trains to the capital he might prevail. But when he walked the imagined routes in his mind, another layer of illusion peeled away.

Father was unaware that when he was considering the Polish capital as a destination in July 1942, mass deportations of hundreds of thousands of Warsaw's Jews were under way to Treblinka, the largest of the Nazi annihilation centers. Here, amid twenty hectares, Franz Stangel, the Nazi commandant, who met the Jewish transports dressed in white riding clothes, perfected a German charnel house that worked with clockwork precision. Ever the "gentleman-aesthete," he cultivated a garden retreat in Treblinka for his and his cohorts' delectation. In the first several weeks of that pestilent summer of 1942, a quarter of a million men, women, and children had already been annihilated in Treblinka—it was the largest and swiftest slaughter of single community yet during the war.

That summer, as Father's escape plans floundered, he was summoned to the German officers' compound and ordered to repair a broken main. Armed with work tools, he was left to his own devices. Inside an enclosed passage, he noticed on the grass a note-sized volume bound in navy leather. He peeked around, stooped quickly, and picked up the book, which a German soldier had dropped. He glanced across the yard again; then, to satisfy his curiosity, he opened it to the blank page and saw the Gebitzkommissar's engraved stamp and an imprinted swastika.

He shut the book, looked about him again, and then stole inside a shed nearby. In the dank air, he examined the volume, tore out the sealed page, and rolled it up as if it were some precious papyrus and slipped it gingerly into his pocket. Walking back to the spot where he had first chanced upon the book, he allowed it to drop from his fingers onto the grass. He toiled at the pipe in a fever of anticipation for the rest of the day.

That night, he kept a candle burning, pretending to read in its shallow pool of light. When everyone around him was fast asleep, he removed the rolled sheet, contemplated it, and then drew out a fountain pen and printed a fictitious non-Jewish name at the top of the page. In the space beneath, writing in a formal hand, he improvised a German sentence giving him the right to travel from Novogrudek to Slonim and then on to Warsaw. At the bottom of the page the official-looking swastika had already been affixed, giving it all a crisp, authoritative look. Now that he had some document, or a facsimile of one, he envisioned the proper attire to make his escape. He trembled at these preparations.

IT WAS EARLY JULY and the scent of summer grass filled the air. The mild evening winds rose and the frailer branches cracked and rattled. Rumors of a planned second slaughter filled the Novogrudek ghetto. To confirm its worst fears, a week later it was flooded with refugee Jews from nearby villages.

Among these new unfortunates was Father's maternal cousin Rashaleh, Rochelle, the irony of whose fate still haunts him today. She had lived in Lubcz with her father and mother. They had once been a family of twelve, but harsh tragedy had already struck during the First World War. As the eastern battlefield neared their town and the artillery duels between the Kaiser's and the Czar's armies became all the more fierce, her father sought desperately to save his ten children and wife. He hit upon the idea of digging a hole in the ground and covering it with a thick steel plate, believing this enclosure would keep them out of harm's way while he would somehow fend for himself out in the open. But little could he have known that his chosen hiding place would prove to be their burial ground. A day later the steel plate sustained a direct hit. The shrieking projectile struck with such concussive force that it killed nine of his ten children instantaneously and left his wife without a leg. Rochelle was the only child to come out alive.

She was now, understandably, the apple of their eyes. But soon after the war, her father died of grief and illness. She was left alone with her handicapped mother, who could hardly make ends meet. Rochelle was a quiet, lovely young woman, her cheeks colored as if by an edenic blush. Father's own mother had supported her sister and niece in Lubcz with regular contributions.

Rochelle's uncle Shepsl had left Lubcz as a young man years earlier and traveled to England. He later moved to the northern city of Leeds, married, and acquired a family. Within a generation, in alliance with his grown children, Philip, John, Sydney, and Raymond, an opera singer, he had established a clothing firm, with hundreds of seamstresses, and stores both in London and in the north. An able businessman, Shepsl found Leeds suited him just fine; already in the eighteenth century, its cloth market had been described by Daniel Defoe as "a prodigy of its kind and not to be equaled in the world."

Once successful, Shepsl befriended a mathematician at the University of Leeds, Zelig Brodetsky. A Cambridge graduate and educator, Brodetsky headed the Board of Deputies of British Jews during World War I, the first Eastern European Jew to do so, and succeeded Chaim Weizmann as president of the British Zionist Federation.

By the mid-1930s, as Shepsl felt his days were numbered, he gathered his family and made his children vow that the fatherless Rochelle of Lubcz would be looked after and that all would be done to find her a husband. After some thought it was decided it would be best to bring her to England.

Travel arrangements were expedited: money was wired to Poland, and a visa was obtained. Rochelle, who had retained the innocence of a schoolgirl, left her sickly mother to try her marital fortunes in Western Europe. The station parting was poignant, made more agonizing by her mother's infirmity and nervous susceptibility, and many tears were shed as the train edged out of Lubcz.

She arrived in Leeds in the flush of her young womanhood and stayed there for many months. She took in the sights—City Square, the new Civic Hall, the river Aire. Perhaps she even came across Haworth, a nearby town which housed the parsonage where the Brontë sisters had lived a century ago and where their literary sensibility thrived. Perhaps she wandered across the wild Yorkshire moors, catching their summer hues and dreaming of a perfect love.

Despite many serious attempts, a suitable match for Rochelle was not to be found. Perhaps she had only met what in the north of England are called blatherskites, boastful fellows, or the equally miserable gobslutches, slovenly characters who trespassed her sense of moral decorum. In time her modest hopes dissolved into disillusion. She yearned for her mother, and so at the end of a year's stay she voyaged fatefully back to Poland.

As August of 1942 approached, Father huddled with the husbandless Rochelle, whose mother had just been killed in the Lubcz ghetto together with thousands of others. Withered to a shadow of her former self, she had arrived with nothing but the tattered blouse on her back. The night sky over Novogrudek, filled with brilliant constellations, starkly contrasted with their brief lives.

Matters worsened again in the Novogrudek ghetto. Different-colored passes were distributed to the remaining inhabitants, an ominous sign portending further selections. Then, in early August, a dark convoy of military vehicles—the heralds of doom—carrying hundreds of Estonian auxiliaries, who collaborated with the German mobile killing units, began to snake its way south to Novogrudek. Father then knew the rumor to be fact: the tide of murder was again in full spate.

The Einsatzgruppen—a fearsome mix of Gestapo, criminal police, and SD (Nazi Secret Service) types, accompanied by a striking force of Waffen SS troops and Baltic auxiliaries—were at work industriously all across occupied Russia. Three of the four Einsatzgruppen heads were men with advanced degrees; one of them, Dr. Otto Rasch, the former lord mayor of Wittenburg, birthplace of the Protestant Reformation, boasted two doctorates. The three thousand sub-leaders of the men who comprised the four mobile killing units that fanned across western Russia counted in their midst noted academics, ministerial officials and entertainers—an opera singer to boot.

Hundreds of thousands of Jews had already been shot within hearing range of villages and towns. By July 1942 Wilhelm Kube, Gauleiter of the region, reported with evident glee to the Reich Commissioner for the Baltic States and White Russia, Heinrich Lohse, that fifty-five thousand Jews had been liquidated. However, something of a loose cannon, he argued for the exemption of German-speaking Jews from mass extermination because "people from our cultural circle are quite different from the bestial native hordes." So heinous were these mass murders that he even found it necessary to write to Alfred Rosenberg, Reich Minister for the Occupied Eastern Territories, in Berlin: "Peace and order cannot be maintained in White Russia with resorting to such methods. To have buried alive seriously wounded people, who then worked their way out of their graves again, in such extreme beastliness," was more than even Kube thought necessary. He asked that Rosenberg inform Hitler of this *"bodenlose Schweinerei"*— boundless swinishness—but to no avail. Indeed, had he not been finished off later in the war by Russian partisans, he might well have been done in by his fellow Nazis, for even this sliver of compassion.

The second enactment of the Nazi solution to the Jewish problem in Novogrudek was readied. Father had been spared during the first selection. He considered it foolhardy to push his luck. With Estonian collaborators pouring in, he vowed to get out of the ghetto until the blood storm had passed. He could not endure a day without the promise of some action.

Death hung in the air like a black cloud; the acrid stench of burned powder pervaded the squalid settlement. Father had already decided to escape the next evening. He wanted to take Rochelle with him, but she feared the forests. She who had seen the shores of England now was impaled to Novogrudek. Since the outbreak of war all contact with Leeds and her loving relatives was naturally cut off. She sensed her end approaching, and her energy and voice had almost deserted her. *"Khotsh rateve zikh du aleyn"*—At least save yourself—she whispered into Father's ear.

The next dawn, as his labor team marched out of the ghetto toward the railroad station, he knew the coming night would bring fresh horror.

The day's usual backbreaking labor, portentous silences, and unspoken fears consumed everything in its wake. As the sun descended behind the pines, Father edged away from his group, taking soft steps toward a great log pile. When no one was watching, he crawled beneath the logs and looked up at the green-veined leaves that gave him cover. By early evening the last human voices had trailed off. He lay so still he could hear his heart thumping, each beat a red tide of fear. This was the first time he'd remained outside the ghetto alone. If he were caught, he knew he would be instantly shot.

In a while, he heard a hubbub of high-pitched voices: carefree children at play. Though it was twilight, a group squealing with delight was throwing a ball in an adjacent field. His heart leaped with the rising din of their laughter. Then, as luck would have it, the ball was kicked hard, and it rolled near him. The pounding in his chest grew as he fought for breath.

Rapid little footsteps closed in now, followed by a skirmish of giggles and chuckles. As one youngster suddenly ran up to the logs and began to clamber to the top, Father felt them shift above him. A moment later two large eyes were fixed on him. The child yelled and then climbed down and scampered away. Just as Father breathed more easily, the scamp returned with a friend whose voice Father recognized. It was Mazurek, a teenager who lived near the tracks and who knew him by name as one of the Jews from the ghetto. The boys were now at the base of the pile.

"Why did you drag me here?" Mazurek demanded of the younger boy.

"Climb up and you'll see," he answered.

Father held his breath, and then Mazurek peered into the gloom of the interior.

"Joseph, what are you doing here?" he shouted in surprise.

Father pressed his finger to his mouth. "Shh," he whispered. "I felt ill and could not go back to the ghetto."

Mazurek winked at him and called down to his young friend, "No need to worry." Then he skipped down the wood pile, and they headed into the fields, their bouncing laughter—a sound Father had thought had long gone out of summer—echoing through the trees. Despite Mazurek's jauntiness, Father knew his spot was effectively gone. Word would spread, and if he dared stay the night, he'd be caught in the morning.

He could not stir till it was fully dark. He stared at the monotonous graining of the logs overhead. As soon as the night sky was dotted with stars, he slid from his wooden berth. He crossed the rails, parted the stalks, and walked into the field. He surveyed the dome of the heavens, then lay down amid the bushes and waited for morning.

As sleep closed in, he felt the burden of what he'd begun. He was frightened, but he also knew it was his only hope if he wanted to slip the noose. That's what it had come down to: one more day, each day. This was the wordless and unspoken reality all the Jews lived through then.

Father's escape was hazardous, for he lacked practical outdoor skills and feared discovery. He wondered how long he could go undetected. As dawn bared its face he left his hiding spot and walked toward the work station, hoping to get word from the ghetto. He sat behind a small outbuilding and waited for hours.

In mid-morning, still huddling behind some clapboards, he heard voices coming from the woods, and when he turned to look about him, he saw a group of Novogrudek Jews flanked by German police and SS, en route to the killing site. Shooting would begin soon.

Out in the open, Father grasped at anonymity. As he stood now, anyone could spot him at a glance. He needed to fade into the air, to devise a disguise. Quickly, he slipped out of his threadbare coat and draped it over his shoulders in peasant fashion. He hoisted a shovel left lying near the tracks and began walking the rail, as though he were on his way to work. He didn't move quickly; neither did he tiptoe. He found the tempo a villager might take on his way to the fields. With artless rusticity, he trekked to the sanctuary of the forest.

His mind toiled in brooding solitude, remembering images of the first slaughter. He knew then, instinctively, that the Nazis meant to destroy all the Jews to the very last. No, not to relocate them, as some still thought; not to use them as forced labor, as still others supposed; but to make them vanish like vapor from the face of the world. But somehow he had to find a way of fighting off fatalism. It was vital to keep walking, step after measured step. Just before the forest entrance, near some rotted birch stumps, he spotted a twelve-year-old boy, Shabakovsky, picking his way through the shrubs. A onetime neighbor, he, like Father, had absconded that awful night when darkness had descended over the ghetto. They were overjoyed to see each other, embraced, and began at once discussing what they ought to do now.

"I'm hungry," the youth said. "Do you have anything at all?"

"Nothing, I'm afraid," Father answered. "I haven't eaten in a while, too."

"What are we going to do to get food?" Shabakovsky said mournfully.

Father lowered his head in shame for them both. They trudged through the brambles in hopes of finding some nourishment, however raw. Then they heard shots in the distance. They stopped. These were their dying townspeople. They continued through the low edge of the woods, once the lyric ground of Polish romantic poetry.

As death pressed insistently upon them, they ran willy-nilly through the forest with no clear direction. But the boy's presence was clearly comforting. There was strength in numbers, and two could accomplish more than one. But by sunset Father was tired and famished as well, his face pale and drawn. The two sat down to rest, and Shabakovsky told him he wanted to go to a bunker in which he knew Jews to be hiding out near the woods.

"Forget the bunker," Father said. "It only provides the illusion of security. We'll go through the forest together and be safer that way."

"No! The bunker is safer, I know it, and anyway they may have stashed food there," Shabakolsky protested.

"Stop kidding yourself. A bunker is a bait trap, a dead end," Father said.

"But how much better are we out in the open? We have no protection at all, isn't that worse?"

"At least in the forest we can move. Life can only be preserved on the run."

The boy persisted in his argument, and Father kept on with his. They whispered as they walked through the darkening shade. When they reached a crossroads, Shabakovsky said, "This is the way to the bunker. Are you coming with me?"

"No!" he said. "And I beg you don't do it."

"I don't feel safe out here—and anyway, they'll have some food."

Father had a premonition that the boy was going to his death. "Believe me, you'll be safer with me. You're walking into a trap," he said. But Father's evaluation of their common situation proved useless against his friend's assumptions. The boy was startled by Father's vehemence, but in the end nothing could convince him. When it darkened, he tore away and ran down the forest path toward the bunker. Father watched him become smaller and smaller, his jacket swinging in the twilight, until he disappeared finally in a dark triangle of green between the trees.

Father now stood in the wooded silence wondering where he could find a hiding place. Although the wilderness provided the best cover, it carried its own special perils: German patrols with dogs combed the woods, tracking partisans and Jews. He walked on dejectedly; he'd lost the life in his step. He missed the boy. He knew he'd seen the last of him.

CHAPTER 3

Into the Forest

THE WIND-RUSTLED BRANCHES scraped against Father's side as he penetrated the green shroud of the forest. A sad melody playing in his ear seemed to commune with every rustling leaf. He couldn't shake the thought that young Shabakovsky, left to his own devices, had gone to his end.

A short distance ahead he approached a crooked line of headstones so defaced by time and creeping moss that he did not at first realize he had come upon a long-abandoned White Russian cemetery. As the sun rose, he opened the rusted black gate creaking on its hinges and wandered amid a wilderness of stones. He bent one knee, cleared the graves of overgrown weeds, but could scarcely make out their illegible markings, which seemed beyond recognition or even vague supposition—no more than chaotic lettering effaced by the elements.

He stooped, cupped his palms, and submerged them into a pool of brackish water that had collected in a nearby depression. He drank with burning thirst and barely suppressed revulsion. He let his fingers pass over the lost language of the gravestones. Then he lay on the ground amid the solitude of soundless things. All that remained was the few square feet under him, and perhaps not even that. He was a fugitive among the dead. And yet, here headlong fear retreated for a moment. Precisely on this ground that had suffered a double extinction—the death of the interred and the oblivion wrought by human neglect—Father found a temporary haven.

As the breath of the wind fanned his cheek, he leaned heavily against the spreading root of a tree. Soon he was fast asleep and dreaming of the first days of the 1941 war against the Soviet Union. Images of Nazi bombers—shrieking and nosediving against the blue sky, bringing murderous havoc in their wake—crowded his nightmare. Black plumes of smoke billowed from houses as shells screamed across Novogrudek's marketplace. In the depth of night, he could hear the crash of falling walls as tongues of flames curled up behind rooftops.

These nocturnal thoughts returned him to September 1939, the time of the Nazi Blitzkrieg, which, descending like a cloud of iron, destroyed Warsaw's air force and entire infantry divisions. When the Polish forces sought to regroup around Lvov in the southeast, they found to their dismay, but not surprise, the Soviet Red Army, rumbling across fields of ripening wheat, pouring in on September 17. Warsaw held on desperately against the Nazis for another week, its lines of trenches wavering for days, but the Luftwaffe finished them off. Clandestinely, the sixteenth-century royal tapestries in Wawel came down and were smuggled out by patriotic Poles, first to Romania and then to France and Canada.

Poland, which England and France had promised to protect, became again Europe's phantom, its symbol of martyrdom ignominiously divided between Berlin and Moscow. German radio crackled with the shrill crescendo of Hitler's foul invective. Hans Frank, the Nazi governor general of Poland, announced that "the Polish nation should be transformed into an intellectual desert," with Warsaw turned into a center of slavery.

Father dreamt of Novogrudek, his hometown, where the Polish colors were lowered and local government officials clambered onto the last trains leaving westward just as Soviet tanks rolled in from the east. Grandfather had been alive then, and life in the town, despite dire portents, still had a fullness and a vigor. From his curbside perch, Father watched in late September an entire squadron of Soviet troops come through town. The tramp of their military step echoed for blocks, the brass work of one caparisoned horse a ringing mass of small bells. When their commanding officer gave his rampant thoroughbred the rein, he tossed the newspaper *The Red Star* in Father's general direction and then bounded into a gallop. Father reached into the gutter to pick it up and spent days deciphering the war gazette's Cyrillic script.

Soviet expropriation began in short order. Within weeks the dreaded political commissars of the NKVD (predecessors of the KGB) tightened supply lines for commercial goods, from silk stockings to tea. Red Army soldiers trooped through town, the Polish zloty plummeted in value and then was withdrawn from circulation.

The commissars made sure that the bullet, not the ballot, was now supreme. Stern monks of atheism, these new Grand Inquisitors of unbelief hounded the religiously observant with special malice. Their dictum was "kto ne s'nami, tot protiv nas"—those who are not with us are against us. Schooled by Lenin, they discovered new worlds of malevolence with the rise of Stalin. How prophetic Churchill had been when he said of Soviet Russia: "Their worst misfortune was Lenin's birth; the next worst was his death."

The Soviet soldiers had been deprived of so much that the paltry possessions of the Jews of Novogrudek seemed to them the last word in luxury. Grandfather soon ran out of inventory and shuttered his food shop once nationalization of commerce was in full swing. He feared what the Soviets would do to him, a store owner, a petit bourgeois. With Soviet prodding, he became a piece worker, spending long days in the local employ of the state lumberyard near the train tracks. He knew all too well that those deaf to Soviet-style dialectical reasoning learned their pointed lessons in the Lubyanka box—an overilluminated casketlike enclosure designed to deprive its inhabitant of sleep and sanity—in the wastes of Siberia, or at the end of a bayonet.

A year and a half later, the Germans, in their fierce onslaught on the Soviet Union, drove the Russians out of Novogrudek in a matter of days and began a chapter of unprecedented terror.

THE WIND RUSTLED THROUGH the White Russian cemetery and woke Father. He reared his head against the gravestones carved with their metaphysical futilities, but soon fell asleep again and dreamt of that spring morning in 1940, seven months after Grandfather had lost his shop. He saw him leave for work and shouted, "Papa, can I join you?"

"I can always use an extra hand," Grandfather called back as he exited the door.

They walked to the railroad station under the blue sky creased by broad bands of gray and pink. Their footsteps echoed in the empty streets, where the stillness of night could still be felt. At Grandfather's work station, they stripped the bark off huge logs. They toiled all day, peeling the skins and then flipping the tree boles on their sides. By sunset they were exhausted, and the last tree was the heaviest. Father thought they should leave it for the next day.

"One more big push," urged Grandfather, who liked completed tasks.

Grandfather's neck cords were strained to bursting, his teeth clenched, and his eyes bloodshot. "That a boy," he said, panting heavily, "you're getting the hang of it."

Grandfather leaned against a pole, stumbled a few steps, and sank onto a log. Father himself sat completely still, relaxing from the exertion. After a few minutes he approached him and said, "It's getting late, Papa. We'd better head home." His eyes were closed and he did not respond.

"It's late," Father repeated, and pulled at his sleeve. "Let's go!"

His eyes opened for a moment, staring blankly. His broad chest heaved in a strange motion, and Father could see his breathing was erratic.

"Papa!" He raised his voice. "Answer me! Papa, talk to me!" he pleaded, but Grandfather neither spoke nor moved. A shiver ran through Father.

He raced to the supervisor at the far end of the station, waving his hands and shouting, "Help! I need help now! Something's happened to my father."

The supervisor ordered a horse and carriage to the scene and then he hurried back. Grandfather had not moved or changed his expression. The cart finally arrived and four burly men tried to pull Grandfather, but they could barely move him. He was nailed to the earth as if he belonged to it already. With two men lacing their arms beneath his and two men heaving, they were able to edge him into the carriage. He was now as heavy as lead. Father climbed in after him and cradled his head in his hands as the wooden vehicle bumped from side to side over the rutted road.

At the hospital they pulled Grandfather from the carriage into the stretcher. A young nurse ran, holding his wrist. "This one's serious," the attending doctor whispered as they wheeled him inside.

The room's single bulb dispensed a pale yellow light and sickly sheen. Father sobbed at the sight of Grandfather's head hanging listlessly and his lips gasping for air. The spittle in his mouth quivered in the setting sun. The doctor said it was a cerebral hemorrhage which caused his loss of speech.

"Go home and return tomorrow; nothing more can be done now," the nurse said.

Father ran through the streets, his head tossing with pain and rage. His throat felt as rough as sandpaper. The night wind's shriek was at his heels. He was out of breath when he tore into the kitchen of their home.

"What is it?" Grandmother cried, marking the horrified look he wore.

"Father is in the hospital," he sobbed.

He was unable to go on. She covered her mouth with her hand and paled, averting her head from Father. When his power of speech returned, he told her that the doctor said there was nothing to do but wait, but they decided to leave immediately for the hospital.

The darkening streets stretched interminably. Lightning sundered the horizon, thunder shook the street, and a heavy rain fell. The vacant wind dragged them along. They arrived at the hospital in a downpour.

Entry into Grandfather's room was forbidden. They stood amid nurses and rumors. They looked at him from the doorway, his head lying on a crumpled pillow. His face was contorted, his eyes sunk like deep craters, and his tongue, heavy as wood, lay glued to his stiff jaw. His eyes stared at them, but whatever his lips wished to say was now beyond utterance. He could no longer murmur the *Shema*, the declaration of faith, required of a dying man.

Father stared at the floor, at the clear drops of water falling rhythmically from Mother's uneven hem. He looked up again at his father. The Soviet nurse stood inside the door and forbade them from coming in.

"Regulations," she said, wearing a scowl. She glanced at her watch and they knew she wanted them to be on their way.

"Please let us stay a little longer," he begged. "You can see his condition, can't you?"

"We have everything under control. No visitors at this time of night. You must go now." Father's pleas seemed to provoke her anger rather than her compassion. She motioned to a physician who looked like a truculent gnome.

Father, at the end of his tether, pushed into the room, which reeked of ether. "Have a heart!" he said with despairing appeal.

She stood ramrod straight, flushed a deeper red, and edged him beyond the door.

"I have only one father," he said loudly in protest. "There is no other like him."

The nurse was impervious to his pleas, and further provocation only made her harsher. Grandmother and he eyed each other in mute interrogation. No choice remained but to leave the dim building in the heavy rain. He pulled her stumbingly from street to street, gently tugging her toward awnings and eaves. They arrived at their doorstep soaking wet.

Their home felt strange and uninhabited. Grandmother sank down in a chair, wrung her hands, and sat up all night, her head bowed at the kitchen table. He opened Grandfather's psalm book and considered the sorrow and beauty within its thin yellowed pages.

Grandfather died that night, the Sabbath before Shvues, the Jewish Pentecost. He was fifty-two years old.

The bright yolk of the sun shone with perverse cheer when they brought his body home. It was at the extremity of grief that Father understood amid the blossoming spring Melville's line he would read a half century later: "All Nature absolutely paints like a harlot, whose allurement covers nothing but the charnel-house within."

Four friends hoisted Grandfather's shrouded corpse and, bowing their covered heads, laid him on a straw mat on the floor, carefully draping him with a black sheet. They lit four candles and placed them above his head. Ten men came to chant David's Psalms, his beloved prayer. Grandmother sank tremblingly to her knees. Father could not get the words out.

Grandfather was not buried in a regular coffin but was returned to the earth wrapped in a white shroud. The sextant smashed black clay pots and placed the shards gently over his eyes. In his sorrow Father remembered the Yiddish adage, *"A kind iz geborn mit kulyakes, a man shtarbt mit ofene hent"*—A child is born with clenched fists in defiance of the world; a man dies with open hands, in submission.

Four wooden planks were set around him, one placed underneath his lowered body, two on either side and one over his prone frame. The sun's hot rays came at them vertically, and discordant cries of lamentation filled the air. Father looked vacantly at the moist, hungry earth. The shovelfuls of soft soil that covered Grandfather buried a part of him as well. At dusk only the wind remained, a mute emptiness with no horizon.

On his way back home, he thought of Grandfather's spirit of adventure

that had driven him across seas and continents and then remembered another Yiddish saying: *"Kol-zman der mentsh lebt iz im di gantse velt tsu kleyn,
nokhn toyt iz der keyver genug"*—As long as one lives, the whole world is
too small; after death, the grave is big enough.

The days thereafter were barren of life's promises. As if to further affirm
the essential absurdity of the human condition, the broad fields and dense
birch groves surrounding Novogrudek loudly celebrated spring, and the
town's street vendors hawked crimson poppies and roses.

WHEN FATHER CAME TO from his night-long dream, he called out
Grandfather's name instinctively. He saw the leaves laced against the sky
and heard the song of birds, whose delicate frames rested on shading
branches. The sun rose and with it the fear of detection even in this remote
spot. And with fear, a renewed longing for life.

He pulled out his mother's knitted cap and pressed it to his cheek, touching its rim and soft fabric. He stared at it for a long time, and then he buried
his tear-streaked face in its folds.

Soon a great storm blew up and the first rain fell through the leaves.
Huge drops splashed against old gravestones, and treetops swayed like bare-
headed worshippers, as twigs and small branches sailed down on him.

It rained for hours and then for days. Thunder boomed above and rolled
away into the forest. A heavy downpour slanted in sheets to the sopping
ground. The wet earth and black sky seemed to stretch endlessly without
another human shadow in the resounding emptiness. Then through the
torrent he heard the whistle of the train that left from nearby Novoyelna
and Novogrudek. But for all he knew it might be carrying German soldiers
ready to dispatch him, if they only knew his whereabouts. He imagined
the sound of their coarse laughter and dug himself a deeper hole in the wet
earth of the cemetery.

On the evening of the fourth day the rain stopped, but by then Father's
strength had ebbed. His stomach growled and would not be silenced. He
had no alternative but to venture beyond the gates of the cemetery.

He rose with difficulty, swayed on his feet, and meticulously wrung out
his dripping clothes. He walked passed the century-old tree trunks. There

was no edible food here, so he headed back in the direction he had come. He feared detection, and every few meters he slouched against a tree, listening for the faintest sounds.

After the buffeting of the rain, he continued treading the dark forest, in search of a seclusion beyond capture. When he accidentally stumbled on a small patch of radishes, whose red tops seemed like the most succulent of fruits, he tore them rudely from the ground and rubbed off their caked dirt, biting into one with relish. He had been brought to such extremes of hunger that he would have chewed grass to stop his pangs. By the time he had gorged on two radish bunches and was about to start on his third he heard a mortar shell in the distance.

He threw himself to the ground, let the radishes roll away, and dug his fingers into the mud as the blood roared in his temples. He wondered if he been tracked into the heart of the forest. Had the Nazis counted the ghetto residents and found him missing? Why, he cried with rage, do the Germans have the greater share of the world? But whatever the answer or lack thereof, he knew he could not slacken his vigilance.

Soon it was quiet, and he moved as noiselessly as a lynx. Again he listened to the wind, but it was an empty noise, carrying no consolation, only a death lament. Night and the forest swallowed him up. The next morning his strength nearly gave out. He felt he was going to die alone, but he secreted himself there till dusk, and then after a while, he willed himself to return to his former work station.

It was five days since he had escaped, and those Jews spared had been forced back to the ghetto. The work station was abandoned. A melancholy air blew through the trees lining the road. Did anyone survive? he wondered.

A Pole whom he knew appeared in the middle distance. Should he approach or hide? His hunger and desperation were such that he tossed caution to the wind.

"Have you seen any of those who used to work here?" Father called out.

"They're all gone, except for you," the Pole said.

"What do you mean by 'gone'?" he said. "Gone where?" he added disingenuously.

"They're gone, finished, no more," the Pole said, drawing his hand across his throat.

"Every last one of them?" Father pleaded.

"Well, all who used to work here with you. But there's a new contingent coming from the ghetto."

"Will you lead me to them?" he asked him.

"If that's what you want," he said.

It was the most troubling paradox Father had yet encountered. To re-enter the ghetto he risked death, but staying alone in the forest was also to invite fatality; it was merely extinction by other means. He would have to enter a prison the more effectively to escape it, but this time with others and with a plan.

He hid out in the forest till the following morning, a prey of wild fears. The informative Pole was as good as his word. The next day some surviving Jews came to the work station, and they confirmed Father's dreaded ima-ginings. What they related was enough to heave the mind from its base.

On the very evening he had chosen to hide out in the woodpile, the German SS and their Estonian auxiliaries had blocked the gates with their trucks.

Arriving from the north with gusto, the Estonians had stood with their guns ready. It was August, and mists of damp heat rose up from the fields. To while away the time, they sported with the Jews, locked some in stables and watched them starve. Trying to stave off the worst, the Jews tried to bribe their tormenters; they pulled off their wedding rings, last precious gems, and brooches in exchange for water. The guards pocketed their valuables and brought just enough water to whet rather than quench their thirst. They watched gleefully as the desperate failed to slake their thirst. The next day the Estonians redoubled their demands, but this time, when they collected their booty, no water appeared at all. Night then hurried to cover the vic-tims' wails. This wantoning with the innocent pleased the Nazi auxiliaries to no end, and they often were heard laughing themselves into a stupor.

The race for life was on again. "Don't obey their orders. It will only end in death," was the imperative refrain. People dug bunkers and constructed special hiding places in the most inventively improbable of places.

During the second slaughter of Novogrudek the Jews suffered a fate no less barbarous than those of the first. Their Nazi killers and Baltic henchmen assembled into small hunting bands and gave full vent to their bloodlust. They tore into the heart of the ghetto, ripped doors off their hinges, smashed locks, and splintered anything that stood in their way.

The scene of entrapment was infernal. The young children in hiding cried and sobbed out of terror as their parents desperately cajoled them into silence. Father heard of agonizing cases where babies were smothered out of fear their cries would betray an entire bunker of cowering Jews.

In the end, parents and children were hounded from their contrived hiding places. Attack dogs were let loose among the innocent, who once captured were forced to lie face down on the pavement. Dragged to the outskirts of Novogrudek, they were made to crawl to their freshly dug graves, as the martyrs of the first slaughter had been. *"Shema Yisrael"* lay on their lips during their last moments before their bodies were gashed by bayonets and torn by bullets. These final Hebrew words bound them to those who slaved and died on the Pyramids, who shed their blood on the ramparts of Jerusalem during the Crusades, and who cried out their faith at the burning stakes of the Inquisition.

When Father returned to the ghetto he saw eerily empty homes, ghostly streets with the possessions of the dead strewn everywhere, the ground spattered with blood. The entire ghetto was a memento mori, a grievous picture of horror that resists paraphrase. Father knew that his cousin Rochelle was among the dead.

The town was haunted by a silence that the Hebrew poet Bialik, writing of a previous massacre, had said, "only God can bear."

Father knew now incontrovertibly that the Nazis were determined to erase Jews from the earth. Their modus operandi were crimes of such magnitude as to make the very conception of human punishment absurd. Yet even with the facts so fresh on the ground, it was still hard for the mind to absorb such atrocity. He had been taught in *kheder* and then in the rabbinical academies of Baranowicze and Kletzk that man was created to imitate God, commanded to be merciful on earth. But here and now he confronted a world closer in kinship with the demonic than with the divine.

After a few weeks in the Novogrudek ghetto, Father began to hear word of a third slaughter in the making. Again Jews were divided into two ghettos and the unskilled were grouped together by the Nazis for extinction. Often their despair was so uncompromisingly pure that they understood their situation entirely. The others, raging at their own powerlessness, threw them compassionate glances as they were led away, knowing they would never be seen alive again. Invocations of divine or human retribution were heard, but in time realism prevailed.

Father's desire to escape again crowded out every other thought. But where to find weapons or accomplices? He careened from one plan to another till he decided to visit Uncle Itche, who had raced into the court-house bleeding from the head during the first slaughter. Father's last living relative in the ghetto, he had lost his wife and daughters—was bereft of everything. He had become increasingly despondent, and every trace of life seemed to have vanished. He mostly stared fixedly in front of him. Father wavered for a number of days, but then, with the time ticking in his head, he sat down to reason with Itche.

"Uncle, you've survived two slaughters. We've lost everything. Let us join together and escape."

Uncle Itche looked down. Deep gloom had descended on him. He hardly ever looked into anyone's eyes anymore.

"Uncle, now is the time," Father said emphatically.

"Where do you propose to go?" Itche finally asked.

"Into the woods. Once there, we'll flee to a larger city and find refuge," Father said, his voice rising with conviction.

"But isn't it the same everywhere?" Itche asked resignedly.

"Don't say that. We must leave soon, before the third slaughter begins in earnest."

"If I am fated to live, let it be here," he said, the mark of death already set firmly on him.

"You're giving up!" Father said, almost shouting. "That's exactly what they want, don't you see?"

Itche lifted his heavy eyelids and stared blankly at him and then into the distance. He did not offer another word and relapsed into his customary torpor. If only Itche's despondency could be turned into anger, rage, and, ultimately, determination! But Father suspected that when disillusionment had advanced this far, little could be done in a hurry. He shrugged, more in sorrow than in anger, then stood up and said, "Good night, Uncle. I'll come to see you tomorrow," and drifted out the door.

Father shuffled through the streets to his quarters. He desperately needed to find a companion-in-arms with whom to flee. Perhaps someone who would be a friend, too, though he thought that might be too much to hope for.

The third slaughter was imminent when Jewish refugees from such nearby towns as Lida and Zhetel began flooding Novogrudek. The Nazis were waiting for a critical mass to perpetrate a new massacre. These latest

arrivals, many of whom were young men and women well acquainted with
the nightmare awaiting them, still felt the ardor for life burning at full wick.
Father decided to approach some and broach his escape plans.

Stealing out of the ghetto as a group—getting past the barbed wire and
the watchtowers manned round the clock—would be an effort, they agreed.
But what choice did they have if they wanted to survive? And so there
were seven now, all schooled in trauma.

Father set to work at once. On Friday he purchased with the little money
he had left a large pair of scissors from a tinsmith in the ghetto. He carefully
wrapped the crude implement in ragged cloth, stuffed it into a shoulder
bag, and then headed toward the ghetto perimeter, where some members
of his escape group were assigned to dig an outhouse, conveniently positioned in an area just in from the fence. Father sat nearby, idling for a
moment. When the guard rounded a corner, he shuffled toward the fence,
unwrapping the scissors slowly as he walked. He dropped to his knees and
swiftly cut the bottom wire, He left the two halves in place to avoid detection, then turned around and trudged back to the courthouse, the center
of the second ghetto.

After a longer interval he was back at the conspiratorial site. He plumped
down on the ground and waited for the guard to move along on his rounds.
When he was out of sight, Father moved quickly to the fence, cut the
second wire, and left it in place, like the first. To the naked eye, nothing
looked changed.

He shoved his scissors back into his bag and was off. After a further decent
interval he was back and worked until dark. Seven trips for seven wires, all
now duly severed, allowing just enough crawl space.

Dusk the next day found the seven at their agreed point of assembly.
They waited in the stillness while evening's first inky shadows made the
ground's unevenness fade. As soon as the White Russian guard turned the
corner, Father crouched and motioned for the first man to approach. While
he scuffled toward him, Father lifted the wires for him to crawl through.
He crouched and ran toward the trees, then dove to the ground and lay on
his stomach.

Father signaled for the second man to come. He ran toward him, bent
low and ungainly, and crawled through the opening in the wires. The
others, watching intently, then passed through singly in quick succession.
Now it was Father's turn, and there was no margin of error. He must leave

no telltale signs of their escape—the wires must be repositioned perfectly so as not to raise any suspicions.

Just as Father was about to bend down, he heard footsteps; he froze in his tracks. He surmised that their plan had been discovered and all was up. He wanted to turn around and see who was approaching, but he thought it wiser to keep his eyes fixed on the ground. To his amazement and relief, the footsteps faded into the distance. Father gulped for air. He needed to make haste; the others, who were on the other side, would be worried if he tarried.

He looked around surreptitiously and then slid under the wires. He turned and rapidly repositioned them. Then he dove into the thickets. When he was safely on the other side, he lay panting on the ground, only then realizing how spent he was. They waited in silence for the cover of darkness, then rose as one and walked away from the ghetto.

CHAPTER 4

Across the Nieman

THE FOREST SPREAD OUT thickly before them. For hours they walked in silence, listening to the faintest noises. Often they felt like shadows scampering along the inclines of the forest path. After many blind turns, they spotted a dirt road that would lead them out of Novogrudek. At its shoulder they crouched and in a zigzag line ran across it to the familiar fields that had once framed Father's birthplace. With the lightest of footfalls, they now headed to Lida, the next large town to the north.

They awoke to the palpitation of morning. That day they lay in the forest's lush green coil. Daylight had become their enemy: to budge when the sun was high was to risk discovery. By nightfall the wind had risen, and they began their trek northward. Before long they reached the Nieman River, stretching in front of them like a great question, and they did not know if any answer lay beyond. Its shores were separated by a stretch of flowing water, on whose surface the moon's bare reflection extended into the distance.

How were they to cross the Nieman's depths? Not one of them could swim. And down a ways a bridge arched above the current, heavily guarded by Nazi auxiliary troops. They walked along the bank for miles, listening to the moving water as to a dirge.

Their eyes searched for a craft to convey them to the other side. In the gathering darkness they spotted the outline of a large raft fixed to a mooring on the opposite shore. In the moonlight, it rocked quietly at anchor. They spent the night figuring out how to board this conveyance.

At dawn the Nieman unfurled its gray-blue expanse. They found a gully to slide into, a secure hiding place in the brush. They crouched close to the ground and watched the morning sun daub the sky.

After dawn the raft began its first crossing of the day. Deftly maneuvering a series of ropes, an unkempt pilot conducted the raft through the channel, ferrying several times a day passengers, beasts, and cargo. At night he anchored the craft on the far side of the river and walked home. Unfortunately, the craft was never moored on their shore, obliterating their plans to steal aboard at night and pull the raft across themselves. They waited in vain for five nights, as the river lay folded in moonlight and framed by a dark mass of trees. With each passing day they watched their hoard of bread dwindle and then disappear.

They could delay no longer. They had to cross that day, for the road back was barred. On the sixth afternoon, Father told the others he would walk to the raft to see what could be done. Dressed in his peasantlike clothing, his blond hair carefully combed, his back pocket bulging with a packet of tobacco, he was ready to take the risk of bribing any comer if necessary.

He crawled out of the brush and headed toward the road that led like a thin ribbon to the river. No sooner had he stepped onto it than he heard a cart and pony trotting behind him, kicking up the soft dust. He slowed and tilted his head in the direction of the driver.

"Do you have a match perhaps?" Father asked the driver.

"Ah!" The stranger smiled. "A man with tobacco, no doubt,"

"You guessed it," Father said in a free-and-easy manner no Jewish refugee could assume.

The stranger's eye sparkled as soon as Father revealed his small stash of tobacco. "Boy, do I need a smoke," he said in colloquial Polish.

"Machorka," Father said, describing the brand. "It's cheap, but it's good."

With brash self-assurance, he handed him some granules, and the Pole's eyes rolled heavenward.

"By the way, do you know when the next river raft crossing is?" Father asked.

"In about an hour. It's the next-to-the-last crossing."

While he spoke, Father rolled the tobacco and lit himself a makeshift cigarette, which he generously shared with his newfound friend. They approached the landing in a cloud of fragrant fumes while the raft was still in mid-passage. They waited as it drifted ashore. Despite his show of sociability, Father carefully kept his distance.

The rafter fixed his ropes, then fell to speaking to the peasant. The passengers then disembarked single-file.

After checking the ropes and washing his face in the river's dark, swirling waters, the rafter shouted, "All aboard!"

Father's smoking acquaintance drove his horse and wagon on ahead and then turned to him, "Well, aren't you coming, friend?"

"Oh, I am crossing a little later. I'm waiting for a relative."

"Ah! Too bad you're not coming now. We could go the marketplace in Lida and get some good tobacco."

"Well, maybe some other time," Father said, waving goodbye.

The raft's steersman slipped its lines, and after the rickety craft had traveled some distance Father returned to his companions.

"The moment it darkens, we're getting on that raft."

They nodded their heads.

At twilight they found a new hiding place in the bank of the river near the landing. Father told the others to be on alert.

"When you hear the whistle, crawl quietly out of the hiding spot and run straight to the raft," Father commanded.

As the twilight shadows lengthened, the raft inched ashore. The pilot waved his cap to Father.

"Still here? You're probably going to take the last passage."

"That's right. Actually, I'm also waiting for a relative."

"Look, buddy, its getting late, and I'm going to make the crossing in a few minutes. So be quick about it, okay?"

"Don't worry. I actually hear him in the near distance."

"Where?" the steersman said as he steadied the raft.

"Don't you see the dust swirling on the road?"

"I don't see a thing," he said.

Father whistled loudly. "Perhaps he will hear me now and not lose his way."

On cue, Father's fellows began to edge out from the trees, one at a time.

"What's taking him so long?" the rafter said impatiently. He was puttering around on the raft and so did not see any of those approaching.

Father whistled once, twice more, while his companions continued to approach silently.

"So long then—I've got to go," the ferryman said.

"Oh, give me another minute or so."

"Look, you seem like a nice fellow, but I've got to get to the other side. I've got no time to waste," he said.

"Please wait another second," Father pleaded as he waved to his companions to race toward the shore. They were still fifty meters away.

"No, no. I'm late as it is. Either you get on now or I'm moving without you."

"Okay!" Father yelled and jumped on. The steersman began to work the ropes the moment he boarded. Father's group picked up speed, sloped down to the water's edge, and as the boat began to drag, lurch, and then drift off, they leaped aboard in one bounding lunge, nearly careening the bark.

"My God! Thieves! Help!" the rafter shouted in an avalanche of curses and imprecations. He was pale, crossed himself repeatedly, and finally let go of the ropes. The raft began to list. Father then grabbed hold of them and began to maneuver the raft back on course. Some of the other fellows then took over while he peered at the streaming darkness of the water.

"Who are these people?" the rafter asked Father accusingly as he continued to cross himself.

"Just ferry us across. We mean you no harm," Father said in a fever of impatience.

"How can I know?" He shot a dark glance at Father.

"You have our word," he said.

"Some word! You said your relative was joining and now I've got a tribe on my hands!"

"Look, we're in a tight spot—just ferry us across!" Father fairly shouted.

"Nothing but thieves," the man mumbled. "My damned luck!" he said, eyeing Father disapprovingly.

Father understood that only a bribe would silence him; otherwise he could betray all of them.

Father collected a few coins from the others, knowing there was no choice if they wanted to turn the steersman friendly.

"Don't be angry," Father said as he turned smilingly to him. "This is for you." He emptied the coins into the man's hand and said, "Buy yourself some good vodka."

Father was anxious to discover what effect this had on him. In a minute the rafter's features softened, and soon he was chatting with them as he took charge of the ropes.

"By the way, fellows, the road over there is lined with police," he suddenly volunteered. "And there are German soldiers coming through," he added conspiratorially.

"Where exactly?" Father asked.

"Well, all I can tell you is that a few days ago, in Bilitza, a posse of White Russian policemen patrolled the area. Probably hunting for Jews."

Father scanned the approaching shore to see where they could hide.

"By the way, where can we rest up once we get to shore?" he asked.

"You're okay guys, so I'll let you in on a secret. There's a hollow among the bushes a stone's throw from the shore. Hide there till it's quiet and move only when it's dark."

"Thanks," Father said, slipping him another coin for good measure.

The raft cut through its final minutes to the shore. A crescent moon danced on the waves.

As Father looked at the shadowy water and then at their white-haired ferryman, he suddenly noticed that in the corner of the raft a pile of rags heaved with life.

"What is that?" Father jumped from his spot and pointed.

"I don't know," the ferryman said.

The shifting rags emitted an inhuman groan and nearly inaudible cries of lamentation. Father's companions stepped back.

They then noticed a strange visage, a living skeleton, among the heaps. A beastly face with an expression of wild sorrow rose from the heaps, its long, matted hair and unshorn beard becoming more visible as the madman's rags fell away.

"My God—it's the pharmacist from Bilitza!" one of Father's companions said, horror-stricken.

They surmised that the educated and once well-turned-out Jewish phar-

macist had lost his family to the Einsatzgruppen and had become this
wild-looking forest creature, whose eyes scarcely moved in their sockets.
He was covered with mud, and grief had dug deep furrows in his brow.
He seemed beyond all charitable prompting, so far had his humanity dis-
integrated. Surely, he was too well-born to bear this kind of world.

He must have scrambled onto the raft under cover of darkness while it
was tied to the shore post. They tried to keep their eyes averted from the
bleak infinity of his face. He shattered something fundamental in them.

The rafter roped the vessel to the standing pole and began to rush them
off the craft.

"Just one thing, boys," he said. "If you're caught by the patrols, just
don't say you've been this way."

"Okay," Father said.

The rafter finished tying his lines to the landing place. They climbed
from the platform in the dark. The pharmacist shuffled off alone toward
the trees. A breach in the woods led them to their shelter.

They reached the hollow and settled there for the evening. But the
blasted image of the wolf man haunted them all that night. There was
something irrevocably fatal about him; it had the harrowing ability to pull
them irresistibly along with it and weaken their strength to resist.

THEY WERE ON THE move again, nearing Lida all the time. In the
darkening shadow they saw dense colonnades of fir. The night grew pitch
black, and they stumbled blindly. Slowly they spotted muddy pools where
leaves had gathered.

Dogs howled in the stillness as they approached a creek. Father was
fatigued and wanted to rest, but the others now urged him on as they raced
against the next morning's sun.

The creek was too wide for them to wade through. To cross they had
to climb up onto a slippery log that snaked high above the water to the
other side, and then crawl along its entire length. The round log was shorn
of its branches and there was nothing to hold on to. To lose one's balance
would mean to be impaled on the rocks studding the creek.

A strong wind blew through their unkempt hair as they fell in one behind
the other. Father's hands, clammy with fear, could scarcely grip the log. He

pushed his arms mechanically ahead of him out onto the damp, cylindrical wood. Below, the moon tossed in the water's tumble. Anxiety drove him as he edged along, his hands trembling, to the end of the slippery log. One after another they crossed. It was only later that he realized the night had turned cool.

They increased their speed, for morning would soon be upon them. Scampering across the thick underbrush, they soon reached a clearing. Behind them the dark wall of the forest loomed. They reached a set of railroad tracks amid a newly risen wind and could see the train station, a dark building set in a clearing. They softened their steps, increased their guard, falling into a silent single file.

They debated whether they should continue down this path. Seeing that they had no alternative, they proceeded.

Suddenly, a window in the small building adjoining the station was flung open by an unseen hand and they heard a shout: *"Halt!"*

"Spread out," Father whispered to his fellows.

They raced across the clearing and shots followed them in rapid succession. The run seemed interminable as bullets tore the ground around their feet. Fear came in waves as they fell to the ground to evade the fire. They felt the approach of death as the Germans would begin to scout the area and unleash their killer dogs.

He wondered how they ever had allowed themselves to walk into this predicament. Father grasped they had invited disaster by coming too close to the train station.

In a few minutes all was silent. It was as if the forest itself were holding its breath. But Father was up a moment later, gathering his shaken friends. The image and sound of rifle bolts snapping into place kept them on the go. They marched till they lost their pursuers.

CHAPTER 5

*Entry into
Lida and Vilna*

THEY WALKED INTO THE gloom of the forest, on the alert for swarming Nazi patrols. They traveled in cadence for five nights, amid the motionless pines, their ears tuned to the subtlest frequencies of sound, their mood one of loss and longing. It was as if the topography itself were heavy with foreboding. Every daybreak, routed by the pursuing sun, they hid in the darkest recesses of the forest. Father had never imagined that a time would come when he would have to curse the sunrise.

They sensed they were now three miles from Lida, once a center of what some considered advanced orthodox thought. As Father trudged through the forest, he remembered once hearing that Rabbi Isaac Jacob Reines, the spiritual leader of Lida at the turn of the century, and a close friend of Theodore Herzl, had founded a modern yeshiva in the shtetl that allowed the concurrent study of religious and secular subjects—a revolution at the time, as well as having established the *Mizrachi* (religious Zionist) movement in Vilna in 1902. In a while a breeze wafted through the foliage, but then a wind blew up in middle of the night. It grew fierce, and swept all before it. The air turned moist and a fine rain began to fall. The wind's velocity increased and it soon howled, the storm-bent branches lashing against the seven and drenching them to the bone. They grew cold and began to tramp on to the main road of Lida.

Before they could enter the city, however, they had to dust themselves off. They were filthy, tired, and limping with pain. In passing through the town to the ghetto they could not afford to appear disheveled and raise the locals' suspicions. To their luck, they approached a pond-studded bog a mile and a half from town. Tall grasses offered a screen from intruders. They trudged deeper into its damp interior, past its matted growth, and then beyond the outlying bog tufts. They lay in its secluded waters for hours. Here they found relief for their mud-caked feet, swollen from walking through the thickets and dense brambles. They removed their battered shoes, rubbed their soles, and soaked their feet in the brackish water.

When the sun set, they slipped out of the bog and onto the lightly traveled road. On the horizon they saw the tapering spire of the town's churches. They walked singly and anonymously, since none of them carried proper identification. The gray ash of twilight drifted down the clouds, and then night was upon them.

Much as in Novogrudek, the wreckage in Lida was everywhere—the magnitude of the disaster that had overtaken its Jews was evident wherever one turned. Members of their group who hailed from Lida directed them to the Jewish cemetery which bordered one side of the ghetto.

They waited amid the ancient gravestones, roofed in by tall trees, until the guard changed and a Jewish policeman manned the entrance. He waved them through in the moonlight. Once they were within its confining walls, his fellow escapees separated, each to find his next of kin, if he was lucky enough to still have any alive in the ghetto.

Father remembered his relatives in Lida, prosperous owners of a boot factory and a lakeside hotel. Were they still alive? he wondered. He inquired, but no one seemed to know their whereabouts till one elderly man, who recognized their names, guided him down a forsaken street.

Cousin Dina and her children, once the envy of their family, famous for their well-bred posture and manners, were crowded in a dilapidated house with other ghettoized Jews. A tall, strikingly aristocratic woman, Dina, now stood bent with age and care. She no longer had the repose born of comfortable country-house living, although one could still trace the delicate veins on her brow as if on the glaze of china. Her son, Mulla, who relatives once said could have passed for a matinee idol, still retained his good looks, as did her daughter, Roza, a young woman who rarely left her mother's side.

They listened to Father with audible murmurs of sympathy. Roza gazed at him with her dark, watchful eyes. He hadn't seen her in many years and could hardly recognize her, although her smile hung in the air like a scar.

"Father was exiled to Siberia by the Soviets in the summer of 1940," Roza explained.

He nodded in commiseration.

"My father is dead on account of them," he added.

She wiped a tear from her lashes as she turned away.

She let a moment pass, then said, "The center of Lida, where most of the Jews live, was bombed last year."

"Just as in Navaredok," Father said. "They have one and one plan alone—to kill us all."

They both looked at the floor.

"Roza," he said, "I'm only staying here for a day or so."

"Where are you going?" she asked with a quiver of hope.

"To Vilna," he answered. "It's our only hope. You must know that Lida, like Navaredok, is a trap."

"What am I to do? What are any of us to do?"

"Let's flee together. Gather everybody and we'll escape."

"But Mother can't go," she said, lowering her eyes.

"Perhaps she can if she realizes how desperate things are here."

"No, she'll never consent, and I cannot leave her. I could never live with myself."

He looked away for a minute. She didn't have to say more. Everything was filled with private grief and silent exclamation.

"But you must do something," he insisted, although by electing to stay with her family she at once occupied the moral high ground and the certain terrain of death.

The next day he took leave of Roza and the others. It was a difficult parting, the final one. They could say nothing more to each other. To be alive now was to be alone with one's fate.

The air was heavy with premonition. Roza's face shone in the late-afternoon light, and the look of death in her eyes haunted Father for a long time thereafter.

Of the six that had escaped the Novogrudek ghetto with him, only a tiny fraction decided to take to the forests again. They hugged the ghetto walls, listening to the swaying branches, and cautiously approached the Jewish guard, asking him the way to Vilna.

"Take the sideroads only," he said. "After some ten miles you will near a vast circular stone wall. Avoid it at all costs!"

"Why?" they asked.

"A posse of Germans are stationed there. You are as good as dead if you fall into their hands."

The two thanked him profusely and wished him well.

They tramped in the forest all night long. A cold breeze had risen, and its breath played cruelly on their faces. They traversed for miles without any clear idea of where they were, always in fear of the whereabouts of the dreaded wall. They treaded softly after marching most of the night torn by the howl of wild winds.

Just before dawn the forest was impenetrably thick and they could see nothing. But they walked on heedlessly, and found themselves facing an inchoate mass. They took another sharp right and approached a forest clearing. In an adjoining field a white horse stood chomping on the grass. In the near distance a few blurry lights burned in the sleepy village.

The animal's placidity lulled them into a false sense of calm. As they scanned the field, they saw that it was roped to a man. They hesitantly edged into the middle of the field where the peasant lay softly in the folds of sleep. They had not taken more than a few dozen steps when a crash of bullets tore the ground all around them.

They dispersed blindly. Father's satchel banged furiously against his side as he darted for cover, and the closeness of death sharpened his senses. After scattering like hares, they lay prone for a long time. When they attempted to rise, the barrage continued, forcing them to the ground. Now they understood that they had come upon the circular wall and how right the guard at the Lida ghetto had been.

The perilous forest made them realize how rootless they had become, creatures trapped between an irrecoverable past and a death-haunted future.

They felt night's departure regretfully. As the sun rose, they trembled, their eyes monitoring every inch of ground like precision instruments. From their forest perch, they saw farmers plying horses with the butts of whips. And at noon golden rivulets of light seeped through the trees, sharpening their fears, and heightening the possibility of German ambush.

They surmised—naively—that Vilna had not yet descended into savagery. In a cultural hub, the Germans perhaps would be shamed into retaining a trace of humanity, a vain hope that gave them stamina to hazard the forest brush.

Father had guided the group from Novogrudek to Lida, but it was now the turn of his fellow—and only remaining—refugee, Leybke ben-Osher, to lead the way. He knew the route from Lida to Vilna from childhood, had threaded through all its secret paths before. If anyone could find his way through Vilna's woods, he could. Alas, his familiarity gave rise to complacency and occasional recklessness.

"Keep your head down," Father admonished Leybke when they reached the forest rim. Only when dark had finally descended was Father able to relax.

After meandering several more days, Leybke neared the house of a friendly Pole he had known before the war. He remembered those happy days when his parents, trusted far and wide, had supplied meat to the Polish army.

They finally tracked him down, a peasant wearing a white shirt with a frayed collar. Now they neared his hut but didn't approach until they listened for suspicious noises. Having circled his hovel a number of times, they crouched among the bushes and saw a lamp emitting a pale yellow glow. In the yard a horse stood grazing in a hollow.

Gingerly for a change, Leybke approached the back window and knocked softly. After a long interval a curtain parted and the Pole, visibly agitated, his eyes looking out of a soft mass of wrinkles, motioned for them to go to the front of the hut, where he would be waiting.

"Has anyone seen you?" he whispered.

"No," Leybke reassured him.

"Then come in quickly."

He sat them down and then bounded to the window. The wind grumbled in the chimney. He knew, as they did, that if he was caught he would be shot.

"Help us find a way of getting into the Vilna ghetto!"

"Not so simple," the Pole answered in a whisper, scratching his forehead and grizzled locks.

Father's face fell.

"Don't lose heart," the Pole continued. "It's not entirely impossible. For example, you might attach yourself to the Jewish labor column that passes at six from the airport on its way back to the ghetto."

As he spoke, they saw the advanced age on the old man's kindly face. With each of his words, he seemed to be in greater fellowship with the angels than with any sublunary creatures. Father recalled Jacob's dream in which angels ascend and descend from heaven on ladders. Getting into the Vilna ghetto now might prove as maddeningly challenging as arriving in heaven.

The rough-hewn Pole coughed and spat on the floor. "As soon as the column of marching Jewish laborers begins to turn the corner on this road and heads in the direction of the gate, you emerge from the bushes. If all goes well, you then join them while the guards are looking ahead. Understand?"

The late-afternoon sun set in bands of orange and pink. Leybke and Father fell into position amid the thick shrubbery and waited. The Pole stood in his doorway on the lookout. He kept nervously glancing at his watch.

After a long wait they heard from afar the tramp of feet. The Pole motioned them to get ready. A long column of four men across marched in unison, their wrists hanging loosely from their bedraggled sleeves.

Dusk gathered as the thud of approaching feet echoed louder. The Jewish column was almost upon them. The Pole cued them to approach.

They stole forward, crouched so low that they could nearly touch the feet of the tired men as they were about to pass them. Just as the tail end of the long column approached, the guards providentially turned their heads away. Father and Leybke edged out of the bushes and leaped into line, knocking into a couple of Jews, who, although surprised and taken aback, kept silent.

—⁂—

VILNA LAY WRAPPED IN an envelope of gloom, soon to be sealed by night. They entered the city to the sounds of horse hooves scampering along cobblestone streets. Worn and grizzled, Vilna no longer resembled the baroque city of the interwar years on which so many superlatives had been lavished—cradle of Talmudists, cauldron of revolutionaries, crucible of Yiddishists and Hebrew enlighteners, ranked with such medieval centers of learning as Troyes, Toledo, and, some would even say, the Sura and Pumbeditha of ancient Babylon.

In the distance the bells of the city's spires sounded as if in mournful accompaniment to their shuffling gait. German guards posted at the ghetto gates would pose the greatest danger. Father's heart quieted when instead he saw Jewish policemen positioned there. But even then the labor column ran the risk of Nazi guards returning without warning, lopping off the end of the line for sadistic sport.

The gates shut behind them like fate itself.

Father milled around like a lost sheep, looking beseechingly at faces in the streets. Leybke had run off to find his next of kin, leaving him to his own devices. He did not know where to turn. He knew nobody, and so far as he could tell no one knew him. As he passed from street to street, posters advertised every kind of public entertainment. Initially, his confidence surged: the situation in Vilna was not as dire as in the provinces. Culture still existed, and so things could not be all that bad. And if theaters and concerts still thrived, then surely synagogues would too.

After all, Vilna, the Jerusalem of Lithuania, could not exist without its fabled houses of prayer and study. This was the city that boasted the House of Rom, which produced editions of the Talmud that were hailed far and wide as works of art and scholarship, and for whom the Navaredker, Alexander Harkavy, the Yiddish expert, had worked. But perhaps most of all it was once the city of Elijah ben-Solomon, the Vilna Gaon, a man of unrivaled Talmudic erudition and scientific learning, often ranked among the greatest of scholars. This prodigal of study was known to have kept the window of his room closed by day and to have studied by candlelight so as to better shut out all distraction. At night he studied the commentaries in an unheated room, placing his feet in cold water to prevent himself from falling asleep. It was said that he never slept more than two hours a day and never more than half an hour at a time. His unsparing application was matched and perhaps exceeded only by Hillel, whose scholarly ardor and material privation led him to brace a winter snowstorm atop a yeshiva's roof, the better to eavesdrop on the learned discussion below.

In his search for a synagogue, Father stumbled onto Strashun Street and mounted the old muddy stairs leading to what once had been a house of prayer. When he opened the door to its interior, his whole childhood came rushing forth. The very walls breathed an air of reverence and learned dispute. There he found prayer books, a Torah ark, age-old lecterns, and worn wood benches. He was seized by an unruly throng of memories. Here, in this sacred enclosure, Jewry still lived, however provisionally. For a brief second he felt freed of the vagaries of time.

He saw a young man hunched in round-shouldered study of a Talmud tractate. He approached hesitantly, tapping him softly on the arm. When his face came into full view, Father shouted in amazement: "Gershon— Gershon!"

"How do you come to know my name?" Gershon asked in a fluted whisper, his forehead creased with worry.

"But Gershon, don't you know who I am?"

"Should I?" he asked inquiringly.

"Of course you should," Father answered. "We were fellow students in the yeshiva at Baranowicze."

Gershon's eyes narrowed and he took a step closer.

"Yes! How could I have forgotten?" he then conceded.

Father was glad to have found a *heymisher ponem*, a familiar face, even if it showed the grievous injury of time. Gershon told Father of Ponar, the killing fields of Vilna's Jews, of the tens of thousands who had been murdered already and the many others who were every day rounded up to satisfy a quota of innocent blood. No one was spared, he lamented, neither old nor young.

Nazi propaganda minister Goebbels had visited the Vilna ghetto and pronounced that "the Jews are the lice of civilized humanity. One has to exterminate them somehow, otherwise they will continue to play their torturous and annoying role."

So much then for Father's deceptive hopes that Vilna might have escaped the atrocities of Navaredok. Indeed, if anything, the opposite was true. Between July and November 1941, when the mass murders were not yet in full swing in Navaredok or Lida, Vilna was already the scene of many *aktions*. Byelorussia, in those relatively early days, was even regarded as something of a haven by the Jews of Lithuania.

"Why are the innocent being slaughtered? Where is divine justice?" Father asked pleadingly.

Gershon had no answer, but quoted God's reply to Job:

> *Where were you when I laid the earth's foundations?*
> *Speak if you have understanding . . .*
>
> *Have you penetrated to the sources of the sea,*
> *Or walked in the recesses of the deep?*
> *Have the gates of death been disclosed to you?*

Have you surveyed the expanse of the earth?
If you know of these—tell Me?

Gershon then fell silent. In matters metaphysical, he, as all of them, was stumped; but to real and present dangers Gershon had ready answers. He told Father that his illegal status in the ghetto made him an easy target. The unregistered were the first to be dragged away to Ponar when the murder quota needed to be filled. Father was saddened yet grateful for Gershon's brutally honest depiction of matters.

"Stay here overnight, and in the morning when Zaguyski, the chief of the Jewish criminal police, comes for prayers, I'll introduce you to him and ask him to register you in the ghetto," Gershon said.

"Ha-lee-vi!" Would that it be true! Father exclaimed.

"Don't worry," Gershon said. *"Bei yidn vert men nit ferlorn,"* he added optimistically. One doesn't get lost among Jews.

He brought Father bread and hot water, which he devoured. Gershon had always been quick with Talmudic learning, and now Father knew him to be a man of compassion as well. Gershon said that rabbis now permitted Jews to work on the Sabbath if their lives were in danger, as they almost always were, even though the ghetto had been "stabilized" with fewer killings. This was an example of the larger Talmudic precept of *pikuakh nefesh*—to save a life you may break a law.

Gershon said that a precedent had been set nearly a century earlier during the great cholera epidemic of 1848. Rabbi Israel Salanter, the father of the *mussar* movement, permitted the devout of Vilna to eat on Yom Kippur after local physicians warned that fasting would irretrievably weaken them and make them more likely to succumb to disease and death. However, when the Jews of Vilna proved skeptical, Rabbi Salanter felt he had no choice but convey his message unmistakably by reciting a *brokhah* (blessing) at the dais of the main synagogue over wine and food on the Day of Atonement and eating and drinking for all to see. He was convinced he had done the right thing and took pride in having been offered the occasion to publicly affirm life.

It was reported that when it came time for Rabbi Salanter to leave this world, he displayed extraordinary stoic selflessness. As he lay dying in Königsberg, alone save for a simple, superstitious attendant who was terrified of ghosts and corpses, Rabbi Salanter spent the last hours of his life soothing and convincing the man not to be afraid to be left alone all night, as custom demanded, with the body of a dead man.

When Gershon extinguished the lights in the synagogue, Father tucked his chin into a soft pillow, and through the cracked and grimy window he saw the moon peering from behind the clouds and then dipping from view.

A quorum came for early morning prayers. Zaguyski, the Jewish police chief, arrived also, as Gershon had promised, and joined their prayers. Their bodies swayed like the flickering of a candle's flame. Like the others, Father beat his chest in an agony of supplication. At the end they all bowed low and recited, "We therefore hope in thee, O Lord our God, that we may soon behold the glory of thy might, when thou wilt remove the abomination of the earth . . . when thou wilt turn unto thyself all the wicked on the earth." They persisted in worship, attempting to reconcile their faith in God with the harsh daily experience in Vilna.

When the last prayers were recited, Gershon approached Zaguyski, who was wrapping his phylacteries. He made an eloquent pitch on Father's behalf. Perhaps stirred more by the intensity of the previous prayer service than by pity for Father's sorry state, Zaguyski consented to add his name to the registration rolls. For a brief moment, Father felt less fugitive.

<hr />

SUFFERING IN THE VILNA ghetto summoned forth a tide of culture to shore up sanity. People read ravenously or attended the theater to escape the thought that they might be killed the next day. On December 13, 1942, the Mefitse Haskalah, the ghetto library, celebrated the lending of the hundred thousandth book with its noted director Herman Kruk giving a paper on ghetto reading habits. Subscribers, it appeared, showed a special fondness for Tolstoy, vicariously delighting in his accounts of Napoleon's failed march on Moscow. Meanwhile, Durmashkin's musical baton kept concerts coming, and directors and actors scurried to mount elaborate plays in spite of life's worst odds. Neatly dressed children recited poetry and sang in ghetto-school choral plays, their performances all the more poignant as they expended their remaining strength in these waning days.

Not everyone in the ghetto applauded these performances. Posters plastered on kiosks accused the organizers of mounting plays in a graveyard, to which others riposted with equal vehemence that only beauty could make hell endurable.

The inferno would not be stilled. True, the Vilna ghetto had quieted since the mass murder of 1941–42, which had claimed forty-eight thousand lives. But at Ponar, once a popular holiday resort, Jews were constantly funneled to their deaths. Marched naked in single file to the edge of fuel pits, they were summarily shot by rifle fire. A thin layer of sand covered their bodies, which laid a human foundation for the next group of naked prisoners led from the waiting area to the edge of the pit.

So-called stabilization in late 1942 meant a more focused kind of murder in the ghetto. Whereas earlier the Nazis grabbed anyone randomly, now the trucks targeted specific groups of victims, such as the inmates from the ghetto's Lukishki prison, who were dragged to the death pits of Ponar. Indeed, Jews were constantly being shot for smuggling food into the ghetto. This is how Liuba Levitska, the beautiful coloratura soprano, met her end. The "nightingale of the ghetto," who had taught singing to children in a makeshift school, had poured out her grief in unforgettable strains. Her moving rendition of "Sand in the Stars" (*Zamd in Shtern*) at the first concert given by the newly organized Ghetto Symphony Orchestra brought the house down.

In the presence of such carnage, Father's thoughts doubled on themselves. He had just come to the ghetto, yet he knew that he had to get out just as quickly. He inquired about work outside the walls of entrapment, and soon he came upon a former Novogrudek neighbor, Mulleh Schelubski. Father told him of his anguished travels to Vilna and how much he now wished to breach its ghetto walls.

"Do you know the attorney Mushkat?"

"I've never heard his name. Who is he?"

"He is involved with the police and has the inside word on everything. A while ago he established a transport brigade that gave hope to ghetto orphans. He may be just the person you need to see."

"Could you arrange it?" he asked eagerly.

"Let me see what I can do," Mulleh said, as they parted.

Father's faith rose briefly upon seeing that his townsman had his welfare at heart. Mulleh still inhabited a moral order, which comprised helping others in need, and he kept his word. The next day, Father sat in Mushkat's room, a small cubicle that the attorney occupied alone. He had fled to Vilna in 1939 as a refugee from Warsaw. He was polite and well spoken, nodding sympathetically as Father related that he had nobody left in the world, no one to depend on. While he pleaded for a way out of the ghetto, Mushkat was more focused on the present, wanting to know how he was getting by for the moment. Father told him he was staying at the synagogue on Strashun Street, but that he did not know how long that would last.

"Why don't you come here for one meal a day?" Mushkat said.

"Oh no! I know how tight things are. I just couldn't," he said.

"Don't worry. I would not have offered it if I couldn't provide it."

Trusting him implicitly now, Father persisted in asking Mushkat if he knew of a way to work beyond the ghetto walls. "We'll see what we can do," the attorney said, standing up and giving Father his hand.

At the synagogue on Strashun Street Father saw Gershon, his fellow yeshiva student, praying, his face hidden and his shoulders softly heaving. All the lights were extinguished save one. The curtain of the Holy Ark hung in ineffable sorrow.

The next day, Father met Mushkat in the street. "I've heard they need a hand at a labor camp in Sorok Tatar, some ways from here," he said hurriedly. "The work is tough, however."

"I'm not complaining," Father said, his voice rising keenly.

"Give me a few days to see what arrangements can be made."

Great perils have the beauty of bringing to light the fraternity of strangers, Victor Hugo once wrote. Here in Vilna, a perfect stranger had furthered Father's plans and come forth to guard his life. A few days later Mushkat informed him to ready himself for Sorok Tatar.

CHAPTER
6

Sojourn in Sorok Tatar

GROVES OF WHITE BIRCHES shimmered against the sky. Their tops melted in the morning mist, encircling Sorok Tatar's brown earth. It was once entirely a Muslim Tatar village, but now was home to a Polish and White Russian majority. Father joined a labor contingent of eighty Jews felling trees in the thick forest and shipping lumber back to the Vilna ghetto. For the moment he had cheated death.

At first Jews in the Vilna ghetto feared Sorok Tatar. They assumed it was another German ruse, another killing ground masquerading as a labor site. But in time this perception changed. By mid-to-late 1942 a host of satellite working camps near the Vilna ghetto arose in response to the accelerated German demand for labor. Sorok Tatar was one of these.

Father worked hard, as did the other Jewish laborers. The sound of their monotonous ax blows reverberated through the forest and at day's end their faces were wet with sweat. But while the others were quartered with the locals, Father had to sleep out in the open because he was the last to have arrived at the camp. There was no light except for the moon peering from the broken clouds. The smell of grass reminded him for a moment of the soft meadows of his childhood. And then he remembered the lurid flames against the night sky, the foliage ablaze, the serried ranks of the SS giving the Hitler salute and the hordes of eager collaborators. How was he to reconcile the words of the Psalmist that the heavens declare the glory of God, while recalling that the congregation of Navaredok had been slain in a forest? The Jews were condemned utterly, Father thought: why did the sun shine radiantly on the wicked, and why did the permitting stars keep their silence eternal? Were they perhaps fugitive, too? Was it rash impiety to say that heaven had now crumbled, its chambers and celestial throne now blackened ruins? Was not Melville right to have allowed Captain Ahab to declaim to Moby Dick: "Thou has seen enough to split the planets and make an infidel of Abraham and not one syllable is thine."

By mid-November the trees were shorn. By early December frost arrived. At the break of each day, Father lay blanketed with snow and chilled by an icy film of dew. His outdoor encampment was through. Stamping his feet to escape the cold, he resolved to find a night's haven. He went from door to door in anxious humility until he found Franzkevich, a poor but kindly Pole full of country solicitude, who offered him a spot in his hut. It was a dim place, but when he lit the corner stove the room was suffused with rustic warmth.

The unceasing work was backbreaking. The harsh weather did not ease matters, and at each day's end Father felt like one of the felled trunks himself. One evening he was alone in the hut of Franzkevich when a stranger called. From his window, he saw a young man, carrying a whip made of rawhide, park his cart and tie his horse to the front gate. He approached and banged loudly on the door, his battered hat in hand.

When Father gave him entry, he demanded loudly where Franzkevich was.

"He's out now and I don't know when he will be back," Father said.

"And who are you? Some relative of his?" the man asked.

"No," Father answered laconically, "I just stay here."

The visitor squinted nearsightedly and clapped his arms for warmth.

"Looks like I'm going to have to come back another time," he said, departing so quickly that Father did not even catch his name.

That evening Father sat quietly and reviewed everything that had happened. The visiting stranger had not identified him as a Jew. Perhaps Father's blond hair and blue eyes had fooled him. Maybe others might be as easily taken in. His fairness suddenly became a kind of illumination, perhaps affording him an exploitable advantage. It was an untried thought, but slowly Father shaped in his own mind the tentative outline of a new plan, as yet uncreated, like the breath of another world, which might lead to freedom.

The Jews at Sorok Tatar met each morning at the home of Kuzminski, a village Pole who doled out their food rations. His yard fence had dwindled to a few naked posts. A fierce dog growled in the corner as they picked up their loaf of bread and cup of coffee.

His son, Bronek, a country-bred lad with a porcine face but a generous nature, greeted them every morning as he warmed himself by the reddish light on the stove. Boyishly garrulous, he repeated jokes till they were worn to shreds. Father would often return in the evening, flushed with exertion, to speak with him.

"Brr! It's frosty out there," Father said, removing his overcoat.

"Listen to this," Bronek said on that cold evening as he spooned hot cabbage soup from a saucepan. "Some folks in Sorok Tatar are signing up with the Lithuanian Auxiliary Army," he added, leaning over confidentially.

"What?" Father asked innocently.

"The Auxiliary Army is fighting alongside the Germans against the Soviets. They're being sent to the Leningrad front," he continued.

"Don't they have a speck of decency?" Father said in disgust.

"Well, they hate the Soviets more than they do the Germans."

"Do they really hate the Germans?" he wondered aloud, but did not press Bronek for an answer. This exchange planted the germ of an idea: If Father could get into the Lithuanian Auxiliary Army, it would bring him to the front and allow him a chance to escape over to the Soviet side.

Winter was frigid. Icicles hung from windows of the snowbound village. Father's fellow Jews logged their daily quota for which they earned their meager bread. Despite his hardiest efforts and a careful husbanding of his depleted energy, his strength ebbed and he failed to meet the quota. His rations diminished and then he grew pale, thinning into a furtive shadow. If he couldn't match the others he would be sent back to certain death in the Vilna ghetto.

He felt lost amid his very own Jews. There was no consolation, no recording angel to take heed of his plight. He remembered Job's cry: "From out of the city the dying groan, and the soul of the wounded cry for help; yet God pays no attention."

Food became imperative. Without it the game was up. To obtain nourishment he would have to go back to the ghetto and buy odds and ends with the little money he had left and then return to Sorok Tatar to barter them for extra food. Necessity had turned him into what in the shtetl was known as a *karabelnik*, a country peddler. Yet, anything that brought him nearer to the ghetto carried him closer to death. But what choice did he have?

His journey took him through the dark wooded outlying region and into the urban forest of blood-red swastika banners. He traveled along snow-burdened roads. He shivered in his coat as he approached Vilna, shimmering with blue frost. Just crossing the street was a walk on the razor's edge, demanding as much luck as cunning. To his surprise, he returned to Sorok Tatar without a mishap.

The Sunday after he returned he set forth. He began at the outskirts of Sorok Tatar, hoping to meet with some bartering success. He spotted an isolated hut ringed by a broken wattle fence, on which a lone cow stood tethered.

He approached softly and rapped on the door as the sun threw a late-day slant on the side window. He waited and knocked again. An older Tatar woman with sinewy hands and a lined face opened the door. Though the sunlight was still visible, she carried a taper with her. She motioned him to a rickety table made of pine slabs, warped with age, at the center of the small room. She nearly stumbled over the hem of her skirt as she wiped dust off the chair with her long apron. She picked up some knitting and worked in silence. Father began to take out some items from his sack— kerchiefs, aprons, and other sundry knickknacks—in the hope of bartering with her.

"Might any of these interest you?"

She rose and walked toward the door of the hut. He tensed in fear. Had he done something wrong? In a few minutes she returned with a cup of cow's milk which she placed on the table. She did not request any payment or barter; for her to gladden the hungry was its own reward. He murmured his appreciation, and she smiled at the chance of doing good.

She reminded Father of his own mother, who always sought to help the poor. When he was a child, she had taught him that a good deed was the choicest of possessions; indeed, it hastened the redemption. It was a sin, she said, to avert one's gaze from the poor. Every Friday Father's mother prepared a basket of food for those too dignified to ask and had Father, then a mere boy, anonymously place it at their doorstep: the unfortunate were not to taste humiliation and misfortune together. Father also recalled that alms collectors at the Navaredok cemetery proclaimed, *"Tzedakah tatzil mi-moh-ves"*—Charity saves one from death.

The lady was Helena Osmanova, a descendant of nomadic Tatars who had migrated from the lower Volga to Lithuania. She eked out a living from her small garden and lean cow and thwacked her weekly wash with a wooden paddle. Her kindness established a bond between them.

Stefan, her gentle son, was just a bit younger than Father and won him over by his simple, unassuming manners. He soon felt as easy with Stefan as with Helena, largely because he never heard Jews disparaged in their house, a rarity in occupied Poland.

SEVERAL WEEKS HAD PASSED, endless in their drudgery, when Bronek and Father took up the thread of their conversation.

"Where did you get your blond hair?" Bronek asked.

"My mother was blond," he said.

"Well, you sure don't look Jewish," Bronek said, flinging his knife several feet, its wooden handle quivering when it landed on the ground.

"Are you kidding me?" Father asked.

"No way. I would never mistake you for one of them," he said.

As the sun set that evening over Franzkevich's hut, Father's misery took on a different temper. Bronek's remarks had struck a nerve in Father, and he began to think along a new set of tracks. Could he pass as a non-Jew? Now that he had been assured by Bronek, he wondered whether he could devise a new identity.

His mind drifted along this current of speculation, but it soon turned into a raging flood. After several restless days, the idea of turncoat expediency finally grew into a nervous obsession. Recalling the death mills at Ponar was the prod that he needed.

Father's aim was to escape the Nazis by reaching the Soviet front and crossing over to the Allied side—surely no easy feat. To accomplish this, he would need to plan far in advance. Posing as a non-Jew, he would make his life-saving escape across battle lines by first faking his way into the Lithuanian Auxiliary Army. But upon closer scrutiny, Father viewed it as an outlandish scheme, fraught with improbabilities.

Day had just dawned; he rubbed his eyes and squinted at the early sun.

It was so peaceful outside that for a moment he forgot his earlier torment. But soon piercing gunshots came in sudden spurts, followed intermittently by the muffled silence of falling snow. The fusillade grew louder as the hour advanced.

He knew Ponar lay close, and he imagined the scene of morning slaughter: arms and legs splayed wildly, the clothing of the newly killed strewing the blood-soaked, heaving ground. The sound of the dying braided with the voice of Bronek insisting that Father did not look Jewish, and his whole frame shook violently.

In time the thought of the Lithuanian Auxiliary Army persecuted him like a relentless tune. Bronek's remark assumed an oracular air, a portent that might carry him to the Soviet front and then to safety. But each time he considered it, he blanched. Would he become a collaborator, even if it only served as a means to an end? Only two years ago he had transcendently ordered his life toward the divine; now he seemed immanently bound to evil. But these were times when only expert dissembling would do.

His false identity, if it was to be at all convincing, would need to be seamless. To pass he would have to imitate to perfection a peasant's bearing and stance. Nothing must betray his ignorance or advertise his former life. To better learn the right cues needed to pass, he began to watch the habits of Franzkevich and his family. These Catholics became his listening post.

During their feast days, he observed them heading to church, whose spires jutted bleakly against the winter sky. He watched processions of choirboys approach the nave. From across the road near the church, Father listened intently to the Latin chants streaming from the interior; he hearkened to the swelling organ *adagios*, the Ave Marias and Pater Nosters, hoping they would yield him a repertoire of melody and ritual, which then could be committed to memory.

But for all its vaunted Catholicism, Lithuanian rural life had a strong pagan foundation. He recalled that Adam Mickiewicz, Poland's Shakespeare, chose Lithuanian peasant ritual for the setting of his great dramatic poem "Dziady" ("Forefathers' Eve"), filled with ghost sightings and midnight incantations. Not surprisingly when one considers that the Lithuanians were the last Europeans to be Christianized. As late as 1382, when Grand Duke Kestutis died, he received the full range of pagan funerary rites: cremation in Vilnius together with his horses, hounds, and hawks, a spectacular leave-taking. Only in 1386, with the monarchical union of Poland and Lithuania, was the latter brought into the church and medieval Latin Christendom considered complete.

Father hoped that these congeries of religious ritual, skillfully combined with literary fragments and a smattering of history, might break the force of disaster when it struck.

It was now November, and Christmas was a month away. Frost covered the fields, and icicles hung from eaves. Wintry gusts had already ripped off roof slats. Preparations for the holiday, muted because of the war, were underway and a buzz of anticipation filled the air. During the long Advent evenings, the women of the house, laboring under the light of kerosene lamps, spun ersatz altar cloths.

No one seemed more animated than Franzkevich's elderly grandmother.

"I'm soon to be ninety, may God preserve me," she would announce, thumping her staff.

"May you live to be a hundred!" came the refrain.

The superstitious Franzkeviches sought to foretell the future by examining animal entrails. Several weeks before Christmas they dutifully clustered around their ancient grandmother as she rolled her sleeves above her bony elbows, bent her gnarled knees, and peered at a newly butchered fowl.

"What does tomorrow hold?" she intoned solemnly.

She leaned her wizened frame over the animal innards and mumbled indecipherably. Everyone bent near in anxious expectancy. A dark shadow fell across her face, and she suddenly rose with a shriek.

"The bones are mottled—woe is me!"

A hush fell over the hut. It all seemed odd to him, but Father decided that as a piece of superstitious folk custom it might stand him in good stead. Of course, he could never forget that to a yeshiva student, all these rites of Polish Catholicism were strictly forbidden and strangely forbidding, as indecipherable as hieroglyphics. Gradually, as he heard bits and pieces about the Incarnation, the Annunciation, and St. Paul's abolition of the physical covenant between God and Israel, he began to recognize the nomenclature. But to him all this adoration appeared highly incongruous. The great cosmopolite and wit, Heinrich Heine, who became a Lutheran to obtain the "ticket" to Western culture, said wisely, "It is true that I was once baptized, but I never converted. It is extremely difficult for a Jew to be converted, for how can he bring himself to believe in the divinity—of another Jew?" Despite Father's hesitation and, even, mortification, he reviewed all that he saw, knowing that no credible imitation could be achieved merely by chance or fitful study.

Despite the Franzkeviches' privations, they threw themselves excitedly into holiday preparations. Everything pointed to their inescapable poverty, almost scriptural in its direness; but they made do, even if the savory smells of Polish sausage, dried mushrooms, and succulent stews were now only a distant memory.

On Christmas Eve a single candle burned on the table, its flame flaring in the draft. Half-empty plates were borne to the spartan table. The chased silver wineglasses had long ago been sold off. From the corner of his eye, Father saw their holiday meal, despite all the Franzkeviches' exertions, was paltry—a sampling of radishes and potatoes. In better days, they had been accustomed to a sumptuous feast: twelve fish dishes as local tradition demanded. But now they could only serve up a dozen variations on water— sweetening, salting, and coloring it—in dim reflection of what ritual prescribed.

The dull bitterness of hunger was on their faces. But they deemed it a holiday duty to keep their mood up. They succeeded, in part, by the savor of memory.

"My children, what wouldn't I give to have some *flaki"*—tripe soup with vegetable—the grandmother piped up.

"I'd be perfectly content with some *pieczony szuz pak z sardenami"*— baked pike with anchovies—her son added, his eyes rolling ceilingwards.

"That's all very well and good, but just give me a *kapusniak"*—sour cabbage soup—her daughter-in-law chimed in.

The paltry meal was consumed quickly after the imaginary contest of palates. But even the fondest reminiscences could not alter the simple fact that they would leave the table hungry. But what saved the evening from total privation was *samogon*, which stood in for finer beverages. The illegally brewed vodka roused their spirits, and they sang till tears welled up in their eyes.

As midnight approached, Father heard the peal of Sorok Tatar's church bells summon the faithful to prayer. The Franzkeviches, rapt in adoration, blew out the candle on the table and the hut fell dark. Their voices trailed away in the distance as they left for High Mass. Father lay on his hard pallet and in the thickening dark saw the moon under the clouds, much like a ship sailing under its banner. The golden hours of Navaredok flowed back to him as if from the dawn of his life: his mother's face cupped in her hands in front of the Friday-night candles, her prayerful chants for the coming of the Sabbath, and her blessings on the gathering thunder and lightning.

How strange it all appeared now. When he was a child in Novogrudek, the Roman Church was viewed by devout Jews as Edom, fated to bring Jewish suffering to eschatological heights. It was a proscribed world, Christmas and Easter signifying danger as Jews lay low hoping to be spared the wrath of merrymaking Poles. Father had bolted the windows against drunken pogromists and rabble rousers. The night lamp, as he remembered it, was extinguished, and they, as many other Jewish families, sat in deathly stillness. And yet, nothing now seemed as rich to Father as the intimate affections of his lost home.

⸺∞⸺

A CARPET OF SNOW lay across the outlying fields in early January. Just after the new year, Bronek spoke again of the recruitment of young men into the Lithuanian Auxiliary to Father, who remained torn between the moral gravity of collaboration and the inevitability of destruction.

It would all have been far simpler if he had been able while still in Novogrudek to escape to the Bielski partisans, Jewish heroes who would win gratitude for their exploits and altruism in the forests. But Father had found no credible way of making contact with them. And in Vilna he was an outsider with no established communal ties, no contact with the right underground groups. For those who counted in this shadowy world, he would always remain suspect, a gun-shy rabbinical student.

Terror galvanized him into action. His plans now assumed a life and strategy of their own. His immediate goal was to reach the Lithuanian recruiting station, as well as a quiet roadside inn where he could stay overnight. Bronek, his faithful conduit of information, was his only resource, but caution was necessary, as he did not want the lad to catch on to his true design.

When he met him next, Father leisurely but determinedly guided their conversation back to the Lithuanian Auxiliary Army.

"Have you ever been to the Auxiliary Army recruiting office, since you seem to know so much about it?" he asked.

"No, but I know where it is," Bronek said.

"Really, where?"

On the ground he sketched the location of the station and a nearby inn, where would-be recruits preferred to stay.

That night Father visualized his way through Vilna's convoluted streets and alleys he had internally mapped. But now the problem of disguises loomed large. He would need to assume the look of a non-Jew, the ordinary gait of a villager arriving in the big city? How, above all, would he devise a way to banish convincingly the look of incriminating fear?

He was tortured by misgivings. Tension squeezed his neck like an iron ring. Though he still was in Sorok Tatar, his mind took up residence in Vilna. In a few days he was worn out by sleeplessness and apprehension, fearing himself unequal to the task and suspecting that the road downward had few landings and no level places. What if his heart and head would not pull in double harness and his plans would go awry? At night he tossed and turned and heard the metronomic tick of the clock.

Toward the end of January, encompassed on all sides, he sensed there was no more time to lose. Spinning the web of dissimulation, he made up a fake Polish name. Once his resolve was fixed, he told Franzkevich that he was going to stay over in the Vilna ghetto for the night and would return the next day. It seemed plausible enough—after all, he had gone on bartering missions before, and in any case, Franzkevich wasn't overly inquisitive.

At twilight Father set off with a sack over his shoulder, mimicking the posture and footfall of a roadside peasant. All he wanted was to cut the figure of a villager with an eye for the contour of the land and an ear for the rhythm of the language. A good sixteen kilometers lay ahead of him. He walked briskly, the pine woods sweeping past him. In a while he rounded the shoulder of a small hill and reached a tiny village, but as night was about to fall, he proceeded without halting. The repetitive motion of walking steadied his nerves.

When he arrived at the outskirts of Vilna, its dark mass of baroque castles and churches loomed in the distance. A wind blew from under the banks of dark clouds. Father tightened his jacket and plunged into the din of the outer city. He blended in with the evening rush of horses and carts, and winced when the drivers lashed at their animals. He felt lost despite Bronek's instructions, but avoided asking for directions, preferring to keep his own company till he found the way. He crossed and recrossed a number of streets, and before it turned pitch black, he approached the low-slung inn, over whose glass window hung a heavy mist.

He unlatched the gate and then shut it quietly behind him. The knob felt cold in his hand as he pushed the door open. A gas lamp shed a faint light on the interior, thick with smoke, forcing him to strain to see the peasants lying on the floor and a proprietress seated in a corner. A fire crackled in the corner, further darkening the room with a blackish vapor. He sidled over to her amid the stale smell of cabbage and alcohol and, in cursory Polish, asked her if he could stay the night. She nodded and he slipped a few coins into her thick hands. She then pointed him to a knot of men splayed helter-skelter on the floor.

Many were splotchy with drink. Their glasses left colored rings on the worn tablecloth and their speech was slurred—every word drowned in warm spittle. The cacophony of grunts, groans, and alcohol-induced shouts set Father on edge. But seeing he had no choice, he wedged himself among them.

As he peered into the darkness, a big tottering fellow—his nose a purple blotch—tugged at his sleeves, inviting Father for a convivial glass. He had reached that point of inebriation where undifferentiated affection is felt for the universe.

Father didn't dare decline, fearing his refusal would be mistaken for hostility or, worse, contempt. He needed friends wherever he could find them, and if comradely tippling and a few round oaths were the way in, then so be it. He first clenched his teeth, then threw his head back and downed the glass in one deep draft, with only a slight grimace. Mercifully, the bottle was nearly drained, and he didn't have to contend with seconds or, even worse, thirds or fourths. Father knew where too many drafts would end. His perceptions needed to be keen and hard, impossible had he had to knock back a few more drinks. Luckily, the others soon dozed off, and for a long while he heard the fluty whistle of their snoring, while the proprietress guarded the door.

Father awoke early the next morning, the blue light of dawn seeping into a room heavy with the men's rhythmic breathing. As they lay wrapped in drugged slumber, he understood that for them drink was their only possession, their last sacrament in a profane world. Silently taking leave, he rose and padded to the door, closing it soundlessly. He descended a few sagging steps and strode along the still-empty sidewalk. As the sun rose over a sea of angled roofs, the city resounded with the clamor of morning traffic.

Without the Star of David pinned to his arm instantly identifying him as a Jew, he had the freedom of the sidewalk, not the humiliation of the gutter. But before he reached the recruiting station, he wanted to give his new identity a test run in the open street, to see if he fit the rustic mold, to try out his newly acquired peasant shadings of speech.

He fumbled in his coat pocket for a cigarette, which he stuck defiantly between his lips. He surveyed the morning throng for a suitable candidate to approach. As Father slowed his pace, a light-haired, well-dressed man, who carried himself with an air of calm self-satisfaction, neared.

"Sir!" He caught the man's attention. "May I bother you for a light?" he continued in White Russian.

The man gazed at Father for a second and asked him to repeat the question.

He stood very straight, then nodded and complied.

"*Natürlich!*" He spoke deliberately, and the cords of his neck stood in high relief. As Father inclined his face toward the man's cigarette, he spotted two tiny gleaming swastikas, one on each of the man's collar tabs.

"*Gut?*" the German asked solicitously.

"*Sehr gut,*" Father answered enthusiastically, though he felt sick from the smoke and revolted by the man's insignia. "Thank you, sir," he continued deferentially.

"*Bitte sehr,*" the German replied and went on his way.

Father's mimicry had succeeded now; but could it stand up to repeated tests? he wondered.

As he turned the corner, still breathless from the encounter with the German, he nearly lost his balance. In the distance Khazan, a fellow Jew from the Vilna ghetto, materialized, walking as prescribed in the middle of the gutter with his Star of David affixed to his clothing.

If Khazan so much as acknowledged his presence by nodding or, perish the thought, by shouting out his name in amazed recognition, the jig would be up. His cover would be blown and he'd be caught, more dead than alive. Father was reduced to the lamentable necessity of avoiding his fellow Jew.

Controlling an impulse to flee, Father imperceptibly turned away and pointed his face and body in the direction of the buildings on the street. By now Khazan's implacable forward motion had them practically level. From the corner of his eye Father saw his drooping shoulders and downcast eyes. What if he lifted them right now? What then? But by some strange miracle he passed unseeingly, mired in his own fear. No sooner was he gone than a stab of regret pierced Father. What if Khazan had surreptitiously seen him and had taken his distance for unfeeling disregard? Father had difficulty restraining a rushed, spasmodic look over his shoulder as the forlorn Jew faded into the distance.

<hr />

GERMAN ARMY TRUCKS HURTLED down the road, tearing up clouds of dust, and honking so loudly as to sharpen his unease. The chill pursuit of the wind was at his back. But he walked steadily under the bleary windows of the gray city.

Within a half-hour he reached his destination, a grim building trembling in the early-morning haze. Guards stood arrayed in the entrance.

Father buttoned his peasant overcoat, adjusted his bundle, and crossed the final street. The sullen eyes of the guards locked with his. Then the wind blew his tattered scarf in his face, blocking his vision, but he shifted it and glanced at the sentinels. To his surprise, none of them stopped him.

A guard spangled with large gold buttons pointed him toward a wooden staircase. He mounted it, the soles of his shoes scraping against a rough, unvarnished floor.

Static emitted by a radio echoed behind a number of closed doors. Raucous voices of a hard-drinking, tough-talking group drifted toward him from the end of a long corridor. These were his fellow would-be recruits.

He took a last drag on his cigarette and entered their midst. Some paced back and forth, others pranced like stallions, the youngest ones gamboling like ponies. He retreated to the rear of the room while they horsed around, spitting tobacco juice and cursing Jews. After a while they calmed down and he waited in anxious silence.

"Here he comes!" one of them shouted.

A tall Lithuanian officer entered the room.

"Line up!" he ordered, his gaze one of calculated ferocity.

They shuffled into position. Father managed in the momentary confusion to end up at the back of the line. The second hand of the wall clock ticked, and through the window the white fog of morning lifted skyward.

The line inched forward till his turn came. The door opened and the officer, whose bearing radiated authority, motioned for him to enter. Although it was still morning, a candle stump sputtered in a bottleneck on his table. He spent a minute putting away the previous candidate's files and then shot Father a sharp look.

"Your name?"

He blurted out a generic Polish name.

"Place of birth?"

"Sorok Tatar," he answered, keeping his voice steady.

The officer stood up and looked at him quizzically.

"Your papers, young man?" he demanded.

"Sir, I did not bring any," Father said, his voice shaking in spite of his best efforts to control it.

"And how is that?" he asked pointedly.

"You see, our village is so small that the German authorities haven't issued any," he said in White Russian, which the officer understood imperfectly.

He leaned forward and asked Father to repeat what he had just said, which he did patiently yet guardedly. The officer listened at first with curiosity and vague suspicion but then seemed to mellow.

"Well, then go back to your village and bring me whatever old Lithuanian documents you have. You do have your Lithuanian papers?"

"Of course! No problem," he answered. "No problem at all, sir."

A clumsy evasion, but he breathed more easily when the Lithuanian did not overly protest.

Father rose and left the room with what little dignity he could muster.

At the landing, the capacious back of the guard greeted him. Hearing the patter of Father's hurried steps, he turned on his heels and rose to a menacing height.

"Where do you think you're going?"

"Why, I'm leaving, of course,"

"Where's your exit permit?"

"I wasn't given any," Father said innocently.

"Go upstairs and get one," he said sternly. "Otherwise you stay."

"But I'd rather not bother the officer unnecessarily."

"Orders are orders, young man," he said, his mouth tightening.

When he gently protested again, the guard's anger curdled into fury. "Go upstairs!" he shouted, the hammer of his gun rising.

Father slowly remounted the stairs. He could almost taste despair beneath his mask. His stomach was in knots. The officer's initial doubts would surely grow once Father reappeared again so quickly. He would see beyond his pantomime and catch on to his ruse.

The stairwell began to spin. Father grasped the banister and then approached the door in a cold sweat. A moment elapsed before he knocked timidly, but no answer came from within. He nearly walked away in relief, but then thought it wiser to knock more firmly.

"Come in!" came the crisp reply.

His heart skipped a beat as he opened the door.

"You again!" the officer muttered. "Didn't I tell you to come back with your Lithuanian documents?"

"Yes, of course, sir. Without a doubt. But I now need your permission to leave the building. The sentry says there is no other way."

"Oh, that's right," the officer said apologetically. He shifted a stack of boxes and took out a slip of paper and wrote something illegible in his elongated script.

"Take it," he said. "And close the door behind you."

"Thank you, sir," Father said.

He raced down the steps, his hands clutching the note.

The guard stood glumly at the landing. He cast a hard look, but this time Father waved the all-important paper, his banner of freedom, in front of him. Smiling thinly but approvingly, the guard relieved Father of the exit permit, then opened the door with an exaggerated sweep and saw him out.

As Father crossed the gutter, he saw the street lined with an ominously familiar-looking row of black-topped trucks. In a moment he grasped their full import. He had seen them before, in Novogrudek. These vehicles of doom were the kind that took the Jews of his hometown to their deaths and tore his mother from him forever.

And undoubtedly, it was Lithuanians similar to those gathered upstairs who had killed Father's spiritual mentor, Rabbi Elkhanan Wasserman, head of the Yeshiva Ohel Torah in Baranowicze. Intent on murder, four Lithuanians had stormed into the house where Rabbi Elchanan was staying in Kovno in 1941. Seconds before his death, the saintly rabbi was reported to have uttered: "Heaven apparently considers us righteous people, for it wants us to atone with our bodies for Jewry as a whole. So we must repent now."

These roughnecks were cut from the same cloth as their Lithuanian counterparts in Berlin, who had issued an infamous promise in March 1941 to those of their countrymen who took part in the Soviet Lithuanian regime: "On the day of reckoning the only Lithuanian traitors who can hope for forgiveness are the ones who can prove that they killed at least one Jew."

Thought and memory suddenly congealed. When Father heard again the coarse laughter of the Lithuanian recruits inside, he understood how quickly they would destroy him should they ever learn of his secret. He could fairly see their eyes alongside the barrel of a gun. With each passing second, the Auxiliary Army reeked of death and betrayal.

On the lonely country road taking him back to Sorok Tatar, his naked terror of the collaborationist army, for whom murder was a pastime, mounted so strongly he decided that he would never go back to the recruitment center, cost what it may.

———— ❧ ————

IN SOROK TATAR, HOWEVER, there was no reprieve from the threat hanging over him and all the other Jews. Every murmur in the forest carried the sound of his demise. Father needed an alternative escape route, and his thoughts began to orbit wildly. The Lithuanian Auxiliary Army was a dead proposition, and he could only hope that it had forgotten his initial approach.

Of one thing he was certain: he needed a stronger false identity, one that he could back up with proof of an unquestionable source—solid papers equal to his interlocutors' sinuous questions. He could no longer do things by halves. Without tangible proof, his double self would be nothing more than the vanishing shape of a mirage.

But where could he turn? The narrowing gyre forced him to search high and low, until one day, baited by desperation, he began to trace a pattern in the midst of the chaos about him.

Stefan Osmanov, Helena's son, whom he was on his way to visit, might just be the person he was looking for. Perhaps Father could forge Stefan's identity, craft it to his purpose and, when suitable, shape the arabesque of a new identity. True, they looked nothing like one another. Father was blond and light-skinned, Stefan swarthy and short. One had the sallowness of the south, the other the fairness of the north.

But the crucial matter was that Stefan, the Tartar, was circumcised. All Muslims were, and in Nazi-controlled Europe that meant the difference between life and death. In the Bible Father Abraham had circumcised Ishmael, his eldest, even though he was excluded from the covenantal promise. Everything would hang on this providentially shared rite of passage.

Father's life had now acquired the mark of a definite plan. He remembered what Adam Mickiewicz had written in a youthful poem, "Measure your strength by your design, not your design by your strength." He worked this vein of ore, the world of the Polish Tatars, till it became as strong as steel. He launched into a period of furious autodidacticism, culling any information about the Osmanovs. His goal was to acquire more than a passing resemblance and he now found that his years at the yeshiva stood him in good stead; they had accustomed him to feats of memorization, once an act of devotion and now a maneuver of self-preservation.

Without letting Helena and Stefan in on his secret, he began to survey this hitherto faint world, and to catch the play of its iridescent colors. He innocently chatted with them, yet focused his questions more directly. Every contingency of their life, ancestry, and folk mythology became as vital to him as breath itself.

He gathered these facts like so many rough, uncut stones, and through the art of daily repetition he polished them into the gloss of a credible identity.

He soon learned that Tatars, the last of a long line of invaders of the Western steppes, following the ancient Scythians, Avars, Hazars, and Huns, were Mongol horsemen whose fourteenth-century empire extended from China to Poland. They had first settled in 1243 in Crimea, the southern land washed by the Black Sea where Stefan's father, Islam, hailed from. Father recalled that this was the very same region that had been ruled several hundred years before the arrival of the Tartars by the Khazars, a heathen Turkic tribe who were said to have converted to Judaism and of whom Judah Ha-Levi, the greatest Hebrew poet of the Middle Ages, wrote compellingly in his philosophical treatise, *Kitab Al-Khazari*, published originally in Arabic.

He also remembered reading that the history of the Tatars was filled with bloody epics. Indeed, their very name had once signified torture, flogging, and mutilation for people in the West. Poles were sometimes heard to describe Russians disparagingly as Tatars, who they insisted were the cruel prototype of czarist aristocracy. Hadn't the court of Basil II of Moscow during the fifteenth century actually spoken Turkish?

This dark reputation largely went back to Genghis Khan, the charismatic nomad chieftain of the steppes, whose brutal military genius and battle mobility made him a genocidal tyrant of millions. And yet it was Genghis Khan who had enlarged his empire by admitting Buddhists, Franciscans, Taoists, and Muslims into his court, thus translating geographical conquest into a cross-fertilization of cultures. And in time Polish princes would grant land to his descendants in return for their military service against the Teutonic knights. So it was that a Muslim tribe came to flourish in Poland while bloody struggles raged between Christianity and Islam elsewhere on the European continent. But most importantly to Father, the Tatars had adopted Islam. As Muslims, they shared that all-important infant ritual that would provide Father a crucial explanation if challenged.

Stefan's stories awoke in him a life of buried memories. As a child he was fascinated by the few Tatars in Novogrudek. Grandfather knew their local spiritual leader, an old and kindly man named Lazarevich, who patronized his well-stocked store. Over the years Lazarevich had picked up some Yiddish phrases and would always bring a smile, even an appreciative hoot, to Grandfather's lips when he used them, and when he indulged in ecumenical comparisons. He would often say, "Don't forget, my good friend, we share many things in common: you have the Bible and Mishnah; we have the Koran and the Hadith. We are also a people of commentary, and believe just as adamantly in revelation and law. Didn't Mohammed preach that the Torah was to be revered and was integral to Islamic revelation brought down by the angel Gabriel?"

During the interwar years, independent Poland had created an autonomous Mufiate (Muslim church body) headed by Jacob Szynkiewicz, a scholar of Oriental languages. In 1930 Mufti Szynkiewicz made the *hajj*, the traditional pilgrimage to Mecca, alone because of the prohibitive cost of the voyage to Arabia. He also helped raise the cultural level of the *imams*, the Muslim teachers, who before the first World War were impoverished and whose knowledge was largely limited to prayer recitation. Polish government subsidies allowed the *imams* to found Arabic schools and to ensure that feast day and fast day were strictly observed. By 1930 a quarterly, the *Islamic Review*, had been founded in Warsaw by Vassdan Guirei Djabagui, a Caucasian journalist related by marriage to Polish Tatars. Four years later, the *Tatar Life*, the official organ of the Mufiate, appeared in Vilna to answer practical questions of daily life. And Father now remembered reading the great *Crimean Sonnets* that Adam Mickiewicz had written during his stay in Odessa and which mirrored the stormy unrest of the poet's mind. His uncommon use of Turkish words not found in any Polish lexicon enraged Warsaw classicists of the period, but in due time his verse-paintings of the original Tatar homelands were regarded as one of the heights of Polish lyricism.

By stringing together pieces of Tatar history and folkore, Father hoped to give his false identity some breadth and extension. He now recalled the sight of Tatar funerals in Novogrudek, whose rear he would bring up stealthily. As a boy, burials appeased his melancholy streak as nothing else could. The veiled Muslim women walked behind their costumed men, wailing their grief. At the cemetery, all the Muslim headstones faced south to Mecca. He remembered a cascade of shouts and pleas as the Tatars interred the body on the first stage of its journey into eternity. Father stood respectfully throughout, as if already following one of Islam's obiter dicta: "When the bier of anyone passeth by thee, whether Jew, Christian, or Muslim, rise to thy feet."

In February 1943 the seeping cold and despair made winter invincible. Wind and rain ate away the wood fence around the Franzkeviches' hut and only a few naked posts stood. Father's only consolation was Stefan and the growing possibility that he might credibly adopt his identity.

It was during this bleak month that Bronek informed Father that local fellows were being sent off to Germany as forced laborers; some, jumping the gun, were even offering to go as volunteers.

What, Father wondered, if he were to steal into Germany as a foreign laborer, thus finding refuge in the lion's den, as it were? What if he sold himself into servitude instead of waiting for others to do so? This at first struck him as madness itself, for how would he exchange the manners of a scholar for the gruff demeanor of a dirt farmer? Could he who had meant to get as far from the Nazis as possible burrow himself into their very midst?

He would have to continue mastering the life of the peasant, learn to use pungent colloquialisms, strike the exact note of rustic dishevelment, in a word achieve authentic poise in an artificial setting. The smoother the surface, the deeper the lie could run. But this time he wouldn't budge without proper documentation. Everything depended on credible identity papers. And here Stefan again provided his best hope, his birth certificate would become Father's new purchase on life.

If he was to stage-manage his fate with cool aplomb and instinctive guile, if he was to flee from Vilna to Berlin, he would have to hurry. Every day that passed was one too many, carrying the possibility of forced re-entry into the Vilna ghetto, and certain death. And yet more than a few days passed before he could gather the resolve to approach Stefan.

As his link with the past grew more covert, Father felt himself losing anchor, drifting between worlds. He now lived in three temporal rhythms: the braided worlds of Judaism, Christianity, and Islam. If his scheme was to work, even the most negligible gesture would count. He paced back and forth in a secluded coppice near Franzkevich's hut, mulling it over. After much thought, he realized that he had a greater chance of survival in the depths of Germany than on the shoals of Sorok Tatar.

The next evening Father went to see if Stefan would lend him his birth certificate. It was pouring throughout the countryside and winter-darkened fields stretched away to the north. He mounted the broken steps of the old hut, rubbing the mud off his boots.

He knocked on the wooden door and drew a deep breath.

No answer came. He knocked again and went around to look through the curtained window in the back of the hovel. Everything was dark and desolate. Father started to leave when he heard the soft patter of steps.

Stefan opened the door a crack and then more widely.

"Come in. What devilish weather!"

"You can say that again. It's torrential," Father said, wiping his boots on a rag.

A chill rose from the wet floor.

"Where is your mother?" Father asked, scraping the hard-caked mud from his pants.

"She's out—imagine, in this weather. We're short on food."

Here was an opening.

"You know, Stefan, I too lack food, and I'm going to go to Vilna to get provisions, even though conditions there are increasingly dangerous."

"What do you mean?" he asked.

"In the past there weren't as many police patrols as there are now. Things are different, and I need more protection on the road."

"What sort of protection are you talking about?" Stefan asked innocently.

Father cleared his throat. "Well, some kind of paper that looks official."

A minute passed and they said nothing.

"You know," he continued, "a piece of identification, maybe a birth certificate."

Stefan sat stock still.

"Do you perhaps have one?" Father begged after a long pause, his voice sounding the base string of humility.

Stefan rose and began to fumble in the closet but returned emptyhanded. Father's heart dropped. What if Stefan had lost it? Nothing was as solid as a birth certificate at a time when racial bloodlines meant everything.

Stefan then moved in the direction of a tin cupboard. He opened it and lowered a worn leather wallet, slowly emptying its packet of yellowed documents onto the table. It lay inside an old mildewed envelope, ready to crumble at the merest touch. It was faded and nearly illegible, but to Father it looked pristine and inviolate.

Stefan unfolded the thin sheet gingerly before Father's eyes. The document contained Stefan's date of birth and, more importantly, his religion:

Islam, a word that then seemed threaded with gold and to Father far more valuable than all the riches of the world.

"Stefan, do you think I could borrow it?" he asked.

He still stood silently, folding and unfolding the document. The paper was so fragile that Father was sure it could not withstand further pressure. What if Stefan tore it accidentally? What if he decided not to hand it to him? Without that certificate, Father's future would be stillborn. Stefan held the mainspring that kept Father's plans in motion—all the revolving wheels of escape.

Just as he was convinced Stefan would withhold the certificate and deprive him of a last chance at life, he thrust it into his hands. Father almost fell to his knees with the gratitude of a mendicant accepting a sacred offering.

Father grabbed both Stefan's hands and shook them for a long minute.

The rain stopped as suddenly as it had started. The trees bordering the puddle-strewn roads were trickling drops.

In the privacy of night he examined Stefan's document. It had the aura of destiny. Father felt like a mountain climber facing a perpendicular ice wall, an image he might have drawn from the poet Mickiewicz who limned an immense frozen landscape in "A View of Mountains from the Kozlov Steppe" from his *Crimean Sonnets*:

> *Yonder!—Did Allah cast that sea of ice as a wall?*
> *Or did he mold the thrones for angels out of frozen cloud?*

With Stefan's certificate, Father at least could wedge his foot into a tiny crevice and begin to slowly scale the glacial block of Germany.

But he now knew that he needed to adopt more than the cover of Tatar history to pass as a Muslim. If quizzed by the Nazis, or by another Tatar, Father would have to know the intricacies of Islamic religious ritual by heart. He would need to quickly assimilate as much as he could about Mohammed and the Koran. He would have to piece together the varying parts of Stefan's religious and ethnic identity, coercing them to his purpose. And above all, he would have to keep all the facts straight; for as they used to say in Navaredok, *"A ligner darf hobn a gutn zikorin"*—A liar needs a good memory.

A Tatar, he soon learned, prayed five times a day facing Mecca, always preceded by rigorous ablutions. Mohammed commanded the supplicant to wash his hands up to his wrists three times, then rinse his mouth, also three times. The worshipper would raise his hands and touch his earlobes, reciting *"Allah Akbar"*—God is great—followed by a recitation from the Koran:

> *In the name of God, the Compassionate, the Merciful*
> *Praise be to God, Lord of the Creation, the Compassionate,*
> *King of Judgment Day!*
> *You alone we worship, and to you alone we pray for help.*
> *Guide us to the straight path!*

Then the Muslim fell to his knees in multiple prostrations, each comprising seven movements with accompanying recitations, culminating with: "I testify that there is no God but the Almighty. He is alone without partner. And I testify that Mohammed is his servant and messenger. O God, promote Mohammed and the members of his house."

The number of regulations initially seemed many and confusing, but Father was relieved to learn that in the end only one congregational prayer was regarded as compulsory: the *saalat al jumah*, Friday midday prayer. Many years later, Father would still be able to recite some lines he had memorized.

As Lazarevich had reminded Grandfather, Islam and Judaism had an almost haunting sense of kinship. Both had elevated right conduct and behavior to the level of spirituality. Indeed, for the prophet Mohammed, "the most excellent *jihad* (holy war) is that for the conquest of the self." Apropos, Maimonides in the Middle Ages and Rav Kook in the twentieth century insisted that neither Islam nor the *hajj*, the pilgrimage to Mecca, were idolatry. One of Mohammed's sayings underscored this parallel: "Do not exceed bounds in praising me, as the Christians do in praising Jesus, the son of Mary, by calling him God and the son of God; I am only the Lord's servant; then call me the Servant of God and his messenger."

So stringent was Mohammed's version of monotheism that he chastised the Jews for calling their religious leaders by the title "rabbi"—my master—for in the Koran it is unpardonable to claim even the vaguest attribute of partnership to God. And there were strains of Islam which exceeded even the strict Jewish concept of providence, arguing that only God can designate which leaf falls at any time from which tree.

Father also could never forget that one of the great texts that hugely influenced the *mussar* movement was the classic work of Bahya ibn Paquda, *Hovot ha-levavot* (Duties of the Heart), the first systematic presentation of Jewish ethics, written in Arabic in 1018 in Muslim Spain and so popular in Eastern Europe centuries later that it was translated into Yiddish. The medieval Jewish philosopher, who fused the light of the intellect with the flame of the soul, lived in Saragossa, served as a judge of the local rabbinical court, and borrowed freely from Sufism (Muslim mysticism) and Arabic Neoplatonism. Bahya ibn Paquda even went so far as to describe the Sufi saints as *perushim*, the precise term used much later for the separatist, ascetic *mussarniks* of Navaredok. Here was another link in the communion of faiths to set Father at somewhat greater ease.

Indeed, Father came to learn that Mohammed in the beginning had not viewed the Koran as an entirely independent work but rather as the Arab version of the Bible. He had intended at first to embrace the Jews of Medina, who constituted in the seventh century nearly one half of the city's population and who controlled the rich oases and important trade fairs of the region, if only they would accept him as the Prophet of Allah. When met by rejection—they were chagrined at Mohammed's unfamiliarity with Jewish rites, although he had borrowed quite a number of ritualistic concepts from Judaism—the Arab seer concluded that Islam must go its separate way. Alas, a lasting enmity for the Jews developed, with periodic calls for a *jihad,* or holy war, and the fateful abrogation of a potential alliance between two similar faiths.

Strategically it could not have hurt Father's plans that Hitler and Mohammed were often conflated in the Nazi mind. Carl Jung characterized the Führer in 1939 as belonging "in the category of truly mystic medicine men. As somebody commented about Hitler at the last Nuremberg party congress, since the time of Mohammed nothing like him has been seen in the world."

Just as Father practiced his new identity, word spread that a new *Aktion* (massacre) was being readied against the Jews in the Vilna ghetto and that the Jewish laborers in Sorok Tatar were to be called back. They entered a period of wakeful death as doom closed in.

Father had to act quickly. He would gamble everything by becoming a "volunteer" laborer in Nazi Germany, if he could only get past the German officials in Vilna. Paradoxically, he would use the rigors of the world of *mussar*—its psychic abrasions and erosions of the self—to discipline himself for the challenges ahead.

Now that his decision was made, he would head to Vilna and present himself to the Gestapo as Stefan Osmanov. His instinct for dissimulation would be tested. Everything would have to fit together neatly: no loose ends, no rough carpentry anywhere. Stefan's birth certificate would be the seal of his new self.

But Father felt guilt-stricken. Stefan had no idea of the risk he was being placed in. If Father was caught, both would be held accountable. He resolved that if the worst came to pass, he would absolve Stefan of all blame, insist that he had stolen his papers or had found them by sheer accident. But even if he saved Stefan, Father would still need his own fallback story if he was to survive interrogation. He could not afford to drift with the tide of circumstance, and remembered Grandfather's saying *"Noyt brekht ayzn"*—Necessity shatters steel.

Outward mutability was now everything; one false self would not suffice—only a marvel of incarnations would do. A series of multiple identities would be needed to stretch like an infinite regress of waves, each shading into one another. He would become like an equatorial lungfish breathing in the air and in the water, moving imperceptibly from one realm to the next.

He decided that if worse came to worst, he would insist on being both Catholic and Muslim, a product of a mixed marriage. The more daring the manipulation of fact perhaps the better the deception. If need be, he would even devise a three-part invention to defy discovery. Perhaps this superstructure of cultures would offer a double-thick foundation and provide greater latitude of movement. In his mind, the lengthening shadow of the Vilna ghetto grew closer. Darkness and chaos advanced by the hour.

The next day, a brisk spring morning, he set forth to the Nazi labor office in Vilna with Stefan Osmanov's birth certificate lodged in his coat pocket.

Plumes of smoke fluttered above the village chimneys. He stopped upon the crest of a wooded hill and looked back to Sorok Tatar, his erstwhile refuge.

A broad tract of blue sky heralded his arrival in Vilna. Scores of outlying rooftops reflected the light of early morning. He negotiated the city streets, his head spinning in a maze of calculations. He finally reached the foot of the Green Bridge of the Vileya River.

Choked with doubt, he began to cross the bridge. His tale had too many flaws. He was about to pass himself off as a Tatar, yet he was almost as blond as a Swede. Surely, this would endanger his tale. And he knew in a fundamental way that nothing that is perceived is exhausted in perception itself. Islam would always, in the end, exceed his grasp, and he would never fully master it. Father could already hear the German interrogator laughing cynically as he saw through his faulty improvisation. What would remain of his web of lies once it was seen as a transparent ruse? This question had assailed him before, but never quite so profoundly.

Suddenly the rushing waters of the Vileya beneath the bridge seemed very close. He halted and leaned on the guardrail while the ground swayed beneath his feet. He could see his drowning body tossed by the tide, as it was swept toward the sea. But then a sound from another world rushed in. It was Grandfather's provident voice, riding headlong on the waves of memory, as if it were a lifebuoy.

He stepped back from the rail, and edged into the crowd, which appeared like luminescent spots with spinning centers. He walked slowly along side streets whose trees cast a riot of shadows on the pavement. The wind behind his back lifted a wet mist that had hung in the air all morning.

A huge swastika emblazoned on the roof of the German *Arbeitsamt* (labor office) loomed in the distance, and his mind settled into singular intent. A Wehrmacht soldier, posted with parade-ground discipline, stood at the gates.

Father reviewed at a rapid clip all the Muslim tenets; he shored up his memory by reminding himself of the similarities between his ancestral faith and Mohammed's. Both believed in a remote and ungraspable God, who just now seemed, indeed, beyond all attainment. Both espoused the efficacy of prayer: the Jews three times a day, facing Jerusalem; the Moslems five, facing Mecca. If he could only keep all this straight, if terror could be sublimated into precision, he might make it out alive!

He crossed the street and stood in front of the building.

"Was wunschen Sie?" the guard demanded. What do you want?

"Arbeit, Germania." He garbled the wretched phrase, not wanting to sound as if he knew German, because how in the world would a Lithuanian peasant know German?

"Gehen Sie ins Zimmer 17!" the guard barked.

Father looked blankly at him, miming incomprehension. Nazis knew that Yiddish-speaking Jews had a fair smattering of German, and he didn't want to drop any hints.

The guard repeated with rising irritation, *"Zimmer 17—verstehen Sie nicht?"*

Father maintained his blank stare and repeated pathetically, *"Arbeit, Germania."*

"Dummkopf—Zimmer 17!" the guard howled in exasperation, and then sketched the number in the air. At Father's gleam of recognition he opened the door for him to enter.

Father mounted the staircase, passing a quick succession of locked chambers. He searched for room 17, sinking his shoulders into his coat jacket.

Two Nazi officers, walking with their hands akimbo, approached as he reached the second floor but turned into a room just before he came face to face with them.

Voices streamed out from room 14 and typewriters clacked away in room 15. He stroked Stefan's identity papers, and rehearsed his story one last time. It still felt strange and uninhabited, still stubborn and foreign, and it would take far more time and effort to make eiderdown out of this hard pine plank.

Room 16 had a plate-glass window, and he could see several desks on which uniformed officers leaned. Its door suddenly slammed, cutting off a strangled cry. Father swallowed hard and knocked at the door to room 17.

A secretary dressed with a portrait neckline opened the door widely. Two Nazi bureaucrats sat at their desks, their hair precisely arranged.

"What do you want?" she asked.

He immediately responded in the most vernacular White Russian he could command. "I have come to register for work in Germany," he said, as the light of the unshaded lamp fell full on his face.

Her large eyes wandered searchingly from the tip of his head to his chin. "Wait here," she said.

He wanted to vanish into the shadows. Short of that, he tried not to teeter restlessly from one foot to the other.

She approached one of the Nazi officials, a thin, well-tailored man, and whispered into his ear. He looked at Father with a reckoning glance. Father's heart beat so strongly that he was sure it was perfectly audible to everyone.

"What brings you here?" the man asked as he approached.

"I have come to register for work in Germany," Father answered, and then stood waiting for the officer's response.

He motioned to the secretary and she opened a drawer of orderly stacked registration forms. "Sit, young man," he said.

The secretary inserted several carbon copies between the pages of the form and then fed them into the typewriter.

Father fingered Stefan Osmanov's birth certificate in his pocket, a thread that might lead him from this labyrinth.

"Name?" flew the first question.

"Stefan Osmanov."

"Where do you live?"

"Sorok Tatar."

"Year of birth?"

"Nineteen twenty-five."

So far the questions were fairly straightforward, and he began to breathe more easily. But now the Nazi's questions took on greater precision.

"Religion?"

"Islam," Father answered quickly, tensing in spite of himself.

"Islam?" the man asked quizzically.

"Yes, I am a son of Tatars."

The Nazi threw his pen onto the desk and bored his eyes into father. "Any Jewish blood?" he demanded, his voice rising sinisterly.

"No!" Father said intently.

A weighty pause intervened. He felt dragged alive to drowning depths.

"Are you sure?" the man insisted.

Father racked his brains for the word that would silence all doubt.

"Quite sure, sir. My family is Muslim from way back. My father was born in Yalta, in Crimea."

"Ah, yes!" the man exclaimed. "The Crimean Tatars are Germany's friends." Father had hit the mark. The questioner thawed; after all, the Crimean Tatars had been Nazi collaborators. Apparently, Hitler had told Martin Bormann the year before: "I am going to become a religious figure. Soon I'll be the great chief of the Tatars. Already Arabs and Moroccans are mingling my name in their prayers. Among the Tatars I shall become khan."

"Where are your papers?" the officer now asked perfunctorily.

Father unfolded Stefan's fragile birth certificate and handed it to him. The man picked it up cautiously, held it between his forefinger and thumb as he examined it. Father looked at his hard profile as he bent over his task. After musing a few seconds, he flung it back.

"Return in two weeks," he said, rising from his chair.

Father felt a wave of relief flowing over him. His ruse had worked.

"Ah, yes, there's another thing we have all forgotten about," the man said.

Father looked at him expectantly.

The officer took out a notebook, tore out a sheet, and hastily wrote a name and address on it. "You are to report next week for your physical." He thrust the paper into Father's hand, which felt as if it had just been seared by lightning.

"Don't forget the visit. It's required. Otherwise we cannot proceed with your application."

The secretary smiled at him, her bright cheeks darkening for a minute. The officer pointed him to the door and Father left promptly.

Terrifying anticipations assailed him in the street. He couldn't possibly go to the doctor without standing revealed; but similarly, he couldn't refuse without ending up at Ponar sooner or later. What he had just been through was surely a pale preview of storms to come.

He returned to Sorok Tatar more troubled than when he left. How had all his studious bricklaying resulted in this impasse? Nothing was enough; the demands doubled with each forward step.

Father's thoughts returned to this same groove all night. Who was this doctor he had to visit? Was he German or Lithuanian? Would he be meticulous—or perfunctory and let him glide through the finely meshed examination net?

He was splayed on the horns of this dilemma. There was no one to ask for advice, and so he kept turning the appointment note over in his pocket for days, unable to decide which road to choose. His thoughts returned to Novogrudek. Who remained of its six thousand Jews? Only a handful of ghosts flitting from one hiding place to another. And surely the same destiny would soon overtake Vilna. He understood more acutely than ever the old Yiddish proverb, *"Yeder tog vos fargeyt tsum keyver baleyt"*—Every day that passes brings you closer to the grave. Should he go to the doctor or not go to the doctor? A decision had to be made quickly; the Nazi order for the Sorok Tatar Jews to return to the Vilna ghetto was imminent. But for days he pushed it off, uncertainty stewing in him like a bitter juice.

He vacillated until the energy of despair drove him out of Sorok Tatar. En route to Vilna and the fateful medical examination, his mounting terror served as a whetstone sharpening his resolve.

On the road taking him away from Sorok Tatar, the morning light quavered on the ground. Father thought for a moment of a magical way out, of epispasm, the surgical procedure Jews underwent in ancient times to reverse circumcision. But he knew that the Talmud forbade it, so much so that even Yom Kippur could not bring expiation. And in any case, it was now a medical figment of the imagination rather than pragmatic reality.

Never before had Father felt his body to be so confined, his freedom so trapped in the folds of his skin. His life, a contracting series of concentric circles, forced him into ever narrower gyres. No matter which way he turned his physical contingence imprisoned him: the hang of his arms, the shape of his hands, the slope of his shoulders, all were defined and, indeed, imprisoned by his circumcision—a sacred covenant before the war, now a stanchless wound.

On the road leading into Vilna, he unraveled his Muslim story thread by thread to ensure it was seamlessly well woven, but doubts assailed him. Beneath his new rusticity lay a tortured assembly of lies, subterfuges, and poses. It was all smoke and mirrors—the brittle instruments of an artless deception. An icy current swept through him again. The faces in the streets streamed by like nightmarish images.

He was now nearly face to face with the door that led into the doctor's office, a mystery whose answer lay within.

He rang the bell, and when a middle-aged woman opened the door he presented his appointment card. She motioned perfunctorily for him to come in and take a chair in the waiting room. He fiddled with his cap, wondering who the physician might be. His life, he knew, was in the doctor's possession.

The same woman who had opened the door now appeared again. She was the doctor. His heart again flew at a rapid canter, his mind bestriding it.

She motioned for him to enter the examination room, which miraculously was dimly lit and made even darker by lowered curtains, thick and dingy and blocking out the waning light of day, which soon decomposed into a mass of shadows. She told him to undress and walked out of the room. He unbuttoned his shirt partway. But he knew he had to go on. He now did so hastily and sat still in the chill air.

He clung to Islam, his shield, his footbridge rising high over the abyss, and remembered all the Mohammedan angels, the intercessors of God, especially Israfel, the angel who calls the souls on Judgment Day, and Mika'il, the life sustainer in times of trouble.

The doctor returned, placed the stethoscope around her neck, and then brought it down on his chest, asking him to breathe audibly. She squeezed his neck and looked cursorily at his eyes. She conducted the exam with an instinctive tact, did not pepper him with questions and did not appear overly inquisitive. After touching his hands and feet, she went over quickly to her table and wrote down her observations.

"You appear healthy," she said, as she glanced up from her notes.

He fully expected her to continue the exam, with fatal consequences, but when she put her note in an envelope and sealed it, a wave of relief washed over him.

She handed him the note. "Give this to the officials at the Nazi labor office," she said smilingly.

He dressed, slipped his fingers through his blond hair, adjusted his shirt, and took his leave. In the street he stood suspended in disbelief. To what could he attribute this unusual turn of events? To her natural modesty? To providence?

He neared the Nazi labor office and his body tautened again. He feared his luck would run out if he was again interviewed by his officer.

He steeled his nerves and walked into the building. The officer's secretary took the sealed envelope, opened it, and read its contents. Father limited himself to a few words, each of which might reveal the stumbling uncertainty of his voice. She finally handed him a slip of paper with the name of Stefan Osmanov and the date and place of his departure for the Nazi heartland.

It was now March 23; in two weeks he was to go to Berlin. He walked along the winding back roads to Sorok Tatar, his anxiety ebbing and cresting.

As he approached its outskirts, the rattling of wheels echoed the waning sounds of the day's activity. It was now just about the time when the Jews congregated at Kuzminski's to pick up their evening meal of bread and soup. He headed straight there, but no Jews were to be found. He felt a mortal chill but still hoped that they might be delayed in the forest.

He waited to no avail. He then approached Kuzminski, who told him that on this very day, the one he went on for his medical examination in Vilna, the Jews of Sorok Tatar were rounded up and returned to the ghetto.

He lowered his head. His hopes soon sank even further. How could he stay in the village of Sorok Tatar and not be betrayed? True, for the Nazi officials he had accreditation as a foreign laborer. But in the village, everyone still knew him to be a Jew.

Under no circumstances would he go back to the Vilna ghetto, a certain death sentence. He'd remain in Sorok Tatar without being visible. That forbade his return to Franzkevich's for the night; even staying in his vicinity was inadvisable. Father knew his Polish host had a relative on the other side of town, who might not even know that the Jews had been ordered back to the Vilna ghetto and thus not realize that his status had been altered. Franzkevich's distant cousin was now the sole answer to his quandary.

He threaded his way to the far side of Sorok Tatar and found to his delight that the cousin, in fact, needed a helping hand in threshing grain. He put him up in a half-abandoned barn, whose walls sloped and roof sagged from the heavy rains.

Father worked hard, and at night he dropped off, weary more from tension than from labor. During the day he thought of the strange convergence of events that had kept him alive. Had he not departed on March 23 for Vilna, he too would have been consigned to a ghetto death.

Two weeks of anxious aloofness followed, and he withdrew further into solitude. He dreaded the sudden and unbidden appearance of Franzkevich or anyone he had known from the other side of town.

He thought again of his own father and how much he was coming to resemble him. He had been a stowaway, a fugitive crammed into the hidden spaces on a ship bound for America. Forty years later, Father was a castaway on the verge of being secreted in the bowels of Germany. A stifling crawl space surrounded by crowded berths was Grandfather's answer to czarist cruelty; Father's haven would be a nook in the dark forest of Teutonia, in the enemy's heart.

The period of expectancy wore to an end. The day of his departure dawned reluctantly, and he woke with a start. He washed his face with cold water, then bundled the wheat for the last time without informing his new host of his plans. He closed the door of the barn, took a last look at the dew that had settled upon the land, and then departed.

In the fog-shrouded distance, where Sorok Tatar blurred into the forest shadows, he saw a materialized phantom approach. It was Stefan's mother, Helena Osmanova, pulling a horse that could scarcely budge an overloaded cart. The animal, with its sobering capacity for suffering, strained until the breath from its nostils streamed like a hot jet of air. Necessity and privation had made Helena a village factotum.

Father's footfall slowed as she neared. Helena looked puzzled but said nothing. They walked together in lockstep with the glacial gait of her horse. She had no inkling of his cunning, so jealously had he guarded the inviolability of his false self that she couldn't have imagined Father was posing as her son.

They parted ways in a few minutes. He passed the jagged line of pine timberland that his fellow Jews and he had felled that winter. Gray stumps stood in the morning air. The spring rains flooded parts of the forest and every ravine seemed liable to turn into a torrent of snow-churned water. The wind rose and cawing crows whirled in broad arcs against the sky, their screaming flight echoing his own, save that they did not need to soar on borrowed wings.

The sun was at its zenith as he neared Vilna. In the distance he heard church bells ringing. The sky was harsh, metallic, and implacable. What was once the city market, a place where Poles and Jews traded goods amid huge baskets of fruits and vegetables, lay under a pall of gloom. He thought of the natural piety and moral order that had once governed their lives.

At two o'clock he arrived at Vilna's railroad station at Zavalna Street. Thousands of Poles, Lithuanians, and White Russians crowded the platform, a varied social patchwork: young cowherds, sowers, farmers, factory hands. He joined the motley crowd, his face a taut line.

Each person carried a bundle for the journey. For Father to have appeared at the station emptyhanded would have been too risky. He had his simple backsack; since he had practically no possessions of his own it contained old papers to give it bulk.

To be convincing, his old self had to be as hermetically sealed as a sarcophagus lid. No one near him proffered a gesture of friendliness, and neither did he. Father discovered yet again how apt the Yiddish phrase *"Vos veyniker me redt, iz alts gezunter"*—The less said, the healthier. The Germans kept the line, and when anyone fell out accidentally some guards rushed forth red-faced to the verge of congestion. Others, more aloof, stood in poses of exalted contempt. Father reviewed his Muslim tale, examining it from every angle. Now more than ever survival meant self-interrogation.

The train crawled into the station, emitting jets of vapor. A tense and nervous mood prevailed. German officers with skulls and crossbones stitched into their uniforms suddenly flashed into view and stood near the rails. The one with a cigar stump tilted in his mouth at a superior angle began calling out their names in alphabetical order. The lists were long and they stood at attention for hours.

Father lifted his eyes and saw the sun sketching an arch of light. The crows cut sweeping parabolas in the air, their shrill cawing sounding like distant cannonading. To his eye they had the brooding menace of condors flying with their gigantic black wings outstretched.

Suddenly the name "Stefan Osmanov" was shouted. It still sounded hollow and uninhabited, and Father's tongue clutched in fear to the roof of his mouth. But instinct forced his arm straight up in a spasmodic burst, and he answered, "Here."

A small ladder leaned against the freight car. He placed his foot on the first rung and looked one last time on the ground patched with sunlight and shadow. He sprang into the car, crawled into its sepulchral corner, and sat huddled on the floor. Though his stamina was about worn out, the journey to the end of night was just beginning.

The freight car filled up quickly with its human provender while the light of the spring afternoon waned. Through the half-open doors he saw the billowing clouds, secure in their elevation. The flight pattern of the birds then broke asunder. The Germans and Lithuanians ran to and fro shouting orders. Father sat still as the doors clanged shut and a whoosh of air shot out from under the wheels. The train eased out of Zavalna Street en route to Berlin.

CHAPTER
7

*Border Crossing
to Berlin*

THE GERMAN FOREIGN LABOR program, initiated by Albert Speer, the Nazi architect and Minister of War Production, enabled Berlin to better conduct a strenuous two-front war. By early April 1943 it had peaked, just at the moment Father was heading by train toward the Nazi capital, one of many foreign workers from across Europe, especially from occupied eastern Poland and Russia, brought to Germany. Speer, who had, in 1934, stage-managed the grand Nazi pageants at Nuremberg, now controlled nearly all German production and was regarded by many as the most significant figure in Nazi Germany after Hitler. Father's transport was to be one of Speer's last from the Vilna region.

Dostoevsky wrote in *Crime and Punishment*, and Father now learned first-hand, how intense the craving for life could become:

> Someone condemned to die thinking an hour before death that if he had to live on a steep pinnacle or on a rock or on a cliff edge so narrow that there was only room to stand, and around him there were abysses, the ocean and everlasting darkness, eternal solitude, eternal tempests—if he had to remain standing on only a few square inches of space for a thousand years or all eternity, it would be better to live than to die. Only to live, to live, to live, no matter how.

The Berlin-bound train raced against storm clouds hanging low over the neighboring fields. The faces of his fellow passengers flowed by Father like the images of sleep, their shadows reeling and staggering in the train compartment. After a short interval he spotted through a crack in the bolted wooden train door a barbed wire gate on which was affixed the word "Ponar," a lonely echo of a departed world.

Like his own father, he felt tied to Polish fields of rye and mustard bloom as by an invisible clasp. No matter how far Grandfather had traveled as a czarist soldier in 1910 across Central Asia, where the medieval Tatar gong had once sounded, he carried the spirit of the *Tehilim* (Psalm-reciting) Jew with him. Even when voyaging across the immense eastern desert or the vast Atlantic abyss, he was borne back on a tide of memory to Novogrudek. And Father would no be less true to his native grounds.

And to think that Novogrudek and Vilna were once the seat of the muses; their fir trees and crystalline lakes said to be inhabited by naiads and nymphs. After all, this was the region that Mickiewicz, son of Novogrudek, had turned into epic. He opens his great work *Pan Tadeusz* with the following radiant invocation to his homeland:

> *O Lithuania, my country, thou*
> *Art like good health; I never knew till now*
> *How precious, till I lost thee. Now I see*
> *The beauty whole, because I yearn for thee.*
>
> *O Holy Maid, whose Czestochowa's shrine*
> *Dost guard and on the Pointed Gateway shine*
> *And watchest Novogrudek's pinnacle!*

A bridesong of praise to a land that evoked a perfect harmony between his characters and their world, these lyric strands now were more poignant than ever.

The Berlin-bound train picked up speed, and the engines were at full throttle. Father breathed in at once the smell of death and the perfume of the flat meadows. How strange that trains, once the conduit of his dreams of travel, were now the vehicle of Europe's nightmarish enslavement.

As Father looked about, instinct warned him that a too austere reserve would militate against him. He needed to mingle with the others, not to draw undue attention to himself by his isolation. But he wanted to select a conversation partner with whom he would feel comfortable. Avoiding knots of roughhousing peasants, he imperceptibly sidled toward a young fellow sitting near him in the freight wagon, an adolescent—almost waif-like—who would not overburden him with questions. Here he could count his words and converse no longer than he had to.

He struck a match and lit a cigarette. After a few puffs, he was engulfed in a cloud of smoke and proffered the youth a cigarette, who nodded eagerly. Father helped him light up and they exchanged heartfelt complaints about their spartan accommodations. He then slid back into his berth, no longer entirely a loner.

Soft rain began to fall as the fog-blurred lights of Vilna vanished into space. Conversations dropped off as night descended. To soothe himself into sleep, Father rehearsed in his mind his mother's tender Sabbath songs, which came to him as from the other side of the world, yet sounded in strict counterpoint to the whistle-wail of the train. Laying in his mother's lap as a child, he had heard her sing valedictory verses to the departing Sabbath, as she scanned the sky for three stars marking the end of the rest day and with it the wondrous division between the sacred and the profane. Her distant lilting voice lulled him into sleep.

The freight train dropped speed, and Grandmother's songs died into a faint sigh. Through the cracks in the wooden doors he saw the shimmering lights in the distance. The others began to stir. The train bore down on the approaching station with ponderous force and then ground to a whining halt.

The doors unlocked and slid open. An array of Lithuanian border guards and German *Feldgendarmes* looked straight at them.

"Everyone out!" the Germans shouted. Their screams burst over them like an exploding shell.

They grabbed hold of their possessions, jumped off the wagon, and assembled along the platform.

The station sign read "Vishbolo." A snarling Lithuanian soldier approached them and said in a rafter-rattling voice, "This is the crossing point into Germany! Before you enter the Reich, you will proceed to the next building to shower! Everyone undress on the double!"

His sentence snapped shut like fate's door. Father's heart leaped into his throat. To stand naked with all the others was to be found out, to be instantly identified as a Jew. He could see in his mind's eye the German guards unslinging their rifles and squeezing the triggers.

What could he do now? He had been caught unaware. Panic-stricken flight would hasten the disaster he wished to avoid. Reluctance to shower could itself raise suspicion among the border guards and incur charges of insubordination. Even if he wanted to protest, his voice was so tremulous that it alone would betray him.

Prior to entering the showers, the laborers' heads were chemically treated to destroy lice. A thin cloth headband was then wrapped around Father's hair to keep the water from running into his eyes.

Shirts and pants were flung on top of long wooden benches. Father stripped his clothes off and threw them on the growing heap. The thick, choking odor of soap struck him in the face.

A sudden wave of shoulders thrust him onto the wet floor. Limbs shot out in every direction, a blur of naked flesh. Jets of hot water streamed down as he clutched his bar of soap, which he used liberally and protectively to hide his Jewishness.

The pulse in his head beat strongly as he desperately sought out corners of the chamber where the vapor curled around him most thickly. Never before had he experienced in the flesh, so to speak, that hell is other people.

The press of naked bodies was such that he could scarcely breathe. But the knowledge that he was no more than a whirling spot in the others' line of vision calmed him.

The pushing was relentless, and in a while Father was forced out of the shower chamber by the sheer numbers clamoring behind him. He toweled himself in the next room, and slipped quickly back into his clothing. He had evaded a reckoning.

The Lithuanian guard who had ordered the laborers-to-be into the showers now reappeared. He waited till they were all dry and then announced, "That wasn't so bad. And now you need to be examined."

Several nurses appeared and led them out of the room. Father passed a huge wall mirror and noticed that he had gone white.

Again he disrobed. The air cooled off and he began to shiver as he waited for the physicians. He pinched his cheeks to give them back color and straightened his posture so as not to betray the bent and haggard look of fear. As the line inched forward, his mind, a bristling armed camp, readied itself for onslaught. A German physician in a white smock wiped and adjusted his glasses and then motioned for Father to approach. Father tensed as he stared at his hard eyes and brutal jaw. The physician sat Father down and began to check his ears and throat. When he was about to bring down his stethescope on Father's chest, the side door opened and a nurse addressed him. "There is a call for you, Herr Doktor," she said.

"Don't move!" he told Father sharply and left the room.

Who could be on the other end of the phone line? The Germans in Vilna, Father imagined. Hadn't they just unearthed the truth about him and relayed the information to the border? The German physician would return momentarily with policemen and guard dogs and have him dragged away. His jaw quivered and his breathing became more labored.

Father touched his forehead and wiped away the sweat that had settled there. Fearing that his agitation would break through to the surface, he strained to keep from falling apart and clung to his Tatar identity as an exhausted swimmer, stroking desperately over the waves, grabs hold of a life buoy.

The side door opened and the doctor reappeared, alone. He looked hurried and distressed as he approached Father and glanced at the long line of waiting candidates behind him.

"Okay, you're finished," he said summarily, and motioned for him to go to the next room.

Father felt as if he had received a special dispensation, not from the doctor but from heaven itself. His arrest, of which he was so certain, had been delayed. The shadow of a pointed pistol that had flickered across his mind's eye disappeared for now.

He retrieved his clothing and combed his tousled hair. The haste of the moment had protected him. But there must be something more to this unaccountable reprieve: his mother's radiant life, whose acts of kindness were now mortgaged to him, allowed him to pass deeper into the iron web without being crushed.

He knew every gesture still carried betrayal as its shadow. Only a conjuror's trick—something on par with the nightly recitation of a life-saving story, à la Scheherazade—would keep death at bay.

After the partially aborted medical examination, Father stepped into the fog- and drizzle-enveloped platform. Trains raced through the station, and he could only wonder at their passengers' debarkation. He felt he no longer had a life but only an undetermined destination.

The others now lined up as the hiss of a steam engine sounded in the distance. Within minutes the pounding wheels of the Berlin-bound train shook the station. These were not crude freight wagons but passenger cars with a modicum of comfort. Their long, rectangular windows were clean and transparent. The laborers entered single file while German transport officials ran to and fro making last-minute checks. The doors finally shut and the train lumbered out of the station.

Gray storm clouds brushed the low-lying hills. Timbered houses and their trimmed gardens plots raced by, receding toward the horizon, their delicacy so incongruous with what had come before. Sunken-headed cows grazed placidly. Here there was nothing of the scorched landscape of occupied Poland.

Ironically, as Father's train hurtled westward to Berlin, another vehicle raced eastward to "resettle" his paternal aunt and uncle in Auschwitz. Henja Stolinski, who had been born in Novogrudek, had left in the 1920s for Offenbach-am-Main, the Frankfurt suburb known for its tanneries and the pungent smell of animal hides, as well as for its martyrdom of the Jews during the Black Death in the mid–fourteenth century. Together with her husband, she had established a leather-handbag manufacturing firm, which initially prospered. But when hard times came, they left for the bustling port city of Antwerp in Flemish Belgium, which even by the turn of the century, years earlier, had become a major embarkation point for the mass migration to America from Eastern Europe. A childless couple, they spent their days running their leather business amid the thriving Flemish guild houses and antique gables. Belgium then had quite a few *maroquinerie*, leather enterprises, which had become a Jewish specialty.

During the late 1930s, Henja traveled from Antwerp to visit her birthplace, Novogrudek, and was welcomed by her siblings and her nephews with open arms. A few weeks after her arrival, she traveled with Father and his cousin Leyzer into the primeval Naliboki forest to visit the legendary "Guter Yid," a centenarian recluse known for his blessings. They journeyed by cart for days, crossed the glassy smoothness of the Nieman River, and threaded through the thick woods. Henja, who had longed for a baby, received a blessing for childbirth, and Father and his cousin got their own special benisons. Upon their return trip through the glowering forest, they came to a lake crossing which they misjudged as shallow. Their horse plunged into the unsuspected depths and began to swim, but their cart would have met with utter ruin had they not miraculously drifted across a huge submerged tree trunk that served as a lifeline. The power of the Good Jew, it appeared, had already begun to work wonders.

But a decade later, the tree trunk was no longer to be found. Compliant Belgian civil servants assisted Nazi overlords, enthusiastically abetted by Rexists, native fascists. Jews were systematically dispossessed, refused entry to places of culture and entertainment and forbidden participation in schools and workplaces. By the middle of 1942 all Jewish property had been "Aryanized." On August 28, 1942, most of Antwerp's Jews were arrested in a sudden *Aktion*. The Nazis cordoned Henja's home on Province Strasse, herded its occupants into a courtyard, where any attempt to purchase release failed. They were marched under guard—passing Antwerp's vaunted streets with their Renaissance façades topped by gilded figures, once their favorite promenade ground on Sunday constitutionals. As the evening lamps sketched ovals of light, they arrived at Centraal Station, the many-spired edifice whose capacious ticket hall evoked the shadowed mystery of a medieval church. The Jewish diamond district extended behind its imposing façade. Henja and Moshe produced their documents for preening, self-satisfied guards. Within hours they had taken their seats on their agonal journey. As the stars traveled deeper into the sky, the locomotive edged out of the station, carrying Henja and Moshe first to the transit camp of Malines, and then to the crematoria of the East.

Father came to discover this tragedy years later. For now, he looked out of the windowed car while his fellow passengers mused dreamily on the Berlin-bound train. His multiple selves could never intersect. Every step he took as Stefan Osmanov must appear authentic if he was to dupe the Germans. No false note could be sounded. No trace of the past—neither the yeshiva pallor nor the singsongy Yiddish accent—must be detected if a deliberate reworking of the self was to succeed. As the train hurtled away from the Baltic, Father's thoughts calibrated just how aloof and sociable he could afford to be with his fellow passengers.

Racing south in the moonlight through the gulches of a pass, the transport car made him dizzy and reminded him of the burden he carried. It now entered a plain of pine forests and marshes. Time, no longer simply registered on clocks, was now imprinted on Father's nerve endings, and the hours dragged.

They now took leave of the soft, undulating farmlands. The first dim

lights of Berlin shone in the distance. The train snaked through the industrial grime and churning noises of the city's outskirts; the screech of truck
tires assailed them through the windows. Those who'd been napping came
to. They passed medieval crenellated walls, grim mechanized mills, and
suburban church spires glistening in the morning sun, and smelled the burnt
petrol in the air.

In a while, after having sped by blocks of tenements, the train approached
a siding and veered left, its engine drawing level with the head of the station.
Father observed that the landing place was large, larger than anything he
had ever seen, but nothing compared to Albert Speer's grandiose urban
fantasies. A tense hush fell upon them as they crowded near the door and
heard loud voices outside.

They leaped from the passenger cars and stood quietly at attention.
German officials divided them and ordered them in different directions.

Father left with a group that descended a strange contraption of mechanically rolling steps, a proto-escalator, whose soft handrails he gripped
to steady his balance. Tables had been set for them downstairs and they
lined up at the huge kitchen. From the corner of his eye Father saw a
number of policemen and soldiers. His appetite disappeared. But like the
others he filled up his plate and trooped heavily to a nearby table and
scrunched his knees under it. He didn't savor his food. His thoughts drifted
off to Helena Osmanova and her pitiful circumstances. And for the first
time he imagined what she might do when receiving fewer rations as a
result of Stefan's supposed departure for Germany. Surely, once her son's
rations declined, she would protest to the authorities. And then in no time
Father's patchwork identity would unravel.

In his mind Father could hear the German officer canceling Mrs. Osmanova's request for a ration-card renewal:

"This doesn't tally. Your son is working in Germany."

"Oh no," she would insist. "Stefan is with me. I can bring him to you.
You must be mistaking him for someone else."

Her words—deafening even though imaginary—unnerved Father. He
then heard the Nazi riposte:

"We do not make such mistakes."

"Sir, if you will permit me," Helena would add, "how can Stefan Osmanov, my very own son, be in Germany when he is right here in Sorok

Tatar? I have never known him to be in two places at once," a thrill of indignation rising in her voice.

"Very clever, Mrs. Osmanova. But our records don't lie. If need be, I'll have this checked out."

What had begun as a distracting uncertainty turned now into a raging obsession, taking on the elaborate contours of the baroque. The self-impelling wheels of Father's mind spun at maddening speed. He now imagined the Nazis in Vilna phoning headquarters in Berlin for confirmation of the whereabouts of the real Stefan Osmanov. Father felt the float-plank of his world sinking and himself with it.

His thoughts whirred like a knife grinder's stone. Father nearly forgot where he was, and for a few minutes he had let his meal grow cold. Was this an objective fear to be taken seriously, or the self-frightening emanation of a tortured mind? he wondered. No matter. He knew he had to halt this train of thought or meet with psychological ruin. It took a fair amount of deliberation for Father to finally shake off its debilitating hold. Only as the meal winded down had he begun to reason his way into a semblance of sanity.

A loudspeaker now blared that the laborers from the East were to proceed to Wilhelmshagen for further instruction. They rose as a single body, collected their few belongings, and headed back up the escalator, a contraption that convinced them—wide-eyed country youth—once again how ingenious German technology appeared to be.

A new train rolled into the station as the day dawned. Father's mind still dwelled on Helena Osmanova and her pressing need for rations. The steady beat of fear made him as restless as the swallows above. In an hour they boarded the train, and he stared out of the window as the sun began its slow ascent in the sky.

The seated laborers watched long, clattering trains enter the station. After shifting in their places, they sensed the train imperceptibly edge out of the platform. From his vantage point, Father saw a band of Hitler Jugend attired in regulation uniforms put through their paces as if in preparatory training for prodigies of battlefield valor.

Many of the faces in Father's car were new, a cause for concern. What if someone from Novogrudek appeared who might blow his cover out of sheer malice? Indeed, ever since he boarded the train in Vilna Father was on the lookout for familiar faces, the better to avoid them. But after over-hearing the conversations near him, he realized that these Polish laborers were from the west and not from the eastern borderlands. For the moment, he rested more easily.

The diesel threaded through Berlin, passing miles of woodland and water. Father wondered if the Brandenburg Gate, topped by a four-horse war chariot of the goddess of victory, was nearby, as well as Unter den Linden, with its landscaped trees planted four abreast. Driven by infernal ambition, Nazi Berlin, it appeared, had recreated itself into a parody of imperial pomp. As if wearing a Wagnerian helmet, the capital was a city flagrantly operatic, openly idolatrous, drunk on its destiny. Yet, through the windows Father saw a sullen man laying about his poor undernourished nag, thrashing it to an inch of its life. From the distance he observed heaped-up wreckage alternate with industrial grime and urban squalor, but he didn't quite know what that meant.

But in a minute Berlin faded from his vision, only to be replaced with Sorok Tatar and the stubborn scenario of Stefan's mother requesting a ration-card renewal again subverting his resolve. It seemed ironic that her son, his lifeline, might just as soon become his death sentence. Survival and extinction were separated by a hair's breadth.

Father saw the approach of Wilhelmshagen, a grim phalanx of barracklike buildings processing thousands of laborers from east and west. The platform was a tumult of multilingual voices as workers from France, Holland, the Ukraine, Byelorussia, and Poland teetered in groups waiting for their work assignments.

"*Achtung!*" the loudspeaker blared.

Quiet fell over the crowd.

Orders were issued in a welter of European languages. Those from north-eastern Poland and Lithuania, who were quickly met by a group of Nazi officials, expanded their eyes with fear.

"Fall into line!" the officials demanded.

Father deliberately found his way to the rear; at least it would give him an extra margin of time to prepare for the unexpected.

They walked for a good stretch amid hilly ground, lugging their bags over their shoulders. At the green painted barracks they halted.

"Get ready for the showers!" a German officer, who had an arched, hooded look of menace, ordered.

This damned delousing business, as Father was coming to learn to his chagrin, was a procedure the Germans, famously obsessed with cleanliness, were to follow to the bitter end. Each time it wasted reserves of stamina he banked on. He felt as if he had been clubbed over the head, awaiting the final betrayal and the slit across the throat.

They surrendered all their possessions before entering the shower, but Father resolved to hold on to the last mementos of his parents. He rolled his father's tiny monogrammed silver cigarette case into his mother's sky-blue cap and fitted them snugly into his palm. He had clung to these objects in the most cramped confines since December 7, 1941; waded with them through swamp, river, and brook.

His clothing was taken to be deloused. His soul again made trial of her strength as he entered the mass showers. No time was wasted on niceties; everything proceeded pitilessly, and indiscreetly. Any stammering hesitation might prove fatal. He tried to appear blithe, but only a will of iron allowed him to wrestle fear to the ground. His parent's talisman-like possessions firmed his fragile hope when all else sought to defeat it.

The next day he was photographed against a blank wall with a number tacked onto his shirt. The camera clicked, and a few minutes later his picture, which he feared betrayed a petrified look, fell into a large basket. The secretary, who had a string of fake pearls plaited in her hair, appeared not to notice. She then asked him a battery of questions, including his place of origin.

"Stefan Osmanov from Sorok Tatar," Father answered obediently. Perhaps because of the number of people she had to process, she absentmindedly categorized him as a Pole and not as a Tatar. She might have assumed that his blond hair and blue eyes were presumptive evidence of Polishness. He didn't argue the point: why draw the bow over tightly if he didn't have to? After jotting down his nationality, she had him fingerprinted.

In a few days he readied himself for a train trip to Schwebus, a small village several hours from Berlin. He again rehearsed his Tatar tale, binding the tendrils of his new identity ever more tightly.

After a desultory ride, the train rolled into the weatherbeaten Schwebus station. The black locomotive belched smoke and its gyrating sidebars came to a stop. A wind whipped the Nazi flags draped around the railroad stop. Father leapt onto the platform, his pants smartly tucked into his boots.

The German labor official ordered him and the other workers against a wall in the full glare of sunlight. Father made out fields of pasture drifting into thick woods, on the horizon.

They waited fatalistically for the Nazi farmers to make their choice, much as slaves once watched their owners auction them on the block. All that was missing was the clang of leg chains.

Father, innocent of farming experience, expected within a day to be revealed for the imposter he was. Time was when everyone knew how to farm; it was the natural possession of mankind. But that age had long passed.

He saw from a distance the frame of a farmer's daughter outlined against the sky, approaching with an eagerness in her step. She hastened her pace and greeted the German train guard. Blond-haired and bronze-necked, she looked them over as if they were tethered animals for sale. For a moment a strange solidarity bound him to the others in their common abject condition. But, skilled in silence, Father said nothing and waited. She walked back and forth, and then leaned over for closer inspection. She squeezed their shoulders, their arms, kicked at their heels, did everything to gauge the life in their limbs. After pinching and prodding she turned to Father and tugged his sleeve. Humiliated, he knew at that instant nothing could appease his hurt.

She nodded to the labor official, and he then motioned for Father and another fellow to come forward. They did so instantly and followed her down the road leading toward her father's farm. Father wondered how he could be treated as an animal by one with so fair a face.

Initially, the other Polish laborer at his side worried him more than the farmer's daughter. She, after all, was unlikely to know much about the East, which she in any case was indoctrinated to despise. While Father's background was remote to her, the same could not be said for the Pole, whose knowingness might betray him. Father feared that he would start to question him about his origins. But, to his delighted surprise, he proved uncharacteristically discreet, not the prying sort.

Father couldn't help but notice that his fellow laborer was too fashionably turned out for the likes of a foreign worker—his pants were professionally ironed and his shoes too well buffed for what surely awaited them.

As they hooked into a final bent of the road, past a tree of gracious shade, a large farmhouse reared up in front of them. Cattle-cropped pastures stretching along the horizon were dotted with oxen lashing their tails. In the distance plows turned up the brown earth and chicken coops clattered and cackled with their crowded denizens.

Margarita, the farmer's daughter, led them to a manure-filled barn. Acting the part, Father buoyantly walked right into it with his boots, uttering no protest, not even making a slight grimace. In strict counterpoint, his fellow Pole, aghast at the scene, held his nose and pointed to his fancy footgear, a posture born of wounded Polish pride. He held on to his *elegancja-francja* (Polish for "fancy-shmancy") ways, acting the titled exile to the hilt.

Margarita fumed with indignation and motioned him to follow her. From afar, Father heard her calling a driver to have the foreigner sent back. "This racial castoff simply will never do," she proclaimed, visibly exasperated at this self-preening Pole daring to raise himself above the Reich.

Later she told her father she had given the Pole the boot: *"Papa, ich habe das Pole kurzerhand von der Tur gesetzt."* He nodded gravely and returned to the farmhouse.

Father envied the Vilna Pole his good manners and aristocratic airs, but he knew he could never share his temerity. Would that he had the luxury of worrying about his footgear! In the end, much as he secretly admired the Pole's chutzpah, a quality that the Talmud aptly described as royalty without a crown, he was relieved at his countryman's disappearance. For Father preferred to work alone. To have had a stranger at his side round the clock would have been unbearable and ultimately would have ground him down. In the wear and tear of daily drudgery on the farm, he might easily betray himself by some unguarded gesture or inexact colloquialism.

Father spent his first night in his assigned hut in Stensch, the farm village, without the prying presence of another. He only heard the grunting of pigs. But he knew his reprieve wouldn't last, since there was another bed flanking his own, which would be occupied in due time. His room was for now his sovereign domain. For hours he sat through the dark watches of the night looking up at the starlight and only falling asleep toward morning.

CHAPTER
8

Blood and Soil

THE SUMMER OF '43 arrived and turned the earth ripe green, wafting the scent of freshly mown grass across the farms of Stensch. Trying to efface the track of generations, Father was masked and padded with lies about his origins, religion, and ancestry. Posing as a farmer, Father had in point of fact never held a plow nor seen the inside of a barn, and knew next to nothing of the required code of behavior.

Three times a day he took his meals with Gustav Steinbach, the Nazi head of the farm, along with his family and the tow-haired Dietrich, a *Hitlerjugend* in training to become a peasant warrior in the conquered lands of the East. Although hardly more than a boy with peach down trailing his cheeks, Dietrich was an integral part of Nazi indoctrination. One could almost trace the budding soldier outlined in his young face. He was part of the *Landdienst* program, designed to turn urban youth into farm workers in the occupied Ukraine. Father could hardly expect much sympathy from Dietrich, whose peasant-like canniness would come to complicate his life.

Father consumed the unfamiliar German food ravenously. He sat wedged between the others, looking at the antique timepiece hanging on the wall and chiming the hour. For the moment he was glad to be alive on this summer morning, to have anything to eat, and to see the foliage cast its seasonal shade on the ground.

Nazi Germany deeply romanticized agricultural life by viewing the peasant as the embodiment of all that was pure, good, and strong. In keeping with party ideology, a large poster with the racial fighting slogan "Blut und Boden"—Blood and Soil—hung over Steinbach's front door. Gustav Steinbach and his fellow Nazi farmers saw themselves as part of a new agrarian aristocracy, training the young for service in the depopulated and ravaged Ukraine, a program originally proposed in the late 1930s by Richard-Walther Darré, an Argentine-born, English-trained Nazi agronomist. A pig breeder who viewed economic life from a strict racial-biological standpoint, Darré—like his fellow *Artamanen* (back-to-the-soil racist group of the 1920s) member and onetime chicken farmer, Heinrich Himmler—saw the local peasantry as the eternal "life source" of the German race. The young were the vanguard, most especially the *Hitlerjugend,* a favored instrument of racial imperialism and *Lebensraum.* The Germans regarded them as biological redress for injuries sustained in World War I. Insufferably wronged, they now saw themselves justifiably storming across Europe in revenge.

Hitler's ultimate aim was to create a German *Volk* of 250 million. His loyal bureaucrats planned to send the first 100 million to the great plains west of the Ural Mountains. Alfred Rosenberg, the Nazi theoretician, also proposed drafting Northern Europeans (Scandinavian, Dutch, and even sympathetic English settlers) to "Aryanize" the East once the war was won. This vast movement of people—the fullest demographic expression of the rage of nationalism—was designed as the most formidable population transfer in history.

SS chief Heinrich Himmler offered fervid explanations for this *Drang nach Osten*—pull to the East. But Hitler, when it suited him, dismissed mystical racialism. As a clear-eyed, merciless imperialist, the Nazi Führer was reported to have said: "What nonsense! We have reached a time to leave mysticism behind, and now Himmler is beginning with his again. We might as well have stayed with the Church. That has tradition at least!" Despite Hitler's murderous sobriety, the SS found ways to invest German expansion with the chthonic weight of myth.

Dietrich was on the farm for precisely this kind of preparatory imperial "nation building." His father, an engineer in nearby Schwebus, hoped that his twelve-year-old son might someday be worthy of managing a huge German-controlled farm in the conquered Ukraine. Dietrich's internship at Stensch thus combined an act of political allegiance with economic self-advancement.

When Dietrich became enraged, crimsoning to the verge of apoplexy—disconcerting to behold in one so young—he would shout, *"Donner wetter noch einmal!"*—invoking Thor, the ancient god of peasants and thunder, who Heine predicted would "leap up and with his giant hammer start smashing Gothic cathedrals . . ." As a member of the *Hitlerjugend*, Dietrich was the kind of youngster Hitler demanded: "a violently active, dominating, intrepid brutal youth . . . indifferent to pain. There must be no weakness or tenderness in it."

Father saw the mythicization of agriculture for the criminal nonsense it was. Farm work, shorn of ideological bombast, was plain and simple drudgery and had little significance other than the grind of hauling bushels of wheat, cleaning stables, feeding cattle, and sundry other prosaic tasks. To be sure, this was superior to a bullet in the back of the head. And the irony of it all was that the crackpot predecessors of Himmler and Darré—such as Willibald Hentsche, a racist pupil of Ernst Hackel, the German popularizer of Darwin, and a champion of polygamy, as well as of the Artamanen with their call for a heroic guild of agricultural workers—had yearned precisely for the removal of Polish migrant workers from the farm estates on Germany's eastern frontier.

THE SUMMER SEASON BROUGHT more trouble in its wake. Gustav Steinbach told Father he was to be joined by a Ukrainian laborer who would share his hut. Gone would be the margin of privacy that had restored him each night to face the trials of the new day. The Ukrainian, he feared, would become the eye of an all-seeing god.

The next morning, as the sun danced around the barn, Gustav Steinbach, accompanied by a stocky, sunburned fellow, approached Father.

"This is Nikolai, the Ukrainian farmhand who is joining us," Steinbach said.

"Abratok ti moy," he welcomed the newcomer in Russian brotherly terms.

They were left to their own devices in the barn, and Father quickly sized up Nikolai's broad Slavic face, strong chin, and huge hands thickly corded with veins. His powerful build, and tenacious jaws fierce enough to pierce the toughest sinews, disclosed that he hailed from a Soviet collective farm. He had lived in Chernigov, near Kiev, until he had been swept into a

German dragnet searching for slave laborers for Hitler's war effort. Father thought him rustic yet not loutish.

But in the confines of the hut Father no longer found repose. Indeed, the first few nights banished any strength-inducing sleep. In a paroxysm of vigilance, he strained to hear Nikolai's regular breathing; like many back country folk, having once vented a loud yawn, he then slept soundly. Although no more than an indistinct shape in a corner of the darkened hut, Nikolai loomed large in Father's sight.

Father wanted to contract into the very bed frame. When he heard what seemed like a ponderous object beating on the roof of the hut—which proved to be nothing more than a branch—he was convinced it was his heart knocking against his ribs. By dawn, Father had spent a night of wakefulness, bone weary when the light of morning slipped through the shutters.

Dark shadows appeared under his eyes after several sleepless nights. His obsessively repetitive thoughts made him familiar with despair. More so than before, he avoided thinking in Yiddish for fear of committing a linguistic mistake. What if he unconsciously blurted out a Yiddish word in his sleep? What if he stubbed his toe and screamed in his native idiom?

He needed to sever his past. Initially, it was painful to have Yiddish, the language of childhood sentiment, bred out of his bones. No language had ever been as sweet. All his dreams and nightmares would now have to be conducted in the lush syllables of Russian or Byelorussian if he still hoped to be alive upon waking. Mutism, he thought, would have been a blessing.

As he came to know Nikolai, who kept reminiscing about his Russian past and filling the hours with jocular conversation, Father's fears abated.

"Stefan," he said with relish, "you should've seen our farm pigs—big as barrels and pink like the dawn.

"So high," he continued, stretching his hand in rough approximation of their size. "And fat, sure as I'm sitting here."

Not to appear outdone, Father extended his hand just a notch higher than Nikolai's and said with good-natured hyperbole, "But ours were *this* high and bursting with fat."

"No!" Nikolai said, drop-jawed.

"We didn't play around where I'm from," Father added for good measure.

Nikolai again gasped at Father's tale, laughing loudly and long.

In truth Father knew as much about pigs as of the dark side of the moon, but since animals were a usual topic of farm conversation, he had to speak knowledgeably and adapt his manners accordingly. Having once been intended for the rabbinate, he could at best dance lightly around this porcine theme.

Nikolai knew only Russian when he arrived on the farm in Stensch. It fell to Father to acquaint him with pidgin German so he could more easily follow orders. Father never let on how much German he really comprehended for fear of rousing the Steinbachs' suspicious. When Father first came to Stensch, he feigned nearly total linguistic incomprehension, although Yiddish gave him a stronger purchase on German than he had even thought imaginable.

In the beginning, absolute caution was his watchword. He acted the complete simpleton when Gustav gave him his first command.

"Stefan, bring me the pail," he said as they stood in the cow stable.

Several implements lay on the ground. Although Father had understood him perfectly, he picked up a broom instead and brought it to him.

"Nein!" Gustav said, his voice rising a notch. "The pail, please."

Father put the broom back and lifted a hoe lying on the ground.

"Ach, Stefan!" he said angrily. "I am asking you for the pail. What's the problem?"

By then the only implement left to choose was the pail. Father clutched it in his hand and brought it to him.

"Ja, gut." Gustav's face beamed.

Father felt safer risking Gustav's momentary impatience than his long-term suspicion.

As time went on, he allowed himself a few borrowed snatches of German. Within a number of weeks he graduated to another few simple sayings. The Steinbachs grew impressed at how much quicker he picked up their language than Nikolai did. But that didn't change his status as a foreign laborer, another statistic among the millions who stoked the engines of the Nazi war economy, much like the great slave populations of the ancient world whose lives were one endless toil.

The Nazis dismissed Polish and Russian as Slavic "sublanguages," the guttural grunt of would-be humans. Father feared Polish because of its teeth-crushing consonants. He deeply distrusted German, the language of the oppressor, suspecting it of irrepressible atavism. Erich Heller, the German critic, would note this elusive phenomenon: "A sober view of the matter may well be that modern German, having become a literary idiom later than French or English, is an adolescent language, malleable and ready to manifest the inarticulate, which lies beneath all languages. . . . It is easily seduced by genius, idiot or villain. Of course no language is immune from the mendacity of rhetoric and pretentiousness, but German has the lowest resistance."

Father had only to think of the "Horst Wessel Lied," the notorious Nazi song, to realize as much. *"Wenn's Judenblut von Messer spritzt/Geht's uns nochmal so gut"*—When Jewish blood spurts from the knife/Then things go really well—was one of many brutal refrains that chilled the mind.

Despite his bearish size and poor German, Nikolai was not all brawn. Beneath his coarse peasant surface, a vein of poetry ran like an underground river, as did a weakness for hyperbole so common among a people for whom geographical size was nearly limitless. He spoke thrillingly of the broad expanse of his native Ukraine, its southern lights, its golden harvests and rapturous song, while decrying the misery of the *kolkhoz* and the humilities of forced collectivization. But for all that, the sun, for him, as well, had descended once he arrived in Germany, and the green fields surounding Stensch had sunk in shadow.

On sluggish mornings Nikolai reviled Margarita's peppy wakeup call, *"Stefan, Nikolai, aufstehen!"* This was typically followed by the insistent *"Morgenstund hat Gold in Mund"*—loosely, "The early bird catches the worm." Her proverbs at the crack of dawn curdled in their ear.

Nikolai hated being dragged off to Germany and did not much care for Gustav Steinbach, whom he regarded as an oppressor. Whenever he spotted him in the distance, he would mutter conspiratorially to Father in Russian, "There goes our Jew," his lips curling in contempt. Father, dumbfounded by his expression, marveled at the irony of a Ukrainian yokel calling a Nazi a Jew in front of a Jew masquerading as a Polish Tatar. Father knew that Ukrainians had long hated the Jews, but this bizarre equation of victim and executioner strained even the rankest credulity.

Father assumed that Nikolai had imbibed a strong dose of Ukrainian populist anti-Semitism, a vile amalgam of repressed nationalism and Soviet ideology. But other than this outrageous remark, which had been passed off with disdainful affability, Father never knew him to have harbored personal resentment against Jews as such, even though he observed Nikolai on occasion reading a viciously anti-Semitic Ukrainian newspaper distributed by the Nazi Party. But in time, they grew much alike in the daily grind.

They worked as one, and at the end of day fell away breathless from their rigorous exertions.

⊶⊷

SOME WEEKS AFTER NIKOLAI'S arrival, Tatyana, a pretty Ukrainian girl from Dnepropretorsk, arrived in Stensch. The Russian farm laborers eyed her flatteringly, and even the Poles admitted she was "goddamned beautiful." Her imperious dark beauty got her what she wanted. For Father she was worlds apart from the chaste girls he had seen in the shtetl. An incorrigible flirt, she appeared hugely amused by Father's pleasantries. And what a cut-up in her nimble use of her eyebrows, reminiscent of the comic expressiveness of silent-screen actresses.

In no time, she corralled a group of other laborers on Saturday nights for weekly singalongs. Luckily, Father had learned a number of Russian love songs by heart and could perform them at the drop of a hat.

In point of fact, he preferred to sing rather than to speak. Conversation was tricky, especially impromptu banter. His Polish was laggard, since he had spent his youth in a yeshiva where Yiddish was the spoken language. He had only very recently improved his Russian. He always dreaded a false note that would give him away, so he made it a point of always using Russian with Poles and Polish with Russians, a language not native to either, thus cloaking his mistakes from close instinctive attention. To give offense to the ear, to lack the natural idiom of speech, could have spelled doom. Verbal concision was everything—the fewer words, the better, in any language.

In song, words were set, never improvised as in conversation. It was like a separate tongue carved out of the larger realm of language. Through meticulous phrasing and inflection, he could master minute tonal shifts. In the isolation of the fields, he managed through repeated practice to find a life-saving virtuosity in lyrics.

Father's hut, alas, became Tatyana's favorite gathering place. Once she overheard a couple of his Russian love ditties, she would give him no peace. After a couple of rollicking songs, she begged him for a few melting numbers, placing her hand exaggeratedly on her heart. The sheer force of contrast between their pitiful condition and their lofty songs at once saddened and seduced her.

At first Father mildly declined her request, but her persistence brooked no refusal. In time he familiarized Tatyana and her friends with songs about puppy love, thwarted longings, and tragic betrayals—the whole panoply of purple adolescent passion. Many of the songs were blithe, others racily exotic, such as "The Girl from Makhachkala," who rides drunkenly, torn between her husband and her lover, through the wild streets of the Dagestan town, as ungovernable as her emotions (*Te yedyesh pyanaya/Ee ochen bled-naya/Pashoomnim ulitzam Makhachkala*). Dagestan, boasting scores of nationalities and dozens of languages, was the most complex patch of the ethnic crazy quilt constituting the spectacular Caucasus. This mountain kingdom, with its capital, Makhachkala, the port city on the Caspian, was notorious, among other things, for its brigands, *abreks*, whose most extraordinarily wicked coup was to attack a wedding and ride off with the bride.

Still other of Father's songs gushed with oily sentimentality or were marred by exaggerated posturing. But some rose to genuine tragedy, capturing the loss they all felt at the time. *"Was unsterblich im Gesang soll leben muss im Leben untergehn"*—That which is immortalized in song must perish in life—Schiller's last lines in "Die Götter Griechenlands," seemed the common unarticulated sentiment then.

Father's chief concern was to bind his listeners into sympathetic accord, so as to better silence their questioning minds. Within a few weeks he had achieved a sweet fluency that surprised him, insinuating himself into his listeners' innermost feelings. Glistening eyes were happy confirmation that his songs had reached their intended target. Some would chime in, and their voices rose and fell as they segued from plaintive croons to stormy ballads. A certain anguished silence would often rise at the center of his songs, the silence of strangled pain that they could barely hear but only he could fully understand. Even as he gave texture to these youths' unspoken desires, he had to guard against the spell he cast.

Love by its very nature inebriates. Now, above all, sobriety was needed. Father could afford neither to be hypnotized nor stampeded by beauty, for to feel was to be distracted. A thoughtless impulse could issue in death itself. It was all very well to sing up a storm about love's ecstasies, but he could never permit himself to be swept by its gale-force winds. Although he had stopped thinking in Yiddish, Father knew the truth of the folk saying "Lunacy without love is possible, but love without lunacy is impossible."

He soon realized, however, the incongruity of his singing amorous songs and not giving at least the appearance of being in love himself, all the more so when everyone was pairing off. Love's natural ferocity was too frightening, yet to achieve proper symmetry he was forced into romantic imposture. The remedy was close at hand. Tatyana had fallen headlong for his ditties, and her avid eyes pursued him.

When they met on Sundays, he learned how to be intimate without being familiar, keeping his secret hermetically sealed. He whispered in soulful earnest about nature and poetry and gave her roses that grew under the window of Schwester Anna, the nun of the village.

Father and Tatyana sang ditties of breathless doggerel. He murmured soft words against the nape of her neck. She ruffled his hair and kissed him under the new crescent moon. Then she would sink into silence as their arms came together in an ecstatic clasp.

But in truth he was innocent of love, and when he first went picking roses he tore his hand among the thorns. Like a baffled youth he was learning everything for the first time. And as a sheltered rabbinical student, love was terra incognita. He had been carefully instructed that unsanctioned passion was sin, a riot of pagan hedonism. He wondered what his former rabbis, many now murdered, might have made of these voluptuous desires, of days and nights charged with fugitive caresses.

Tatyana's eyes shone like moonlit lamps. While she provided him company, she could never, under these circumstances, fill his solitude. As he became more practiced, he wove enchantment with passion and mastered the right rhapsodic tropes—misty lakes, ruined castles, and uncharted seas—without divulging his private fears.

One Sunday evening when they were apart from the others she seemed pensive. Her normally bright face turned pallid.

"Stefan, I bet you didn't know that Tatyana is not my real name."

At first Father didn't know how to react. Whatever he might say he feared would fall flat. For a wild second he imagined a frank exchange where he would reveal that he wasn't Stefan either, but he thought again and restrained myself.

"Stefan, I would do anything to return home and be Taïssa Gretskaya again," she said, and then sobbed bitterly.

Father was puzzled at this disclosure, so suddenly imparted. Is she Jewish?

he wondered. A name like Gretskaya set him thinking about Jewish surnames. But he said nothing. The whole topic of conversation was a minefield best left untrodden. It was too dangerous even to ask.

He took her into his arms and consoled her under the full harvest moon, gazing at her features of such poignant charm. He longed to share his solitary secret too, to put down his burden of the triple life even for the briefest moment and bind himself to another human being in utter trust. He remembered the wise men of Navaredok saying, *"Tsum shteyn zol men klogn nor nit bay zikh zol men trogn"*—Better share it with a stone than keep it to yourself.

But in the end he did not. He maintained his silence, smothering the murmur that rose from his buried life. Was Tatyana's confidence in fact sincere, or was it coquettish entrapment? Best not to find out. Why allow the careful work of months of concealment to be erased by a sudden impulse? Everything had to be subordinated to the mind's considered purpose—love as well, disputing Ovid's dictum *amor omnia vincit*. Anything that subverted reason would now be cast away.

The rabbis, after all, had taught that passion undermines order. Father understood that in Nazi Germany he could not know exalted love, only self-conscious spontaneity at best. That evening he left Tatyana lonelier than ever, his footsteps echoing in the distance.

Father feared attracting envious attention, which soon shadowed him. Two weeks later a Ukrainian SS guard at the Bretz punishment camp near Stensch rode into town on his motorcycle, a revolver protruding from his holster. Athletically built, roguishly good looking, he swaggered around town, tearing up the pavement. He was coarse and rank. One Sunday, as Father was readying to meet Tatyana, he spotted her flirting with the guard in front of Unter den Linden, the popular beer hall where song and drink flowed in equal proportion. The light glimmered on her dark hair as she flirtatiously moved her shoulders and smiled invitingly. Soon they were passing evenings around the *Stammtisch* engaging in ribald talk while raising foaming jugs of beer to their lips.

Father disdained the Ukrainian who was spending time with Tatyana. Angered by what he saw, he was astute enough in assessing the dangers inherent in such rivalry. His career as Tatyana's troubadour and lover was over. He had no intention of contending with a Ukrainian SS man and thereby lost his taste for cavorting with Tatyana, who was only sensible to her own newfound pleasure.

But what he forfeited in love, he acquired in his fellow laborers' sympathy. They commiserated with him about his loss; they muttered that she heartlessly toyed with her admirers and drove them to despair. He now cursed the treachery born of false love, hinting that while the tree of beauty displays fair leaves, it conceals bitter fruit. In truth, he felt radiant at having extricated himself from so dangerous a situation.

Though Tatyana ignored his singing, he continued to vocalize, remaining popular with the others and keeping suspicions at bay. But soon he learned that even the armor plate of song had its chinks. It was on a Sunday, and the laborers had again gathered in his hut for their weekly entertainment. Tatyana was absent, and everyone cynically assumed she was gallivanting with her new muscled boyfriend.

Father began with a poignant Russian song, "The Nightingale Sings," about an orphan boy expiring alone and ungrieved in a foreign land and whose dying hope is to embrace his native valley one last time. For a second he was so mesmerized by the verses that he seemed to be describing himself.

Just as Father repeated the last refrain, "He remained a luckless orphan abandoned to his destiny"—*dolya*—a Ukrainian laborer, Ivan, grumbled in chilly disapproval, "Don't say '*dolya*'; Jews like to use that word." He labored under the delusion that Jews prefer this emotion-laden word for destiny.

Father imperceptibly shifted to another song, but thereafter his mind began to watch itself even more deliberately.

Father's shaken confidence allowed the worm of doubt to bore more deeply into him. How on earth could he guess that such an innocent word as *dolya* carried such a freight of meaning? He made sure never to sing that tune in the presence of the Ukrainian.

WINTER'S APPROACH BROUGHT THOUGHTS of Christmas in their train among the community of laborers. The holiday, even in these straitened circumstances, was a cause for celebration for Poles, Lithuanians, and Russians; but it was a tricky time for Father, demanding extra caution. After all, to have fully mastered all the Christian rituals in Sorok Tatar would have solicited an alchemist's patience and luck.

For the holiday season, a four-hundred-pound hog was to be slaughtered on the farm and its carved flesh to be jarred and pickled for the Wehrmacht. A messy business, the very thought of which made Father shrink with horror.

On the sacrificial day, a rope was tossed into the animal's maw and as soon as it clamped down on it, it was pulled out of the stable by Nikolai. Dietrich and Margarita as well as Father walked behind the hapless pig. The short grass swayed against its stocky legs when Dietrich brandished a sharp pick and slid his finger across its thin-edged point. With his other hand he grabbed hold of a hammer, bent his own body level with the pig's head, placing the sharp point of the pick between the glistening eyes of the animal, mercifully unaware of what awaited it. Then Dietrich slammed the hammer against the pick, piercing the animal's brain. A full-throated howl of pain tore out of its mouth. The animal fell back onto its rear legs and the massive folds of its flesh rolled toward its hindmost parts. Yet there was still life left in the beast. Dietrich ordered Father to grab hold of one the animal's hind legs and Nikolai of the other, and hold it down as it lay dying.

Margarita drew a long knife and handed it to Dietrich, who, in one clean stroke, slit the pig's throat. She placed a bowl under the animal and drained away its hot smoking blood. She used a big wooden spoon to mix the broth so that it would not congeal.

In ordinary times it would be unthinkable for a rabbinical student like Father to touch a swine, dead or alive. How different biblical sacrifices in the Pentateuch were from this ghastly sight! He recalled passages describing the ancient Israelite priests, standing near the altars arrayed in white vestments and jeweled Urim and Thummim, the divine breastplate, and how they brought fattened animals to the Lord. These burnings were sacred offerings for the remission of sins and for atonement. Had not the scribe Eleazar resisted unto death the Hellenic Syrians who tried to force him into contact with the unclean animal, racking and torturing him when he refused?

But for the moment, Father felt strangely drawn to the slain animal. Its inglorious end spoke with uncommon directness of their kindred destiny, if he were caught and his true identity revealed. For the Nazis every Jew was a *Judensau.*

Several weeks hence, Father and Nikolai traveled to a Christmas party thrown by Russians and Ukrainians in a nearby village, a paltry affair the Germans cast a blind eye at, especially around the holidays. The two borrowed farm bicycles, and at the first narrowing of dusk they peddled through the woods, the dark outlines of whose trees lent the journey an air of mystery.

In the distance the lights of the neighboring farms shone feebly. They spotted a low-slung farmhouse from whose shaded interior tapers flamed. They braked their bicycles and wheeled them to the front of the wooden gate that fenced off the farmyard.

"Stefan and Nikolai are here," Pyotr, a convivial Russian, announced at the doorway.

A smoky room bursting with celebrants, whose lusty bellows and cacklings rang from every corner, greeted them. But the poverty of the place echoed even more loudly—old tinsel bells hung forlornly from the cracked ceiling.

Father was hailed by vodka-induced shouts of acclamation. Someone slipped him a drink, which he sipped cautiously, fearing that a sudden draft of alcohol might loosen his tongue. For the others, the holiday hedonists, life was turned into a sacrament by consuming it, for Father by repulsing it.

"Styopka," said a village girl with a saucy expression, using a colloquial variant of his name, "we've heard you're a famous crooner."

"No, not tonight," he begged off.

"We'll see about that," she laughed with sweet assertiveness and walked away.

"What's your name?" he called after her.

"I'll let you guess," she said, turning her head coyly.

At some point that evening his protest would be of no use. He'd be expected to beguile their hard-won leisure with festive song, to drown their cares in a carouse of drink and music. He was a convenient instrument at hand. Bemused by his aura of musical authority, he consoled himself with the thought that at least song did not carry the perilous contingencies of conversation, the precarious shifts and reversals of colloquial speech.

He approached a group of partying laborers hunched over a stash of photographs, which they examined with whoops of delight. Although he minded his business, a Ukrainian girl handed him a batch. He eased into a chair and two girls sidled over and joined him in looking at the snapshots, which at first were nothing more than a wild succession of unknown faces and places.

A sudden clumsy motion of his hand made him fling a few photographs to the floor, and he quickly bent down to pick them up. When he sat down, a Hebrew holiday card incongruously topped the pile on his lap. Its lettering burned into his eyes. As he locked into a stare, the voices around him seemed to grow indistinct. He was almost afraid to touch the card, which gleamed like an apparition, a phantom of another world, whose faded letters took up arms against an engulfing silence. But just when he forced himself to proceed and to turn over the card, the girl on his right stayed his hand and said, "What's that?"

"Beats me," he said matter-of-factly.

She plucked the card from him and passed it on to the girl seated on his left.

"What do you suppose this could be?" she asked.

The other shrugged her shoulders.

"Hey, Pyotr," the girl on his right called to the fellow who had greeted Nikolai and him so expansively when they arrived. He was reluctant to leave his cronies, who were enjoying themselves tumultuously. "Come here!" she motioned vigorously.

"What is it?" he demanded.

She slipped the card into his hand. "What's this?"

"I don't know," he said, puzzled, as he ground a cigarette into the earthen floor. "It must be the devil's own script," he guffawed. She flung the card back into Father's lap and drifted off with Pyotr and the other girl. Alone with his thoughts, he did not dare to take a closer look at the card, though nothing was more compelling.

How on earth did a Jewish New Year's card turn up here? Yet upon reflection it seemed fairly obvious. It was plunder, part of the looted remains of a Jewish home, dragged off to Germany. These sepia-toned pictures and cards had survived, but their bearers had not.

Just then he was borne back in a rush of recollection to the High Holidays of his early childhood, when life was inhabited by symbols and portents. During the hours preceding Yom Kippur in the mid-1920s when he was a very little boy, his parents were on the verge of sitting down to a pre-fast meal when they heard the ground creaking outside. Father spotted a shadow stealing past the window, near a rotting stump. His mother stopped ladling the soup and his father started to investigate. Then their front door flew open and an old man clothed in a great shabby coat, his shrunken face webbed with wrinkles, staggered in. His worn shoes tracked mud on the floor. Father paled, but Grandfather kept his head. He grabbed his own coat and fumbled through its pockets for the rare zloty. He then slipped the coin into the man's gnarled hands. The old man bowed, retreated a few steps, and left, closing the door softly behind him.

They sat motionlessly for a while, the sweet smell of *khale* in the air.

"Who was that?" Father asked in boyish wonder.

"A messenger," Grandfather said.

"A messenger? From where?" Father continued.

"From heaven. That was Elijah the Prophet," Grandfather said gravely.

"Yes, my child. That indeed was Elijah come to bless us, for we need his prayers," his mother added.

This memory now stood on the far horizon of his childhood. The world had never been the same for him after the old man departed; for then Father had come upon the essential doubleness of life, a duality whose deeper meaning he now discovered.

The song-cajoling girl reappeared, wrinkling her face into a provocative pout. "Guess what would make me happy," she said.

"What's that?" he asked ingenuously.

"Don't play stupid!" she demanded.

"I'm not," he insisted.

"Okay, okay! All I want is a song."

Her friend chimed in, "We all want a song. Is that too much to ask?"

To sing was risky; not to sing might carry even greater danger. Father had to choose between the painful and the intolerable as the Jewish New Year's card lay cradled on his lap, each of its letters a tongue of flame.

Without bothering for his response, she assembled the other girls on the floor and grouped the fellows around them. They looked at him with up-lifted faces. She then clapped her hands and shouted, "Quiet, everyone, Styopka is going to sing for us!"

He understood as never before that one can live down anything except a good reputation. He decided on two of his best songs, whose lines would not trip him up and whose accompanying gestures he had mastered.

Father launched into verses about the moonlit sea and the star-sown sky. Note by note, he poured out his anguish, which they interpreted as the anguish of love. His lyrical poignancy compelled the others to join in, and their voices entwined like gold thread.

As he took his bow and began to retreat to a corner, some fellow in the back shouted, "A Christmas carol!"

"Yes, a carol," another seconded.

A chorus now heatedly insisted on a holiday song and would not be placated. If he resisted their demand, would he be found out? he wondered.

"Come on now! I've done my part. Someone else take a turn," Father responded. An unacquainted tune could only highlight the falseness of his position.

"No, no!" they kept on shouting, raising their beer glasses in unison. Father was bemused how music which ordinarily charms anger was actually stoking it.

When some party revelers turned hotly impatient and demanded then and there that he regale the crowd with a holiday carol, he feigned a sudden lacerating coughing fit. After roughly clearing his throat, he pleaded with them that if they didn't ease up, he would damage his voice, and then all songs would stop.

Finally they relented and began to hum a carol together. But soon some other hard-partying Poles approached and shouted, "The night is still young." Interjecting a loud note of frivolity, they started a patter song of inspired silliness. What luck to have begged off further performance, Father thought. This tongue-twister, demanding daring agility, would have been a virtual death sentence for Father, its knotted consonant clusters heralding extinction.

The Poles sang their tune at such demonic speed that Father could practically hear the devil in its breakneck sibilants. They finished in a roar of laughter to which he added his hoarse-inflected hoots.

After Father and Nikolai had taken their leave, they could still hear from a distance the faint strains of the diabolically quick music.

Father greeted the passing of Christmas with more than a bit of joy. He would now have to face only the customary ordeals without the special holiday burdens. But other minefields were always plentiful.

After the strain of holiday merrymaking, Father caught a cold. His head throbbed, his legs dragged, his knees felt heavy. He longed to lie down and rest, but he knew that would not be countenanced. He remembered how his mother had hovered over him whenever he took ill in Novogrudek. She would prepare a *gogl mogl*, a healing village concoction of raw eggs that cleared the worst throats—even strep, some would say optimistically.

Then the doctor would arrive, bustling through the kitchen, a stethoscope sticking out of his satchel, and the chill north wind blowing through the open door. Grandmother led him to the young patient lying in bed. Bending his knees, he began the auscultation, the first of many procedures.

But Father in Stensch was on his own. All he could do was throw on an extra layer of clothing and wait it out.

LITTLE DID FATHER IMAGINE that a day would come when he'd have to answer for the transgressions of his assumed family members, the Osmanovs. But that day was upon him when Janek, a Polish laborer he had recently met, accused him of a "hereditary" affront.

They had fallen into conversation when in passing he had asked Father for his surname. Upon discovering it was Osmanov, he unaccountably reddened.

"What did your father do for a living?" he demanded.

"Dad was a baker," Father said.

"And where did he work?" Janek continued, tensing.

"In various cities. I think Warsaw must have been one of them."

"Aha!" Janek shouted, as he leaped to his feet.

"Aha what?" Father asked perplexedly. He could not understand why Janek was lashing himself into a fury.

"Now I've got you!" Janek fairly bellowed as he approached.

"What in heaven's name are you talking about?" Father persisted.

"A baker in Warsaw! I'll show you," Janek shouted, about to take a swing at him.

Father's heart was racing. Had he penetrated his tale? How had he tumbled into this trap?

"I don't know what you're imagining, but you've got it all wrong," he said.

"Look here, you good for nothing!" Janek said, grabbing a chair menacingly. "I happened to have worked with your goddamned father!" he screamed, his mouth a mass of froth.

"Excuse me!" Father rose to his full height in defense of his assumed honor. "You're speaking about my father and I won't have him talked about in this way."

"Well, let me tell you, wiseguy, that your father beat me bloody while we were working together in Warsaw!" Janek said aggrievedly.

"It can't be! My father would never have done that. You must take my word for it," Father said. He was dumbstruck how in a city as large and as anonymous as prewar Warsaw, Islam Osmanov, his assumed father, could have had a run-in with Janek, an event that now had come to haunt him.

"Oh yes he did!" Janek persisted, his fists tightening and the reek of alcohol emanating from his lips. "All I know is that I worked for a man named Osmanov in Warsaw and he beat the daylights out of me."

"Oh, come now," Father said soothingly. "Warsaw is a big city and has many bakeries. You're surely mixing them and their supervisors up."

Janek's eyes still emitted glittering sparks, and his mouth frothed with spume. Father saw he had no choice but to insist that he had misidentified the city.

"Did I say Warsaw was where Dad had worked? No no! It was Lodz."

It took several rounds of denial before he could dampen Janek's anger, which sputtered before it died.

That evening while he lay in his cot, Father scolded himself for befriending Janek in the first place. To proffer a slap on the back, a sympathetic laugh, a ready smile, Father had naively hoped, would make a go of it, smooth the rough and jagged edges of living in Stensch. But just when he thought he was getting a hold on things, the rules changed. Stensch, he then understood, would always remain a shifting kaleidescope of misery and chance.

BRETZ, THE PUNISHMENT CAMP near Stensch, shadowed Father. A re-education facility, where the tools of instruction were the whip and the rack, it filled every foreign laborer with dread.

At harvest time, Father obtained quick intimations of what Bretz meant. The Steinbachs needed extra hands that season. All of them had pitched in, but their numbers were too few to cover the tasks. Gustav Steinbach, a Nazi Ortsbauenführer, was entitled to extra workers supplied from Bretz by the SS.

The Steinbach crew set out for the fields shortly after breakfast. Nikolai and Father sat on the lowest rung of the rubber-tired truck while the SS men, who had arrived earlier, sprawled on top, trading salty jokes with

Dietrich, the budding *Hitlerjugend*. Staccato bursts of laughter rang out as they clutched their sides, their mirth finally terminating in wheezing gasps.

Earlier that morning the SS men had deposited their human cargo from Bretz in the fields. When Nikolai and Father arrived, the prisoners were hard at labor, gathering mounds of potatoes and loading them into huge sacks. They worked on the double, nervously eyeing the SS guards. Once they filled a bag, Nikolai and Father heaved it onto the wagons for transport back to the farm.

The prisoners wore striped uniforms and coarse hats to match. Although none were treated gently, one especially was manhandled. Whenever he bent down to gather his quota of potatoes, he was viciously kicked in the rear by an SS guard, and no degree of obedience ameliorated his situation.

At noon they broke for lunch. Nikolai and Father dropped to the ground and filled their flasks with hot tea. The SS men sat near them at the edge of the field.

Gustav Steinbach looked puzzled. After digging into his sandwich, he asked one of the adjoining guards, "Why do you beat this prisoner more than the others?"

"Oh, you must be referring to Hermann," he replied. "It's a long story."

Without betraying his curiosity, Father overhead everything they said.

"Herman was a soldier in the Wehrmacht, fighting on the eastern front—" the SS man continued.

"Well, that's certainly not a reason to beat him!" Gustav interrupted irately.

"I haven't finished!" the guard snapped. "You'll understand if you'll let me explain."

"Okay," Steinbach said sheepishly.

"Hermann's father and grandfather were German, or so we thought. But when he was on the eastern front we discovered to our disgust that he had a Jewish great-grandfather. He was brought back and sent to Bretz."

"What's going to happen to him now?" Steinbach inquired.

"He'll be dead after the season is through," the SS guard said, sketching a noose in the air.

"Yes—a clear conscience is a soft pillow," Gustav sighed in relief, verbally caressing his own unblemished bloodlines.

The sunlight dappled the grass, as Hermann stood forlornly in the distance, baffled at fate. He was forced to confess a faith and kinship he considered foreign. In spite of himself, he had fallen victim to Nazi ideology, which demanded his death as part of its iron law of necessity. Nothing could help him now: he would go to the gallows as a Jew.

ONE SUMMER AFTERNOON NIKOLAI sat peeling onions in the shed alongside Father, who was equally busy peeling potatoes, his back against the door and, as always, on his guard. Nikolai's onions were so sharp that Father eyes began to tear, but he tried to suppress it. He then heard the door open behind him, but did not see Margarita step on the threshold. Suddenly, without warning, he felt from behind a hand on his back and heard her ask, *"Bist du Jude . . . ?"*

Certain his cover was blown, Father felt trapped like a minnow in a cranny. His heart contracted and he felt pain crashing through his chest. Margarita had discovered he was a Jew and was confronting him now.

Gripping the peeling knife, Father was ready to use it against her or himself. His fingers tightened around the handle. What should he do? There wasn't much time left. Perhaps she had already alerted the local Nazi police.

As his breathing seemed about to falter, Margarita repeated, *"Bist du Jude . . . Nikolai?"* and burst into peals of laughter. "Ha! Ha! Jews love onions!" Nikolai smiled and Father then turned around and could see the jocular expression on her face and hear the drollery in her voice.

If only Father had immediately noticed her smiling or if she had uttered Nikolai's name on the spot and not tarried in mid-sentence, he would not have assumed the worst, understanding this to be her feeble attempt at humor. Nikolai, not surprisingly, having far less to fear about pedigree, took it easily in stride.

"Jews peel onions! If you're paring one, you must be one, *nicht wahr?*" she cried, doubling over with laughter. She grabbed an onion, and began peeling it too, giggling all the while.

Quickly rallying, Father joined in the general good cheer. "Oh, that was a good one!" he said, slapping his thigh and clutching his sides. "You're a real comic!" he added, clapping his hands for effect.

Margarita, proud of her wit, chuckled and sat down with Nikolai and Father, regaling both about the Jewish love of onions. She left later that afternoon in a warm glow, delighted by her own cleverness.

At night, lying on his cot, Father thought of the peculiarity of rural German humor and the dangers it carried for him. He might well have agreed with George Eliot's remark a century earlier: "German humor generally shows no sense of measure, no instinctive tact; it is either floundering and clumsy as the antics of a Leviathan or interminable as a Lapland day." For its clumsy antics Father could now easily vouch.

On Sundays when he put on his finery—a blue Polish gymnast's jacket and riding boots—he even spied Margarita eyeing him as he made for the streets of Stensch on his day off. When she was especially buoyant, she'd say to him and to whomever was standing around, for no reason at all, "When the war is over, Stefan will marry in Berlin." Father smiled graciously and acknowledged the compliment. This was high praise indeed for her to offer. And for a moment he relaxed in the encouraging sun of her good opinion, though he was inwardly repulsed by her suggestion. The quick contrast seemed numbing: one moment she had jokingly belittled Nikolai as an onion-loving Jew, the very next she thought Father suitable for marriage into the German race. Despite the momentary reprieve, entrapment and capture continually cast shadows upon him.

WACZEK, A POLISH LABORER from a nearby farm, came to regard Father as his best friend. He was only seventeen and had fallen for a Ukrainian girl named Ilyana, who after a brief romance dumped him for another. This only inflamed Waczek's infatuation, and he would talk about her at length. Father's infinite fund of patience in no time won the boy's gratitude.

As a trusted buddy, he shared many things with Father. Waczek had apparently once landed in a punishment camp near Frankfurt-an-der-Oder for leaving his work station.

"Stefchu," he said one Sunday, as one Pole to another, "do I have a story for you!"

Father leaned over to listen intently.

"You know the camp I was imprisoned in. Well, I saw with my own eyes how three Jews caught with false papers were handled."

"What did you see?" Father asked, dreading what was to come.

"You should have been there for the sight alone," he said, the savor of anticipation full on his face.

"Those three Jews thought they had pulled the wool over the eyes of the Germans. Ha! They thought they had it made with their false papers. But the Germans outsmarted them."

"Get to the meat of the story," he said.

"Boy, I see I've whetted your appetite."

Waczek spat a few times and continued.

"They dragged out the first kike—what a sight he was! He was laid out on a box placed between two Gestapo men, each wielding a leather whip tipped with a shard of iron."

"Where were you?" Father asked.

"I and the others were made to watch. We had the best seats in the house," he smiled.

"Then they pulled down the Jew's trousers. How he howled! I'm telling you again, you should have been there to see it for yourself." Waczek stopped to catch his breath, trembling with excitement.

"Take your time. I'm not going anywhere," Father said, now trying to appear interested and yet offhanded.

"The Gestapo policeman on his left placed a wet rag over the Jew's buttocks. Then they took turns—the guy on the left coming down with his whip, then the fellow on the right. *Eins, zwei, drei . . .* " Waczek, wishing to give the ring of authenticity to his account by imitating the harsh sibilants of German, began to count the number of times, over and over, the Jew was whipped.

"Listen to this, Stefchu," he added, smacking his lips and spitting out a common Polish curse, "dog's blood."

"Well, let's have it," Father said.

"This . . . this Judas, whipped to an inch of his life, cried out to his tormentor, '*Herr Gestapo, ich kann nicht mehr*' "—I can't take anymore.

"What happened then?" Father asked.

"The Germans were infuriated and redoubled their energy. They kept on whipping him till he passed out," Waczek said, beaming. "You should have seen with what joy the Germans brandished their whips."

"They probably brought out one of the other Jews at that point," Father added.

"Ha! That's what you might think, but not so quick! They poured cold water over the wretch in order to start the procedure all over again."

"He must have been a bloody mess," Father remarked, an icy current racing through him.

"That's an understatement. He was beaten beyond recognition, past revival—he was dead."

Waczek cursed and spat. His expletives came thick and fast. His obvious relish nauseated Father. He could not bear to listen anymore and succeeded in moving their conversation onto another topic.

Later that day Waczek returned to his farm. The Pole was obviously unaware of the terror he had instilled, and, to be sure, Father did nothing to dissuade him that they were the best of friends. But it intensified his moated psychology of isolation.

Adam Mickiewicz, while exiled in Rome in 1848, had affirmed in his *Political Declaration of the Polish Legion*: "To our elder brother, Israel: we offer respect, fraternity and help on his way to eternal and earthly welfare, equal rights in every matter." Three years earlier, in a sermon he gave in a Paris synagogue on the Ninth of Av, the saddest day in the Jewish calendar, commemorating the destruction five hundred years apart of both temples in Jerusalem, the Polish Catholic poet declared his sympathy for suffering Jewry and its longing for Zion. He had turned the character Yankel, an old Jewish innkeeper of Novogrudek, a cymbal player, into a Polish patriot and a hero of his epic *Pan Tadeusz*. Yankel's music captures Poland's fight for freedom and its undying chord of hope. It is from his instrument that "A well-known song floated to the heavens, a triumphal march, 'Poland has not yet perished; march, Dombrowski, to Poland!' " Mickiewicz would in yet another work compare the Polish emigrés in Paris to Israel marching across the burning sands in search of the Promised Land. And in a supreme Byronic gesture, Mickiewicz, succumbing to cholera, died in Istanbul in 1855 trying to organize a Jewish legion in the struggle against czarist Russia. Drifting in memory back to his hometown, Novogrudek, Father thought of the promise of Polish-Jewish friendship the national bard had longed for. The contrast between then and now could not have been greater.

With each passing day Father sensed that the hour of his own trial would soon approach. He felt that some horror, the German initials "NN," which stood for *Nacht und Nebel*—night and fog, execution and oblivion—would in the end seal his fate.

CHAPTER
9

Gestapo Interrogation

MONTHS OF DAILY DRUDGERY inured Father to farm work. He now forked the soil and wielded the chisel plow and the hand hoe with greater ease. Slogging through horse manure no longer revolted him but while other laborers sought solace in drink, he sought it in sobriety. Any other means would have him stunned and blindsighted.

One day Gustav Steinbach, chin thrust forward, came toward him in the barn. "Stefan!" he shouted as he approached with a heavy step.

"Yes, sir," Father answered, with a slight formality he always reserved for Herr Steinbach.

"You are going to Schwebus in two weeks," he said.

Father tensed but remained outwardly calm. "Whom am I to see?" he asked.

"Gestapo," Herr Steinbach said.

His words lanced the air and tore through Father like a lead bullet.

"In two weeks?" he asked.

"Yes, don't forget."

After Steinbach left, Father looked at the sky and the drifting clouds, a gray primordial chaos. Fate was fixed, and nothing could undo it now. The Nazis traced everything to its ultimate source and followed every lead to its remotest corner, and so it must be with him.

He had spent months living in the infinitesimal gap between spaces. But things were to be different now. There was no way to benevolently construe this turn of events. He was sure the Gestapo was closing in and could almost hear the wooden door splintering as their approach neared.

As the nights wore on, his capacity for suffering was tested again. He began to sum up his life, seeing that by all indications it was soon to end. A vein of sadness ran through his memories of childhood, of the hills and meadows of Navaredok where he saw the world for the first time. And then, as he had done as a child when facing great fear, he murmured under his breath in secret supplication, "In the name of the Lord, the God of Israel, may Michael be at my right hand, Gabriel at my left; Uriel before me; Raphael behind me; and the Shekhinah of God be above my head."

After the first wave of panic had passed, he forced his mind to focus on what might concretely lie ahead. He began to review every detail of his forthcoming visit to Schwebus and what its larger meaning might hold for him. He knew that every daring deed demanded a deep act of concealment.

If the Germans had detected his traces, why had they not come for him right away? he reasoned. It seemed only natural that if he were a marked man, they would have quickly finished him off. Why did he have two unaccountable weeks in which to stew? Surely the Gestapo had not gone into the business of politely deferred interrogation. Was this then perhaps some new sadistic sport, the latest refinement in Nazi cruelty?

He reviewed the arc of his journey, the farrago of lies that had brought him to Nazi Germany. Where had he slipped along the way? He weighed every possibility, sorted out every occasion where he might have given himself away. But he refused to cave in to the inevitable. Instead of brooding, he decided to act. Perhaps he wasn't alone in being summoned to the Gestapo. Maybe other Poles were also called. If he could only be sure, he might blunt the edge of his fear.

He had his task cut out for him: to question other Poles in the vicinity. Of course he could not appear too eager; he must query them indirectly, to avoid the risk of inciting their curiosity.

After giving it some thought, he decided to seek out the fastidious Pole with whom he had arrived in Stensch. Yes, that would be it. He must find him, the very one booted out of the Steinbachs' farm when he haughtily declined to step into the cow manure. Whatever had happened to this finicky stylist? Perhaps he had been reassigned to a neighboring farm and was now the recipient of just such a summons.

To go to an adjoining village or town required a special permit, one that

Gustav Steinbach would undoubtedly have to sign. Father toiled like a helot in the days before he made his request. Convinced that Herr Steinbach was well pleased with his work performance, Father approached him.

"Sir, I would like to visit the neighboring town."

Steinbach appeared curious at first and asked him what purpose he had in mind.

"You see, a friend of mine has not been well and I want to check on him," Father said matter-of-factly.

In a few days his rail pass arrived. Yet he was now too uneasy to travel by train, suspecting that the station would be the scene of his entrapment. Safety lay in taking the side roads and making his way across the woods.

He wondered if he was not aggravating matters by trying to improve them—what the Germans called *Schlimmbesserung*. But the imperative to go was too strong to halt.

En route he felt as if he were walking on a burning plain under the blue of the sky. He hacked his way through tall grass and trudged across the marshes, whose silence was more racking to his strained nerves than the most discordant noises. How much fear, he wondered, can a spirit bear?

Upon arriving in Schwebus, he inquired where the Polish laborers lived and headed in their direction. But despite his best sleuthing efforts, the man from Vilna was nowhere to be found. He wondered if sartorial habits and the mocking glint in his eyes had finally done him in. Too dapper for these times, he was assured a messy end, Father thought.

The Poles he did meet in the area came from other regions, and from all indications they had not received a call from the Gestapo. Father, driven into a dangerous corner of frustration, felt like a phantom pursuing empty clues.

Hope waned as he realized that he was in all likelihood the only one summoned. His eyes traveled along the wraithlike trees that lined the route back to Stensch. Suddenly a wave of menace broke over him and an equally sudden loss of will.

It was as if an evil spirit were rustling the trees. With each passing step he came closer to a fir from which a large branch jutted out. Leering at him like a gargoyle, in a few seconds it beckoned him and his thoughts turned to death. A magnetic pull, something stronger than himself, dragged him to the branch. The leaves turned into a swirling mass of green and soared above him like a great ghastly cover.

"Remove your belt," a voice whispered into his ear. He could no longer stop it; it raged like the tide.

"Wrap the belt around your neck," the voice persisted like a persecuting tune.

He fought the thought of annihilation, but for the moment it stupefied all other claims. The tree carried death within it, and he was convinced it would soon carry his own as well.

The ground burned under his feet and his mind seemed to fail.

But then unaccountably a buoyant surge of anger at fate and at his own sudden weakness broke over him. He struck out blindly, screaming, "No! I want to live!"

"Flee this accursed spot!" another voice echoed in a far corner of his brain. Two voices, two discordant sounds, battled within him as ancient antagonists.

He finally wrested himself free from the magnetic pull of the branch and retreated in the direction of his newborn desire.

He did not look back for fear of being drawn once again into the swallowing vortex. He had coerced death into a tight corner and vowed he would not permit it to expand its fatal sovereignty. Never before had he understood as now the Jewish affirmation of "choosing life" as the greatest good in the world.

The rush of the wind lifted him. He looked up and saw the swallows rise and circle the air. He walked briskly back to Stensch, feeling life once again coursing through his veins.

HE RESUMED HIS DAILY round but the dark penciling of fate reappeared a few days later. He was at lunch with the Steinbachs, Dietrich, and Nikolai, eating a common dish they called quark, a dairy concoction prepared daily on the farm. Father had just helped himself to boiled potatoes and was about to dip them into the quark for a more palatable bite. Suddenly he heard a loud knocking at the kitchen door.

"*Ja, bitte,*" Gustav Steinbach said, rising expectantly.

The door opened and three young SS men strode in as one, conscious of their audacity and possessing the hard fixity of stone. They halted and then shot out their arms in a Nazi salute, shouting, "Heil Hitler!"

"Heil Hitler!" Gustav Steinbach responded, his less vigorous arm rising somewhat hesitantly.

Father's dish looked congealed and inedible. The potato fell off his fork and his mind pitched as in a storm. They were here to arrest him. He wouldn't have to go to the Gestapo; they had come for him. He already felt flayed alive, though a drop of blood had not yet been shed.

Steinbach flung his napkin on the table and hastened to greet the SS men and lead them into an adjoining room. Fear absorbed Father in an ever-expanding radius, but he nibbled at his food as if nothing untoward occurred.

The *Hitlerjugend* Dietrich peered at the two well-attired SS men retreating into the other room.

Margarita's face was taut with anticipation. Turning to Dietrich, she said, "I can see you now, all fixed up in an SS uniform!"

He beamed, a look of unarticulated pride spreading over his fair face.

"Dietrich will someday fight for the glory of the Reich," she added for emphasis.

Father sat with an almost frantic air of alertness. He waited for the SS to bolt into the room and drag him away for interrogation and worse. The precipitate beat of his pulse made him fear mental collapse and loss of consciousness. If only the end would come quickly, Father thought.

But, as luck would have it, the SS visitors dallied. Why were they taking their merry time? Why didn't they just get it over with? Father thought. They must be delaying out of sheer spite. Why not let the Jew agonize before he was finished off? But minute followed excruciating minute and they still didn't reappear. Could they have come for some other purpose?

Father looked out the window at the cattle-cropped pastures, but he couldn't stop his heart from racing. Nikolai sat undisturbed, chewing calmly and gazing out the window. Father continued to survey the horizon, the world outside the farmhouse looking wide and beckoning while the room he sat in grew more claustrophic.

His puzzlement increased as the lunch hour passed and Steinbach and his visitors did not reappear. He tried to imitate Nikolai, to appear equally imperturbable, but he couldn't shake the vision of the SS men grabbing him by the collar and taking him away.

The SS men departed in the wan light of late afternoon. They gave Gustav Steinbach a final "Heil Hitler!" salute and he responded in feebler kind. An ample smile spread across Steinbach's usually somber face as he watched his visitors leave, their uniforms laundered and pressed to a fault.

The remains of that day broke Father's mounting fear. But this reprieve he was sure would not last long.

Few days yet remained till his appointed hour at the Gestapo. He imagined rough questioning and brutal beatings. Would he be able to hold out? He knew that the only thing that might see him through was his fictionalized identity, the Stefan Osmanov story, which more than ever was the central act in the drama of his survival.

Again he trudged out all his Moslem references. After reviewing all of the customs of the Tatars, he recalled his own father's tales about being stationed in Tashkent after returning from his sojourn in America and his memory of its graceful mosques and minarets. Grandfather was bewitched by the hypnotic arabesque of Uzbek textile art and the dazzling splendor of its calligraphy. Indeed, like many a romantic traveler, he was fascinated by what often struck the Westerner as the havoc of Asia, finding its mix of geography, history, and pageantry a heady draft. And Father, ever the faithful auditor, had vicariously marveled at Central Asia's fabled cities and a harsh desert landscape that carried traces of God.

The inevitable day dawned miserably, with breakfast lasting an eternity. It took effort to swallow the tepid tea. The morning bread tasted ashen and the sunlight seemed to fail. From the stable he could hear the snuffle of the feeding horses, whose placid life he envied more than ever before.

In his hut he made final preparations for the trip to the Gestapo. Amid eerie stillness, he honed his knife to a keener edge, its cold blade a balm to assuage his fear. In his final moments, he would either use it against his tormentors or turn it against himself.

He gave the hut one last sweeping look. It seemed lost in the white shroud of morning, glued to the very body of death. From afar he saw Margarita driving the cows to their milking. As he was about to leave, Belu, the farm dog, bounded to the door. Father patted his furry neck and the hound barked affectionately, which he sensed must be an uncanny act of indignant sympathy with Father's plight. What wouldn't he give to exchange places with Belu, who was freer that he could ever know and more beloved by the farm owners than any of their imported laborers!

The countryside was in bloom, but he saw none of its color. He traversed an endless solitude as he walked toward the station. The shrill crescendo of the Gestapo's shouts played in his ear until it merged with the joyless sound of the oncoming train's clattering wheels.

The wagons snaked into the station and came to a halt. The doors swung open and he took his seat as Stensch receded into the distance. Flat green fields stretched to the horizon. A ribbon of mist marked a lake beyond his view. The train slowly passed clear bodies of water and he thought again how to give his new identity an ungraspably smooth surface.

The outline of the next station appeared in the surrounding mist. He seized his sack and headed to the door. In a little while he would be a statistic, a fragment of life swept away as so much "racial refuse."

On the platform a German policeman asked for proof of his identity. Father tried to take his measure at a glance as he handed him his pass, but the official kept his face buried in Father's papers.

Who could tell him how to get to his destination? he wondered. Better not to ask the gendarme for directions to the Gestapo office and thus encourage further conversation and possible suspicion. His eyes swept the length of the platform and landed on an elderly man struggling with a heavy package. He walked over and offered to relieve him of his burden, which the man accepted with vocal relief. Only when they were out of earshot of the gendarme did Father ask for directions. The old man gave them to him quickly and courteously, although Father secretly hoped that he would misdirect him, perhaps staying his execution.

He walked past children scampering across the street and adolescent girls walking in twos and threes, their cheeks blushing in the cool morning air.

His courage dissolved as he neared his destination. If only he could call down the four winds of heaven to destroy the Nazi citadel of evil. He gritted his teeth and the hard glaze of his features stiffened even further. A few more yards and the road would give entry into the Gestapo building. All he could see in his mind's eye were its huge darkened windows, behind which lay blood, fire, and smoke.

A guard stood at the gate and raised his gloved hand to block Father's entrance. The rifle slung on his back was shiny along the whole length of the barrel. Extra cartridges hung on his belt. His eyes darted all over Father's face as he demanded his pass. He handed it to the guard and felt anew a mortal chill.

He then motioned for Father to enter a room on the ground floor. Glad he hadn't been frisked, as his knife was still on him, an instrument he now caressed like a lover, he walked quickly, almost as if he were carried into the chamber by the swift, unsparing current that had forced him to come there.

A Gestapo man's brooding eyes fastened on him.

"Are you Stefan Osmanov?" he asked.

"Yes," Father answered.

"Come this way," he said quietly, his peremptory gesture pointing Father in the direction of the backyard. Father followed him like an animal fastened by a rope around its neck.

"Sit down on that chair," he said and then left.

Father threw a fugitive glance in the direction of the door. Was the Gestapo man loading his pistol to finish him off?

Everything breathed danger as Father sat on the low backless chair, trying to still his nerves and not draw attention to the falsity and extremity of his position.

Suddenly a German shepherd dog rushed at him from the building. It bared its teeth. Father was certain he'd be mauled, and as he was about to bleat a final protest, the cur began to run in circles.

He then heard a click from inside the building. He stiffened with fear, waiting for a bullet.

But no gun went off. Father waited several seconds, conscious of his back and suspecting that a slug might soon be lodged there, trying to discipline his raging mind. The hound then raced away like a rough beast crashing through thick woods.

The Gestapo official reappeared. Father had expected to be killed by now, and here the Nazi had returned and was leading him back with a firm guiding hand into the building. What strange command was the German obeying? And why was he experimenting with Father's emotions? It all seemed inexplicably menacing.

He then approached Father with a sudden movement. A fierce look on his face forced Father's heart into a gallop again, as if he were flung into hell's innermost circle. He tried to keep his balance on this dizzying crest where all could be lost in a moment.

Father stood but two inches from him when the Nazi demanded, "Are you from Vilna?" a gleam of impatience in his eyes.

"*Ja, gerne,*" Father answered promptly, checking his inward start. The Gestapo's blue eyes darkened with sudden wrath and his question now sounded like the stropping of a razor whose keening sharpness could kill as it cut.

"No question I'm from Vilna!" Father repeated.

The Nazi then grabbed hold of the letter *P* attached to Father's jacket and tore it off violently.

He was done for, a rock breaking beneath the fury of oncoming waves. This was the first stroke; the second would be death.

"Then you are no longer a Pole but a Lithuanian," the Nazi declared, a furtive smile of confidence spreading over his face.

"Yes, sir," Father said with polite acquiescence.

The moment had the aura of a resurrection. Father expected to be consigned to death as a Jew, only to be pronounced by sheer bureaucratic grace a Lithuanian and raised a notch on the racial totem pole. A more radical tilting of the scales could not have been foreseen.

"As a Lithuanian," the Nazi continued, pleased to be observing such fine racial distinctions, "you are entitled to a special passport that allows you travel privileges within a 150-mile radius."

Tension broke inside Father and the rushing waters of life buoyed him up. The seal of fate had come ungummed.

"Your passport will be mailed to you once the negatives have been developed," he said.

Father nodded. Newly badged and ticketed, he now understood that the click he had feared emanating from within the building had been that of a camera.

"You may go now." The Nazi motioned to the door.

The sun poured down the street. Father's soles pounded the pavement as he returned to the train station. Astonishment had not faded, and he could still feel his breath coming in quick pants. In the endless weave of intrigue, losing his Polish identity was a stitch Father had neither planned nor foreseen. And even more outlandish was his sudden elevation from Slav to Balt, to a Lithuanian, a kind of neo-Aryan. In a split second his so-called racial inferiority had been expunged, as he was promised a ticket out of the netherworld of servitude.

How to fathom a realm in which the Gestapo served as the blind instrument of providence? German precision, which pervaded every step of Nazism, had unwittingly taken Father's pursuers farther from the truth.

On the return train journey he looked out of the window and saw the tapering edges of the green fields receding into the distance. Though vastly relieved, he still felt hollowed out by the interminable duration of the day's events.

As the train rattled toward Stensch, he wondered why he had been so fortunate. It must be his mother who loomed large within the suddenly expanding circuit of his life. It was on account of her merit that events had taken a kinder turn. Again he saw in his mind's eye the crush of Novogrudek's collapsing buildings. At that moment it seemed as if he stood on the shores of a distant sea whose expanse was pitched alternately into darkness or illumination by the revolving searchlight of grace.

He walked toward the gate of Steinbach's farm. The green grass seemed more alive than before. In time his Lithuanian passport, with an embossed swastika on its bright red cover, arrived. Some time thereafter he also received a pack of cigarettes—a "racial" fringe benefit—which came monthly. Father understood that man's most miserable tragedies, just as his sudden dispensations, had now, as Camus wrote, "the smell of the office and . . . the color of dirty ink."

With the Lithuanian passport tucked into his pocket, Father could cut a wider swath. Soon he won the admiration and the envy of other laborers, and his spirit rose proportionately, but in time the old imprisoned feeling returned with the nagging certainty that, as the Germans would themselves say, *"Aufgeschoben ist nicht aufgehoben"*—The day of reckoning can be postponed but not banished.

CHAPTER 10

Enlistment in the Waffen SS

Unbeknownst to father, 1944 saw the dual emergence of the United States and the Soviet Union as great powers. The *Stavka*, the Soviet high command, had finally come to display a formidable level of imagination, flexibility, and mastery of logistics. After Stalingrad, and surely after the battle of Kursk, the largest tank engagement in history, the Red Army won strategic and tactical initiative on the eastern front, while the Americans and the Allies, revving up for the Normandy invasion, soon acquired it in the West.

Ten Soviet offensives cleared Russia itself of enemy troops in 1944. The most impressive was Operation Bagration, whose last-minute details were finalized in the spring. Named after a famous Russian general who died stopping Napoleon's invasion of 1812, this massive Soviet assault wrested Minsk, Lida, Novogrudek, and Brest-Litovsk, the region of Father's youth, from the Nazi grip. Twenty-eight German divisions lay encircled in Byelorussia, and within a three-week period Nazi casualties soared to three hundred thousand.

Heinz Guderian, the architect of Hitler's early blitz victories against Poland, France, and the Soviet Union, understood the situation to be hopeless, further aggravated by Hitler's maddening military doctrine of "not one step back." As the war worsened for Berlin, some of its leaders descended to new levels of the bizarre. Marshal Goering was said to employ a rainmaker to help him improve his battle strategy and was seen by close associates swinging a diviner's pendulum across war maps.

On July 15, 1944, Hitler ordered the ever-faithful Heinrich Himmler to raise and equip fifteen new Waffen SS divisions for the eastern front, on the assumption that the vaunted brutality of these units might yet turn the tide of battle. Himmler and Gottlob Berger, chief of the Nazi Replenishment Office and the architect of the Waffen SS racial selection process, had to fight the Wehrmacht for scarce recruits and resorted to every subterfuge in the book to bolster the Waffen SS: recruiting underaged or overaged men, Volksdeutsche, or even Muslims from Bosnia/Herzegovina, who had their own SS division and wore field-gray fezzes adorned with eagle and swastika.

By recruiting "Aryans" of different nationalities, Himmler foresaw the expansion of "a German Reich of the German nation," based on the feudal-like allegiance to the Führer of its geographically diverse but racially unitary community. Berger, a blunt and unscrupulous Swabian with many German relatives in southeastern Europe, easily fell in with this scheme. He had seen to the publication of the instructional pamphlet *The Subhuman*, which called the people of the Soviet Union "the afterbirth of humanity, existing spiritually on a lower level than animals." Indeed, it was he who originated the idea of the Waffen SS as an international army, and as president of the German-Croat Society and the German-Flemish Study Group, he sought to mold a European union under the Nazi aegis.

By mid-1944 genocide in Europe had reached its immolating crest, as Hungarian Jewry, the last major Jewish community still alive on the Continent, was swept into the maelstrom in a matter of seven weeks. Any hope that Auschwitz would be bombed was laid to rest by callow indifference. Sir Charles Portall, British chief of the Air Staff, blocked Churchill's suggestions to bomb extermination sites, writing that Hitler "has so often stressed that this is a war by the Jews to exterminate Germany that it might well be, therefore, that a raid avowedly conducted on account of Jews would be an asset to enemy propaganda."

ON A CLOUDLESS SUMMER'S day in 1944, Father suddenly felt the hopelessness of all his endeavors. As he approached his hut, tired and winded from a long day of labor, he saw Sergei, a burly Russian laborer, sitting and talking with Nikolai inside. The window was open, and he could hear the sound of their voices, though they could not see him. When he was about fifteen feet away, he heard Sergei growl, "Only the devil understands Stefan, a Polish-Lithuanian Tatar who jabbers in so many languages. Makes you wonder."

Father stood transfixed. The full implication of this sudden disclosure rushed in on him: Sergei's words were a death sentence, a burial vault snapping shut.

"That venomous tooth!" Father raged inside, quickly realizing that Sergei possessed the mortal persuasiveness of the biblical serpent.

Ever since Novogrudek and Vilna, Father's life had become a story of dispossession. For a while he had nearly lulled himself into the belief that tireless vigilance and self-control would halt hostile conjecture. But now Sergei, he was certain, had deciphered the palimpsest's faintly visible underwriting. With vulgar cunning, he had seen through Father's disguises, had debunked the myth of his assumed identity, and was proceeding to contaminate the mind of Nikolai, with whom Father shared the hut, and with whom till now he had gotten on tolerably enough. If Nikolai came to believe these harsh innuendos, then Father would be through. Once the foul wash of gossip spread, he'd be done for. He knew that hasty, ill-conceived explanations he might offer would only dig the hole deeper. Why could he do to save himself now?

There was no choice but to halt Sergei's further aspersions. He would have to walk right in on them and thus, by his very presence, cut short their deadly confidences.

Father grabbed hold of the knob and flung the door open.

Sergei's shrewd face hardened and his silence darkly hinted at far more. He gave Father a quick stealthy look as he slithered out the door. He seemed like a coiling viper ready to strike again.

Father spoke volubly to Nikolai to better distract him, anything to fill the menacing silence.

That night passed in troubled dreams. Father thrashed around, his life caught by an unseen current. Was Sergei merely jesting, or was he setting a trap for him? Whatever his motivation, something irrevocable had occurred: Father's cover could be blown at any time.

Stensch could now only be a temporary haven. Lingering would run the risk of betrayal and the swift arrival of the Gestapo with German shepherds straining on the leash. Gone would be any possibility of retreat. This was the end of the road.

As a foreign laborer he had no existing rights, even considering his new-found Lithuanian status. He could not ask to be reassigned to another work-place, and if he had the temerity to abscond, he would end up in Bretz where the regimen was brutal.

A week after Sergei's revelation, Father took his Sunday stroll through the village of Stensch, looking more haggard and crestfallen than ever be-fore. He greeted several raw-boned foreign laborers in bedraggled and ill-fitting clothes, squinting in the sunlight. A Lithuanian, with whom he had spoken briefly a number of times, approached him.

"Stepanos, how goes it?" he said, using the ethnic variant of Father's assumed name.

"Not bad," Father answered.

"Didn't you say you're from Vilna?"

"You bet."

"Well, then, we're both Lithuanians."

"I can't argue with that," Father said, secretly unimpressed by their al-leged consanguinity.

He approached a bit closer and lowered his voice. "Listen to me. We Lithuanians don't have to slug it out on the farm. We're quasi-Aryans, you know, and that means we can join the Wehrmacht or even the Waffen SS."

"The SS?" Father asked. The very word sounded like the hiss of a de-scending blade.

"You got it," the man said, straightening his rough collar and adjusting his rope-belted pants.

"You must be kidding," Father said.

"No way. I'm dead serious. The word is they need volunteers, and I'm joining up."

"They're actually taking Lithuanians?" Father said in astonishment.

"Would I lie to you? Why don't we join together?"

"Um . . . I don't know . . ." he said, his voice trailing off.

"But it's the chance of a lifetime! Don't let it slip by!" the Lithuanian said, laughing wickedly.

"Let me think about it," Father said as they parted.

The SS, the strictest guardian of Nazi "racial purity," was the murderer of his mother, aunts, and uncles and the thousands of Jews of Novogrudek. Images of their prostrate bodies lining the mass graves filled him with tears and rage. The Lithuanian's very suggestion of fighting for the Nazis revolted him; but then he had only to hear Sergei's sneering remarks spinning in his ear to know that something must be done if he was to avoid being swept into night and fog. Would the SS be the bridge over the gulf? Father figured that entry into its ranks would abolish the remotest conjecture that he was a Jew.

Father's stomach turned at the thought of collaborating in murder. He considered alternate avenues of escape, however quixotic, anything to avoid the Lithuanian's importunities. Near the farm Father had espied military trains stacked with rows of German Tiger tanks on their flatbed platforms heading east. Perhaps he could steal aboard one of these and hide out until it reached the Russian front. Once there, he would scramble to the Soviets and avoid German capture. But the more he contemplated this scheme, the more harebrained it seemed. The SS option returned like a persecuting tune, like a foul shadow that he couldn't shake.

All that week he lived in a continuous state of alarm, caught between two abysses: Sergei and the SS. The following Sunday, amid the bluish mist of morning, as he took his typical worker's constitutional, the importunating Lithuanian reappeared, his worn boots scraping against the pavement. Father now dreaded the fellow's geniality, and his head thudded as he saw the lowered visor of his cap.

"Stepanos!" the man broke out in a shout of delight. "Take a look at this!"

"What is it?" Father asked.

He meticulously unfolded an application, brushing a speck of dust from its surface.

"This form is going to get me an induction interview with the big guys," he said proudly.

"Which big guys?" he asked disingenuously.

"The Waffen SS, you know. Look here—I've got one for you. Once we've filled in this application, they'll know we're interested."

"I don't believe it!" Father suddenly shot out.

"You wanna bet? Sure, there'll be medical exams, racial inquiries, the whole lot. But I've nothing to fear, and neither do you. After all, are we Lithuanians or aren't we?"

"I can't argue with that," he said.

"So what's the point in losing time?" the man thrust the extra form into Father's hand. "After all, they need us. They need volunteers."

"Wait a minute!" Father protested.

"Don't tell me you're chickening out!"

"But I've never been a soldier," Father protested feebly.

"So what? Neither have I, but that's not stopping me. Anyway, what've you got to lose?"

"Well, I don't know," Father said falteringly. "I mean, this is not the sort of thing you jump into."

"Stepanos, we're Lithuanians, don't ever forget that. The Germans consider us to be almost like them."

"Look, I'll take the form, but I've still got to think about it," Father said.

"Don't take too long about it. Strike while the iron is hot! They need us now!"

Father returned to his hut that night in renewed uproar. He would again have to step out of the protective shadow into the blinding light. He stayed up poring over the form after Nikolai fell asleep. It seemed like the monstrous growth of treason itself, certain to shut him out from the blessing of the world to come.

Signing the document would set in motion forces whose consequences he could only guess at. Where could he find the moral sanction to join the SS, even if it might paradoxically mean survival? Could he commit this deed in the sight of heaven, even a silent heaven? It was surely an abomination, starkly opposed to everything that he had learned since his childhood, and would upend the foundations of his life.

Navaredok, the city of his birth, swam before his eyes. This was, after all, a vital center of *mussar*, which encouraged supreme worship of God, modesty, and asceticism. After his bar mitzvah Father was sent to Baranowicze, where as a young acolyte he was urged to examine his innermost promptings, to discover the serpentine motion of evil and self-deception— its every detour, shift, and loop.

He recalled the life of cloistered study, the halls of the yeshiva Ohel Torah in Baranowicze and Etz Chaim in Kletsk, filled with a sea of black skullcaps and swaying shoulders, men and boys with grave brows loudly debating in Yiddish the finer points of law and quoting medieval commentators on the Talmud. Black-hatted rabbis walked solemnly back and forth with their hands clasped behind their backs, and at holy dusk, that impressionable hour, warned their students against the sins of pride and other insidious vanities lying at the heart of seeming virtue. Father soon discovered that regret and sorrow were man's second nature.

Could all this now end in service in the SS? The SS, even more than the Wehrmacht, exemplified the Nazi mission of annihilation, its deadly brutalization and the cult of the Führer. Is this where Father's shifting scenario of otherness would finally lead—to a solitude more absolute than death? And what would his mother have said, whose chief desire in life was for him to be a rabbi? She had begun training him for the religious life when he could barely speak. One autumn evening in the mid-1920s, when the air was cool and the tree leaves were thinning, lightning flashes rent the sky above Navaredok. He ran toward her, rubbing his eyes with his small fists. She lifted him on her lap—the most lulling seat he knew—drew the white muslin curtain aside, and scanned the storm clouds through the leaf-strewn window. In a clear and loud voice she recited the Hebrew prayer over thunder and lightning, which he stumbled over. Each of her words tightened the delicate web of trust he had in God.

"Nothing is more moving than a child's lisping benediction," his mother said to herself, wiping his tears away, combing his tousled blond hair, and whispering him to sleep in her soft, floating voice, fine as the drift of flowers. With the passing of the thunder, the quick rains fell across the outlying fields of Navaredok.

Who better than his own mother to understand that the distance between the yeshiva in Poland and the Waffen SS was more than one life could encompass? Yet it was she who had urged him to defy the German command of death. She would have realized compassionately the shuddering logic under which he labored.

He sank weakly onto his bed. That night he lay awake shifting the application from one hand to the other. His resolve struggled to take shape. Was his scheme a piece of inspired legerdemain or the sheerest folly? His decision, he feared, would haunt his life to ruin. But then Sergei's words returned like a ticking bomb of encroaching time. Wearied to exhaustion, he felt himself standing at the outermost boundary of the world with no abiding for refuge. He had to fling himself into the future with no familiar landmarks, to leap into the roiling core of the inferno.

By morning he had wrestled his mind into submission. He would press his scheme with all the vigor he could summon. Everything would be subverted to his goal. He crawled out of his cot and amid the first gray beams of daylight he hastily signed the SS form. As he affixed his name, he feared that to delay sending it off would again weaken his resolve. A grimace of revulsion lay etched on his face when he let it drop into the local mailbox.

All summer, waiting for a reply, he restitched the weave of his false identity into a pattern as sinuous as that of an oriental carpet. Even now it still felt foreign, all outside of him. He waited impatiently, hoping against hope that the SS would put him on the far side of vulnerability. But when no answer came, he suspected that the Lithuanian either had been misinformed or, far worse, had deceived him. He cudgeled his brain for new methods of escape, but nothing credible came to mind.

Towards the beginning of autumn the SS recruiting office in Guben finally sent word.

He was knee-deep in cow manure when Margarita ran to him waving a letter in her hand.

"Stefan, Stefan! Stand up this minute!"

He rose immediately and looked at her radiant smile.

"This looks important—it has the SS return address on it. Open it immediately!"

Father's hands were flecked with the waste of animals and the grime of work. He ran outside and washed them at the water pump.

In one violent movement, he tore open the envelope and read of his summons for an interview and an examination by the Waffen SS in ten days.

"Well, what does it say? Don't keep me in suspense," Margarita cried.

"The Waffen SS wants to see me," he said.

Margareta applauded enthusiastically and then slapped him on the back. *"Dem Mutigen gehört die Welt,"* she declared—The world belongs to the brave. Father stood ten feet tall in her eyes.

On the day of his recruitment appointment, the morning dawned as if ready for dusk. He came to in fear. All of his life stood in front of him in a shroud of blinding accusation. Herr Steinbach had arranged for a cafe proprietor, heading in a similar direction, to transport Father to his destination.

Father's driver arrived in a horse-drawn wagon crammed with empty beer bottles emitting a pungent odor of past revelries. Father hopped on board, and as the horses trotted off amid stalks of tall grass, he again wondered if he had made the right decision. Only a command performance would save him now.

They rode for a long time. Father heard a calf lowing in the fields as the beer bottles clanked in angry discord, their acrid smell of alcohol mingling with the verdant fragrance of freshly mown grass.

The wagon rattled into Guben before noon. Father alighted in the center of a town swarming with carts, dray horses, and buses. The town casino, a kind of off-duty officers' club where the SS recruiters were based that day, was visible from only a block away, and he could see the swastika flag flapping in the wind.

Father's fears shadowed him again as he wondered whether he had too loosely woven the web of deceit.

He opened the gate to the building and the guard gave him a discriminating glance before letting him in. Father understood that to survive this descent, he'd have to become a face shaded under an iron helmet sent to do the murderous bidding of Heinrich Himmler.

At the yeshivas in Poland he had been instructed in benevolence. The SS's close-drill mentality, its worship of mindless servitude, and glorification of death were a brutal assault on every truth and precept he valued. How could he, a student of the top-league of Talmudic academies, join such ilk when his rightful place was with the hapless victims, not with their zealous tormentors?

Inside what seemed like a house of nations, fifteen-to-eighteen-year-old Hitler Youths crowded the front of the chamber, their eyes light blue, their skin a raw pink. Joining them were a rabble of Ukrainian nationalists, Baltic and Romanian fascists—miscellaneous outlaws from every land ready to join a "knighthood of race" and glowing in eager expectation of battle.

SS officers in well-cut uniforms stood all about, as if encased in tough armor. The Lithuanian enthusiast who had set Father on this course stood at the side of the room, regaling a group of other Baltics with stories. When he spotted Father, he waved exuberantly, and although Father had little desire to join him and his friends, he knew he had little choice.

"Stepanos! Stepanos! Have you forgotten your friend?" the man called.
"Of course not!"

"Good guy!" the man said, as he clapped Father on his back.

Father managed a feeble smile.

"Can't wait to get into a SS uniform. What a picture I'll make!" the Lithuanian said, hopping with excitement.

"Don't be so impatient," Father said.

"Ah, Stepanos! You can't imagine how much I want to get even with the Jews."

His heavy-shouldered fellows, standing all around him, grinned. All broad smiles and good cheer, the Lithuanians thrust out their chests in patriotic delight.

As Father watched the Lithuanians gleam with pride, he never felt more alone, more dangerously poised on the edge of a precipice.

To the side some *Hitlerjugend* flung themselves to the floor, stretching, twisting, and extending their limbs to heighten their muscle tone. Young, cold-eyed, and hard-jawed, their faces betrayed a blood lust sobering to anyone but themselves.

Dozens of black-booted officers with SS insignia stitched into their military caps gathered in an adjoining room. Their blunt massing against the door made Father's throat go dry. Two entered the waiting room and ordered the would-be recruits to line up. In the shuffle the Lithuanians raced ahead of Father, their heads bobbing up and down in a fever of anticipation, as if ready to be shot from a cannon.

Within a few minutes the ground was a heap of shirts, socks, and boots. Many of the now partially clad volunteers glowed in robust health. Father saw a boulderlike fellow babbling to the man in front of him and when both louts burst into husky laughter, he sought somehow to screen himself from their view.

Father's row twisted into the adjoining room. At one o'clock his turn came. He proceeded into the chamber, where storm troopers lined the walls. Stern-browed Waffen SS doctors and functionaries sat behind a phalanx of small desks stacked high with forms and questionnaires. Medical orderlies stood behind them, and at the far end of the room sat the racial suitability examiners.

A young SS officer posted at the first desk summoned Father. A white chalk circle had been drawn on the floor in front of his desk. From the corner of his eye Father saw another SS man with the double-lightning insignia on his collar brandish a riding crop. The odor of his polished leather boots mingled with the stinging fumes of a strong disinfectant.

"Undress completely and then enter the white circle," the young officer said.

The sun struck prismatic hues off the glass-topped table. Father unbuttoned his shirt and prayed silently. His fingers resisted the officer's command, but he forced them to do his bidding. A sputtering candle on a nearby desk emitted dying smoke which drifted their way. Father feared that his mournful eyes, which had seen more than anyone should witness, would betray him as well.

He slid out of his pants and stepped naked into the void, his back facing the SS doctor. The intense light condensed on Father's unclothed figure.

"Turn around," the officer demanded.

Father remembered the verse in Genesis: "God said to Abraham . . . You shall circumcise the flesh of your foreskin, and that shall be the sign of the covenant between me and you. And throughout the generations, every male among you shall be circumcised at the age of eight days."

Would the doctor let him proceed, or would he stop him dead in his tracks?

If he were discovered now, Father would be like the bound Isaac brought as a burnt offering by Abraham, but without the miracle of God's restraining hand.

Circumcision, meant to protect the child, would here, Father feared, sacrifice the man. Nazi terror turned an ancient holy compact into a horrible tribal scarification. He listened to the measured click of boots in the next room and guarded his facial movements from betraying involuntary changes of expression. When the SS doctor nodded and told him to put on his pants, a jet of warmth ran up Father's spine. How grateful he was that Islam had carried over the ancient Jewish rite of circumcision. Just then the old steam pipes which lined the walls began to clank. Never had plumbing sounded so musical.

At the next desk his height and weight were measured. Father was now informed that anyone less than five foot seven was barred entry into the SS, but that he had nothing to worry about on that account.

Another SS doctor listened to his heartbeat but did not hear the reverberant sound of his fear. He passed him to a neurologist, who had him stretch his fingers while standing on the tips of his toes. Father held his breath, fearful that the thin, tearing membrane of his sanity would burst. But he did not stumble and was told to proceed further. With each stepwise progression of the line Father could almost hear the beating of those angelic wings that had stood guard over him from the beginning.

Suddenly, as he was waiting for the next doctor, the Lithuanian approached him, pale and near tears. "Stepanos," he moaned, "I'm destroyed!"

"What's happened?" Father asked with feigned concern.

"They won't have me in the Waffen SS," he said.

"Why not?"

"I'm too damned short. It's all about regulations," he said exasperatedly, his illusions now in tatters.

"But why aggravate yourself?" Father responded, trying to salve the Lithuanian's wounded pride.

"But you know I was dead set on getting into a SS uniform. Now all I'll get into is the Wehrmacht," he whined.

"But the Wehrmacht's no shame," Father consoled.

"Maybe you're right, but I'm disappointed as hell."

"You know how rules are. But I wouldn't get too upset about it."

"And how about you? How do you stand?" the man demanded.

"I'm fine," Father said matter-of-factly, trying not to exacerbate his so-called friend's sour mood.

The most treacherous ground lay ahead: the racial suitability exam. Only a miracle of persuasion would serve. An SS interrogator held blank racial questionnaires in his hand and tapped his pen on his forehead. Behind him boxes of files sat neatly arrayed in stacks. His secretary, whose hair sat coiled over her ears like two exotic shells, brought her boss black coffee, which he sipped deliberately. Father strained to overhear the kinds of questions the others were being asked, but he couldn't make out a word.

To bolster his confidence, Father quickly rehearsed his Islamic tale, ticking off all the details he needed at his fingertips. His lie had to be solid and unmovable as a brick wall, his face grimly set as if to defy the cleverest of physiognomists. Yet for all that, Father sensed that the racial examiner would see past his convoluted tale, would hear the creaking stage machinery and know it for what it was.

Father's turn arrived. The racial tester picked up a fresh questionnaire form. The room began to spin, reel, and pitch like a boat caught in a swell; soon he would plummet off his tightrope.

"You! Come forward!" the SS examiner said.

Father managed to do as he was told.

"Nationality?" came his first question.

"Lithuanian," Father answered.

A page-long form unfolding like a fatal decree lay in front of the examiner. How many lies would Father have to fabricate, how many lives to dissemble? As soon as he began to slur over details, the SS would untangle the skein of his tall tale and just wait for him to betray himself.

The racial examiner pinned Father with a cold stare. "Any Jewish blood?" he spat, as if referring to the larval condition of subhumanity.

"No," Father responded, keeping his voice even.

"Are you sure?" he said as he dropped a closer look at Father.

"Yes!"

"Any Jewish blood going back three or more generations?" His words rang out like a pistol shot in an empty chamber.

Father's chest tightened and his throat felt torn by glass splinters. "No," he repeated. In another minute he was certain to stammer.

"Are you sure?" the SS examiner insisted.

As the questions became more finely deliberate, Father's safe passage narrowed to the thinness of a blade.

"No!" he repeated emphatically. Did the SS examiner hear the subterfuge in his voice? he wondered. He could feel the ripples of hysteria just below the surface of his skin. To strengthen his case, he prepared to tell the story of his Islamic background and origin, though he knew how fraught it was with factual and logical inconsistencies.

Just then, a strong ray of sun—"a golden deluge"—pierced the window, illuminating and highlighting his face and his abundant head of hair. As if dazzled by the gilded shaft of light, a German *Feldgendarme* sitting immediately across from the SS investigator smiled and leaned over to Father's tormentor and said, "Look at the fellow's blond hair. He's okay."

The SS racial examiner appeared impressed. He took his pen and drew a long diagonal line through the questions that remained unanswered. Each movement of his hand brought Father a fresh arterial flow of blood. When he came to the end of the page Father knew the sheltering angel that had hovered over him from the beginning had opened its wingspan to its greatest width.

The suitability examiner then straightened out his papers and after putting them in one pile affixed a swastika on Father's application. The SS man rose, offered Father a wide congratulatory smile, and informed him that he had the honor and privilege of being drafted into the Waffen SS.

War, Father was now informed, was the forge in which his destiny would be hammered into shape, the finest educational experience of youth, the great gardener, pruning mankind on its racial road to perfection. War would make the recruits hard, toughen their mettle, make them harbingers of a new world. The weak would fall by the wayside while the strong would lead to victory, and other such racial blather.

In front of Father's eyes stood the mournful tenderness of his mother. Sundered from his past and from his people, from the old continent of his childhood, he was stricken by a wave of guilt. How could he, a former rabbinical student, deliberately forget who these men were and what they had done to those he loved more than anything in the world? Had he blotted out the sound of rifles snapping into place? But he knew that whichever way he turned lay either moral repulsion or physical annihilation.

He moved forward along the line. Another functionary asked him which branch of the SS he wanted to join. Did he wish to be a tank driver, parachutist, anti-aircraft launcher, or infantryman? For a second Father couldn't figure out which would serve his purpose.

"What will it be, young man?" the SS man asked impatiently after Father hesitated.

"Infantry," he replied. The choice would afford him access to the front line encumbered with minimal military baggage. Perhaps in the confusion of battle he would slip to the Allied side.

The hallway mirror reflected the blond sheen that lay on his sun-stroked hair. A summer's blanching had given it a blessed hue, had made it lighter than ever. The late-afternoon sun cast its shimmering net on the windowsill near him. It was the gratuitous quality of light, even more than the bits of myth, mixed dialects, and makeshift genealogical trees Father had thrown together, that had saved him.

Twilight enveloped him on his way back to the railway station. He walked as a haunted man. For a moment Father felt weighed down by his sorrow, too pinioned for flight, but he knew he had little alternative but to stay aloft.

He arrived in Stensch as dusk deepened into evening, his ears filled with the sound of the train's shunting metal and pitched whistles. Sleep came reluctantly, and he only yielded to it toward morning. His bed seemed nothing more than a box in a shallow trench, and it was now that he dreamed of the SS initiation-cum-solstice-rites—a kind of baptism in pagan blood in which Caspar David Friedrich meets Wotan.

A HEAVY MIST SHROUDS a steep hill in Germany, toward whose summit Waffen SS recruits march. With each step the lowlands fall away. Smoke billows from torches carried aloft by Hitlerjugend, *singing harsh songs of loyalty and honor—*Treure und Ehre—*of blood and valor. Their hair is wind-swept and their cheeks reddened by the cold air. They gaze upon the peaks of farther mountains and watch the haze rising from below. Flanking SS officers tread forward, their footfalls echoing in the valley below. The mountains slope and then plunge darkly into the abyss where the rumblings of thunder die away.*

At a new plateau, they halt, and the Hitlerjugend *hoist their torches, invoking the names of ancient pagan gods as other torchbearers approach, their faces shadowed by the light of the flames. A* Hitlerjugend *kindles his torch with that of one of the SS, and then draws near the central bonfire. As their flames rise into the night air, the recruits swear eternal fealty to Adolf Hitler.*

WHEN FATHER AWOKE, THE phalanx of torches and the fire and smoke they emitted were redolent of the sacrificial flames of a new heathendom, of a Germanic romance of paganism skillfully stage-managed by Nazi propaganda, with fascism's requisite glamorization of death, of prodigal effort, of the massing of bodies, and of the heroic endurance of pain.

How vastly different these petrified elevations were from the heights of his childhood, when he had studied in *kheder* the Psalms of David: "Who may ascend the mountain of the Lord? And who may stand in his holy place? He that hath clean hands and a pure heart."

Ernst Jünger, the literary fascist wounded seven times in World War I and the bard of the *Fronterlebnis*, or front experience, could have been writing of the SS rites when he said: "Like divine sparks the blood pulsed through the veins when, conscious of one's own audacity, one crossed the fields in clattering arms. The cadence of the storm blew away the values of the world like autumnal leaves. What could be more sacred than the fighting man?"

For Jünger, the German stylist, the SS, at least in its earlier years, was comprised not of soldiers following professional standards and codes, but of fanatical fighters embodying a brutal attitude toward life. Those who had endured hell were destined to rule. It all came down to pitiless force, lust for war, the worship of harshness and cruelty. The SS fighting force would always be on the alert, enjoined to bind its helmet on tighter when the struggle was over.

CHAPTER 11

Liberation

Father waited anxiously for the SS mobilization orders to send him straight to boot camp and the battlefield. This would be the natural sequence of an unnatural beginning. Once he had chosen the last road of dissimulation, a Jew's entry into the Waffen SS, he had to traverse it till the bitter end.

Weeks passed, and life on Herr Steinbach's farm continued apace. Agriculture's unalterable rhythm marked his days, but even so, something had fundamentally changed within him. He no longer belonged to the world of the farm. He had crossed the border into the unknown, a frontier he feared he would never be able to recross.

The Steinbachs regarded him differently now that he was readying to fight on their behalf. As a future combatant, he came in for approving nods, and even slight deference, but not for any diminution in his workload. He still danced attendance on their pleasures. Their military pride in his new role was tempered by doubts about losing a farmhand even in the name of the Reich. In the struggle between patriotism and privatism, the latter would always win out.

The farm laborers were kept in the dark about developments on the eastern front. Stray parts of the *Volkische Beobachter*, the rabidly anti-Semitic rag that the notorious Julius Streicher had founded in the early 1920s—the only newspaper Hitler read from start to finish—would accidently find their way into the barn. Father would surreptitiously pick them up to glean any information, but to no avail.

On a Saturday night in late October, Nikolai and he were cleaning up and looking forward to some much-needed rest, only to find their routine strangely interrupted. Herr Steinbach ordered them not to return to their hut but to await further instruction. They had never known him to issue such a command.

Around midnight a tractor arrived pulling a wagon with a number of other foreign laborers from the surrounding region atop it. The tractor's engine was powered by wood, and the fires it emitted gave the night a ghastly illumination. Father and Nikolai jumped on board without uttering a word.

Driven for a number of hours in the quiet of the night, they finally dismounted at the edge of a forest, and saw vast numbers of foreign laborers guarded by the notorious Nazi Brown Shirts. One of them led Father to a hillock, thrust a shovel into his hands, and ordered him to break the hard earth with it. Nikolai was assigned similar duty. At first Father didn't catch on to the significance of their assignment, but soon enough he grasped that they were digging trenches, the very idea of which suddenly sprang open a door in his mind. If the Germans were marching from victory to victory, as Father had supposed, why would this defensive maneuver be necessary? Perhaps, then, the war had turned decisively against Nazi Germany and this was a last-ditch effort to stem the tide. This glimmer made Father dig with zeal. He craved more information, but he did not want to appear overeager in obtaining it.

The laborers dug till the break of day and then were ordered to stop. On their return journey to Stensch, they passed towns and fields, and Father caught every image, as if the land itself could reveal the shape of the future.

They were kept in total ignorance, and none could summon the nerve to ask Gustav Steinbach the purpose of their night journey. If Nazi Germany was cornered, it was better not to importune him with questions or to display anticipatory keenness. But to Father's chagrin, they were not called to that distant place again, and he considered it the better part of wisdom to keep silent.

Autumn ran its course, and the puddles lay strewn with fallen leaves. The Waffen SS still had not called him back. Had they found incriminating information requiring further inquiry, or had their headquarters been bombed by the Allies, preventing them from mobilizing their newest re-cruits? Whichever was the real reason, the SS continued to remain his fulcrum.

———∞———

IT WAS NOT UNTIL the second week of January 1945 that the long-awaited confirmation of the collapse of the thousand-year Reich grew im-minent. Father and Nikolai were seated at the farm lunch table, a ritual set in stone, waiting for Herr Steinbach. As he stumbled into the dining room the Nazi farmer mistakenly left ajar the door to the living room. The radio blared: "... *starke Einbruch am Weisel Bogen.*" Father wanted to leap with joy on hearing that there had been a strong Soviet breakthrough on the Vistula, but he kept a strict rein on his emotions.

They finished the meal and he left the table at his usual pace, although his brain was ablaze with a new vista of hope opening before him. If the radio report was true, his life would once again catch the glimmer of the sun.

As soon as he was out of their earshot, Father wanted to give himself over to the elation of the moment, to shout his relief at the top of his lungs. But he knew that silence was the best herald of his newborn joy. Any public display of happiness might tip off the Steinbachs and the other laborers as to his real identity. Why was he, they might surmise, so much gladder than the others? Ecstasy, much as fear itself, he kept telling himself, needed its own quiet mastery. If people were born with two ears but only one tongue, it must be for the reason that they should hear twice and speak once.

Who could imagine the number of reverses still standing between him and freedom? All his accumulated sorrows and deferred prospects needed to be corked; nothing could tumble forth. The last lap of the race was the hardest and often the most easily lost. It was precisely now, when his thoughts were whirling in a mad and beautiful confusion of hope and doubt, that his guard had to be the most stringent.

At meals the inscrutable Steinbachs betrayed nothing. They were im-perturbable, showing no outward emotion at the tumultuous turn of events, and Father began to fear that perhaps he had misheard or misinterpreted the radio announcement.

It was now a Sunday in mid-to-late January, and Nikolai and he had just attended to morning chores. They were tired and looked forward to having the rest of the day to themselves. After resting up a bit, they took their customary walk through Stensch and beheld a sight they never thought was humanly possible: endless wagons streaming from the east, loaded with German refugees draped in huge overcoats, their bundles corded with rope and their faces lined with worry. For Father a German refugee still seemed a contradiction in terms.

A week later, on the very last Sunday of the month, January 28, a stern tranquillity settled over the farm. Herr Steinbach was glued to the radio as to the lattice of a confessional.

At noon, as Nikolai and Father were in their hut, a tank shell whirred across the farm. Crouching near the window to get a better view, they saw Herr Steinbach and Dietrich pushing a lumbering wagon to the doorsteps of the farmhouse and begin loading it with hastily sewn bundles. Emma, Herr Steinbach's wife, was crying, "My furniture, my home—woe is me!"

Dietrich, angry and bewildered, piled the wagon on the double, and Herr Steinbach harnessed the neighing horses for the journey west. Dietrich then ran toward the green gates which gave onto the road and threw them open. With Margarita and her parents on board, Dietrich hopped in and the wagon bounded off, the horses trotting in the distance, tugging till the blue wintry silence enveloped them.

Father and Nikolai stayed put in their hut, fearing that the Steinbachs might yet return and finish them off. In the heat of departure, the Steinbachs had left them unharmed, but now they might turn around to deal with them decisively. But when no one returned, they emerged outside to a messianic scene. The village of Stensch was one mass movement of German refugees stretching to the horizon.

The unfolding drama was as incredible to Father and Nikolai as it must have seemed to the refugees. To Father at least it had something of the biblical symmetry of the retributive sea that drowned the pursuing ancient Egyptians, although this latter-day settling of historical accounts came far too late to save the hapless descendants of the Israelites.

But even in defeat, the Nazis fought ferociously on the eastern front to escape falling into Soviet hands. Almost on the very day that the Steinbachs fled, eight German divisions halted the advance of Soviet troops near Marienburg. But these were temporary setbacks; the Red Army, sweeping all before it, soon breached the Oder.

Berlin was declared a fortress city with the entire population assigned to build fortifications—trenches, earthworks, and tank traps—in a vain effort to stop the thundering advance of Soviet generals Zhukov, Rokossovsky, and Koniev. On Berlin's walls and buildings the old martial slogan "Wheels must roll for victory," which Father had first seen in Königsberg, was replaced by "Victory or Siberia."

Yet, amid the mounting chaos, German order and discipline appeared calamity-proof. Even with the Soviets knocking at their gates, Berlin postmen delivered mail and the Berlin Philharmonic played on. Goebbels's propaganda ministry wore on tirelessly, and on January 30, 1945, it released *Kolberg*, the most expensive color film ever made in Nazi Germany, with more than 185,000 troops specially withdrawn from the battlefield or active service to shoot one scene in this declamatory film depicting the miraculous triumph of the Germans in the Baltic in 1807. Although present-day Kolberg was in imminent danger of falling, the film proceeded without interruption.

But Soviet heavy artillery spoke decisively and broke the most hard-bitten resistance. Hitler continued to grasp at every straw. Against the better judgment of his generals, he placed Heinrich Himmler, chief of the SS, at the head of an emergency army designed to stop the main Russian threat on Berlin, with disastrous results. Indeed, the SS remained so central to Hitler that he did not consider the war lost when Germany was rubble, but only when he learned that the SS troops were no longer trustworthy.

When all was indeed lost and Germany lay in smoking ruins, Hitler had only one satisfaction left: the knowledge that Germany had destroyed European Jewry. In the concluding months of the war he had told Martin Bormann: "Well, we have lanced the Jewish abscess; and the world of the future will be eternally grateful to us."

⎯⎯∞⎯⎯

FATHER'S LIBERATORS HAD NOT yet arrived, and in the chaotic interlude, caution continued to be his motto. The front lines were fluid, and there was no knowing how often they might shift. In time German counterattacks withered, but for the moment they still spoke too persuasively for comfort. Father's assumed identity would need to remain tightly in place till the end; and yet he felt something unarmed expand inside him.

Perhaps for the first time since he had arrived in Germany, the ice floe that had locked his being begin to thaw.

Nikolai and Father left the hut to seek better protection. They ran to the now abandoned farmhouse and hid out there: Nikolai in the loft and he in the cellar amid stacks of potatoes.

Later that day the green gates giving onto the farm rattled with such force that Father rose amid the heap of potatoes. What should he do now, hide deeper or run for his life? A voice rang out, or what seemed then like the music of the spheres, shouting in Russian to open up.

Father peered out of the cellar window into the dark landscape. He leaped outside in one bound, something greater than himself urging him on.

He ran towards the haggard soldier, his face smeared from the heat of battle, his helmet gleaming in the moonlight. The eastern horizon was aflame with light. Father could no longer disguise his feelings. He approached the Russian soldier, bent down with all his accumulated pain and tremblingly kissed the soldier's grimy boots and the ground on which he stood. For that brief moment Father understood that there are times when a man does not have to be a saint to be considered an angel.

When he rose he shouted to Nikolai, still hiding in the hayloft, "Our brothers are here!"

"Are there any Germans around?" the Russian soldier asked him in a voice that at once commanded attention and conceded bewilderment.

"The Germans have fled," Father said. "Take me with you," he added, in a low, awed tone, his voice as expectant as a child's.

Nikolai stood near him, facing the soldier, who warned them to exercise the greatest caution because the Soviet army was still a ways back. As part of a reconnoitering team staking out the area, he knew how dangerous the situation remained. Pockets of fanatical enemy soldiers posed a special hazard. This was, after all, the first time in the twentieth century that the Germans were fighting on their own soil, and their last stand promised to be gruesome. Hitler had made it clear that he would tolerate no withdrawals and that disobeying officers and soldiers separated from their units would be tried by a "flying court martial" and shot.

An hour after the Russian soldier had left and Nikolai and Father had returned to the safety of the cellar, a car screeched to a halt near the farm and several German soldiers leaped out. Father heard their footsteps near the cellar window. What if they marched right in and caught him red-handed? To be so close to freedom and yet so near to death was intolerable. Father's life passed in front of him, a tableau on which all the horrors of the last five years were violently scrawled.

He grabbed a pail that lay near the potatoes and placed it on top of his head as a better disguise. The German troops, however, stayed just long enough to set up a flame thrower and hurl their ammunition at the oncoming Soviets. Within minutes they jumped back into their vehicle and sped off. Father and Nikolai spent the rest of the night in the cellar, shuttling between hope and fear.

By morning, an endless stream of Russian soldiers had brought up their heavy weapons, an image Father had lovingly nursed during the dark watches of the long German night.

Father saw a high-level Russian officer borne along by a horse-drawn sled suddenly rise from his seat and gesticulate angrily. Spotting an escaping German soldier, the Soviet military man bellowed for him to stop in his tracks. The German turned around reluctantly, looked narrowly at the Russians, and lifted up only one hand; the other remained in his pocket. He kept the incriminating posture despite the officer's repeated demand that he raise both hands. In a few moments his rank insubordination had cost the German soldier his life. Soviet vehicles rode blithely past the body, which a steady layer of snow had already covered.

Another sled-driven Russian officer pulled over and asked Father for directions to the next village, and he excitedly hopped aboard to better convey his instructions. Before he knew it he was racing into nearby cannon fire, giving the officer a running list of turns and twists he should take to reach his destination.

At first he had no perceptible fear, so secure and childishly trusting did he feel in Russian hands. The thrill of being part of what he mistakenly took to be an advance patrol blinded him to the precautions of war. But when the officer failed to offer him an armed escort back to Stensch, Father came to experience the unmediated terror of the front. He had no choice but to set off on his own, expecting to be ambushed by retreating Germans. The wind stroked his face, and after a while he was lulled by the woodland scene. But just when he let down his guard he heard the crackle of gunfire and a bullet whizzed past his knees. He fell to the ground unhurt and lay waiting for the next barrage, which, surprisingly, never came. As soon as the fire had stilled, he wended his way back through the death-haunted woods.

———— ∞ ————

FATHER'S UNALLOYED HAPPINESS AT the arrival of Russian soldiers was not matched by the other foreign laborers, who feared the Red Army, especially its political commissars. These ideological enforcers traveled with each corps and, invoking Stalin, regarded Soviet POWs and foreign laborers as betrayers of the motherland. The latter could expect the severest penalties to be meted out, to be falsely and deliberately condemned as "Vlasovites," renegades who fought on the side of the Nazis against the Soviet Union under the leadership of the turncoat Andrei Vlasov, a onetime Soviet defender of Kiev. "Vlasovite" had become so predictably elastic a term that it could be stretched to include every kind of perceived collaborative sin.

As a Jew long targeted for certain annihilation, Father could not but view the Russians as liberators, but to hedge his bets he still carried his Waffen SS papers in case of battle reversals. His vivid apprehension of sudden German offensives blinded him to the dangers he ran if the Soviets caught him with this incriminating document.

A day or so after playing guide to the Russian officer, another Soviet soldier banged on his cellar door. This time it was for a rougher reckoning. He entered with gun in hand and looked at Father suspiciously.

"Welcome!" Father said in greeting.

"Keep your distance," the soldier said sullenly.

"Why are you angry?" Father asked. "I am one of you."

"I don't know about that," the man said.

"Whatever do you mean?"

"You're a Vlasovite like all the others!" he bellowed, his finger on the trigger.

"What are you saying?" Father shouted with emotion. "I have waited four long years for you! My whole family was killed. I was forced to come here."

Father spoke with such dramatic conviction and with so marked a tone of palpable hurt that the Red Army soldier finally lowered his pointed gun. "Well, maybe you're different, but there are a whole lot of betrayers of

Mother Russia, and we will know how to deal with them," he said heatedly and left.

Even in so tight a corner, Father still did not concede to being Jewish, deliberately refusing to emerge from the shadow world. He surmised enough about Soviet anti-Semitism to suspect that not every Russian soldier would cheer his ethnic identity. And there were still the Germans to worry about. What if they returned and the tables turned once more? Why forfeit his protective shield? His triple identity still had a ways to go before he could renounce it.

Nikolai and Father left the farm, as scant protection was to be had there. They headed for a larger location where more Russian laborers lived, hoping to find security in numbers. But getting there when the contrary winds of fortune blew in every uncharted direction was formidable indeed.

They persevered through fire and smoke. At their new quarters, they were eight in one room. But Father continued to fear the Russian laborers as much as the retreating Nazis. What if during the confusion of war's end they discovered his Jewishness? Surely they wouldn't take kindly to having been duped for so long. Amid the general lawlessness, who would be the wiser if he were dispatched? Father continued to keep his Tatar story alive; the time had not yet arrived to unearth his secret.

Dangers sprouted like rank weed from the least accountable places. Misha, one of the eight in their new quarter, a former tractor driver, possessed somewhat darker features that once led Father to fleetingly wonder if he might be Jewish. At first he appeared the last person he needed to fear; but matters shifted rapidly. While Father was still half-asleep one morning, Misha whispered to the others: "Hey, guys, don't you know Stefan volunteered for the Waffen SS? Now's the time to finish him off. No one will know the difference."

Each of his words stabbed at Father. How had he found out, he wondered. Father had sought to maintain his SS induction a secret from the others; after all, it was merely a pretext, a means to survive until he could steal across to the Allied side. But word had spread, and Misha, suspecting the worst, tried to foment a lynch-mob atmosphere.

Father was strongly tempted to confess his Jewishness and decisively squelch further malicious speculation. But something urged him against it. Others coming to his defense could only strengthen his case.

Spearheaded by Nikolai, the other Russians did vouch for him and told

Misha to stop barking up the wrong tree. Father, they announced, was a good sort, but Misha was not so easily assuaged. He continued to cast aspersions at Father, who distrustingly eyed the revolver Misha carried, the instrument to polish him off. He could not help being bemused by the irony of his situation: His SS identity, once a necessary shield, had now nearly turned into his nemesis. But in the end the persuasive clamor of the others forced Misha to retreat into sullen silence. From then on Father gave him the widest berth.

More and more Russian troops poured into the area as the battle entered the very heartland of Germany. Under the flail of heavy artillery, the German lines steadily eroded, but Father knew the defeated Nazis were certain to drag as many others with them as they possibly could.

An arc of fire blazed on the rim of the horizon. The laborers marched eastward to escape this burning ground, no place for unarmed civilians. On the road they passed the bloody wages of war—charred corpses, overturned vehicles, wrecked tanks. The grimmest image was of an anonymous Russian soldier who had apparently jumped out of his flaming tank, his uniform on fire. He was now past saving, his last moment frozen in a contortion of agony.

Row upon row of half-destroyed, abandoned buildings accosted them on their road back to Poland, yielding them fresh glimpses of the widespread devastation of the war. Food was scarce and the Russian laborers complained loudly of hunger pangs which would not be silenced. It was a squalid life on the grim edge of indigence.

In the chaos of shifting boundaries, they had crossed unknowingly into Poland. Here, amid the wreckage, one of the Russian laborers spotted a cow lost in a meadow. Riotous appetite now gleamed from every eye. In no time, the others fell upon the wretched cow and dragged it to a shed. One of the heftier men clutched a board and slammed it against the hapless creature while the others held it down, saliva drooling from their gaping mouths.

Her protracted death agony made Father avert his eyes and shrink further into himself, quickening his resolve to break free of the group. If they should discover that he was a Jew, could he expect a lighter sentence than that of the condemned animal? He still trusted Nikolai, but amid the gluttinous reek, who could be sure?

Next morning a film of ice lay on the Polish marshes. He awoke earlier than the others. While they were distracted by their morning rituals, a Russian military vehicle drove by. He rushed outside, flagged it down, and pleaded with the driver, "Take me with you."

The driver stuck his head out of the window and shouted, "Let's go!" In a second Father was on board, and the Russian laborers rushed outdoors, perplexedly. They lunged forward shouting, "What about us?" The car picked up speed; their voices faded as the landscape receded into the morning mist, and the rows of firs and birches lining the road stood like sentinels guarding the approach of a new day. Father had crossed the meridian into a different world. Henceforth, the triple life was to be a question of choice rather than of necessity. As the sun ascended, Father understood what the rabbis had meant when they quoted the great second-century sage Rabbi Akiva, who said, "Everything is foreseen by God, but the right to choose is given to man." Human experience was, in fact and in paradox, at once predestined and free.

CHAPTER 12

———❧———

Return

THE WAR WAS TO last for several more months, but Father began tentatively to discard his masks and to re-enter the ranks of the living. Yet his assumed identities, like foreign skin grafted to his own, were hard to shed, and it would take effort to do so.

Once back in Poland, his singular goal was to return to Novogrudek and mingle his tears with the ashes of his mother and her fellow martyrs. But passage across the devastated countryside was arduous and demanded weeks of planning. In Lodz, Poland's second-largest city, he needed permission from the Soviet authorities to travel eastward. But here a new challenge faced him. He still retained his Nazi foreign passport and feared to part with it. The past held him inexorably. But to enter the NKVD headquarters with it would be a mortal risk. He had to dispose of it.

Moments before he neared the Soviet-run building, he stepped into a nearby lavatory, took out the swastika-emblazoned Nazi passport from his jacket pocket, looked at it one last time, and tore it to shreds. He flung the fragments into the toilet and pulled the cord, sending the remains of his false identity into the netherworld of Poland's sewers.

Burly Soviet officials, manning the desk of the NKVD in Lodz, had the look of confidence born not only of military victory but also of ideological triumph that comes from being on "the right side of history." Father identified himself as a Polish foreign laborer in Germany who wished to return to his home in Novogrudek. They glanced suspiciously at him from the corner of their eyes.

"What proof do we have that you were not a Vlasovite?" they asked, adding some expletives for good measure.

"But I'm no collaborator, you must believe me," he insisted. They looked unconvinced, and his eyes darted despairingly across the room. Would the Soviet security service office be his fatal snare? But then he recalled the civil war story, the tale of Bolsheviks bursting into a Navaredek yeshiva, aiming their guns at the head of the chief rabbi, and demanding the immediate closure of the talmudical academy. The spiritual leader rose from his dignified seat, unbuttoned his shirt, and in a composed voice said "Shoot," prompting his younger students to do the same. Miraculously, the Bolsheviks retreated.

Something equally dramatic needed to be done. Now, at last, was the moment for Father to reveal his Jewishness and obliterate all doubts. It was time for him to drop his false self, which felt as ponderous as a Tatar lance. What could serve as better evidence that he wasn't a Vlasovite or an SS recruit? How ironic that he would unveil his ancestral faith in the bastion of atheism, inauspicious for any kind of religious avowal.

One of his NKVD interrogators, shorter and swarthier than the rest, had a lurking ethnicity written on his face. Was he Jewish? Father wondered. He had no way of knowing, but at this desperate juncture he had to assume the man was.

Father then rose from his seated position and voluntarily recited in a loud and clear voice the Hebrew profession of faith Jews have uttered throughout history on the road to martyrdom: "*Shema Yisrael,* Hear, O Israel, the Lord our God, the Lord is One."

As these holy words rang out in the austere sanctum of atheism, the short NKVD officer visibly straightened his posture. He looked at Father, and with each passing word of the avowal of God's unity, a glint of recognition grew in his eyes. Father assumed rightly that the Jewish declaration of monotheism might still be recognizable to him even if it had been forbidden by Stalin. Now he knew he had hit the mark; in no time the officer thawed considerably and called the others into a corner, after which all loyalty questions ceased.

Father's voice quivered as he spoke of what had happened to his mother and the thousands of his kinsfolk from Novogrudek. Language, that "cracked kettle," could hardly convey what lay beyond the measure of human speech. Yet, even these hard-bitten men stood silently and listened grimly. He said that his purpose was not simply to surrender to sorrow and grief, but rather to take part in the final dismantling of the Nazi murder machine. This he meant to do by being in the stir of things, by entering the ranks of the Allied forces, which had been his first desire when he insinuated himself into Germany. In the end he won them over with words ripped from his living flesh. His return to Novogrudek would now have to wait till the end of the war, but in the good fight he was working out his own salvation and was returning to what was best in himself.

AFTER FIVE LONG YEARS, peace descended on a tired continent. Life in Poland would revive for the Poles, whose soul Churchill had described as "indestructible": it would "rise again like a rock, which may for a spell be submerged by a tidal wave; but which remains a rock."

But for the Jews, a more ancient martyred people, it would play differently on that devastated plain. Father returned to Novogrudek with a fellow soldier, Pavluk, arriving at midnight at the deserted railroad station on the small compact train that had once been the vehicle of his sweetest childhood dreams.

The town lay enfolded in darkness, hardly a light anywhere to illuminate their path. Novogrudek seemed abandoned of human presence. Pavluk and he groped in the dark till they found their way to Castle Hill, from whose summit Father had once surveyed the world. They lay down on the wet grass and tried to sleep, but Pavluk, who had trouble breathing, coughed incessantly. They then descended the hill and in the thick of night sought out police headquarters.

After stumbling blindly they came upon their destination. Just as his hand turned the knob, someone opened the door from the other side. The moment Father saw who it was, he shouted, "Dovid!"

A thickset man in a military policeman's uniform looked at Father with unseeing eyes and asked, "Who are you?"

"Joseph of Yiddisher Street," he said, his throat tightening with emotion.

"Joseph who?"

"Joseph Skakun," Father repeated, "the yeshiva bokher."

A dim light of recognition dawned on him. He, like many others, Father would come to learn, had assumed that he had been consumed in the fires of the war.

"Is anyone alive?" Father asked. "Are my cousins here? You remember them—we prayed in their home after the first mass slaughter," he added.

"To be truthful, I cannot remember, but perhaps the fellow next door, Tzirinsky, will know more."

He led Pavluk and Father to a house behind the police station. It was two o'clock in the morning, and a horse with sunken, mangy flanks was tied to a post, neighing softly. In the black-sooted structure Father shook Tzirinsky's hand, posing the same question to him. He led them outside, past a gutted wood hut, and directed them into the night. Father said nothing, his mind a confusion of thoughts as he followed the metallic click of heels, Pavluk trailing a few feet behind them. The noiseless steps of wandering souls filled the empty streets. They then approached a house lit by a weak lamp. As soon as Tzirinsky opened the door, Father saw a man lying on a bed in the next room, enveloped in a big quilt. He left the two others at the threshold, crossed a kitchen with broken utensils, and walked stammeringly toward the recumbent man.

The closer Father came to the bed, the more terrified the supine man grew. Father recognized him instantly as his cousin, who had fled to the woods on that fateful Friday in December 1941 when the Nazi curfew went into force, the moment that marked the final hours of Novogrudek's Jews. This was Leyzer, with whom he had spent those terrible days after Grandmother, Aunt Rivke and Uncle Shloimke were killed and despair had descended like the pall of night.

Leyzer's eyes opened widely and he began to sit up as if he were seeing a phantasm.

"A ghost . . ." His pale lips trembled. He rose imperceptibly, as if against his own volition, the quilt falling to the side of the bed. His brows arched wildly as his frame shook. He too assumed that Father had been killed in the ghetto, a rumor that spread in middle of the war once all trace of him was lost.

Leyzer walked toward Father and in a low, gasping sob asked, "Joseph?" He looked at Father again as if he were emerging from a distant dream or from a winding sheet. "Is it you?" he cried.

"Yes, it is I." Father nodded vehemently.

"Joseph! My God! Joseph still lives!" he shouted. "Blessed is the hour!" They fell into each other's arms.

⁘

FATHER'S LONG JOURNEY BACK to Novogrudek still had one un-fulfilled promise: to pay final respects to his mother, torn from him by the exterminating angel. The next morning, as dust whirled through the town's streets, he made his way to the mass gravesite in Skridleva, where she lay in the unquiet earth with five thousand of her townspeople. An other-worldly silence hovered over the space—a latter-day *emek ha-bakha* (vale of tears). Something broke inside of him as he gave vent to his long-deferred grief. His gait was unsteady, his soul exposed as he approached the makeshift marker. He dropped to his knees and read in the strong light of the noon sun its Russian commemorative words. Then he saw, as if in a blinding light, his mother reposing in God, basking in the radiance of the Shekhina. There, as it were, she was sitting in the innermost circle of celestial paradise among the souls of the blessed—the biblical patriarchs and matriarchs and the long line of martyrs arrayed around her. He remembered how every day of her life she longed humbly for the hereafter, how she spoke raptur-ously of her desire to die on Friday so as to be gathered into eternity on the Sabbath.

He knew then as he had known throughout every day of the war, that his survival hinged upon her merit. He lay rooted to the grave at Skridleva, wishing to remain forever nailed to that ground of ashes.

As he finally rose he stretched out a penitential palm and cried, "*Mameh*, my spirit was too weak to join you. Forgive me!" He bent down again and knew guilt to be the condition of his soul, an internal hemorrhage that would bleed into all the days of his life. Neither the burden of remorse nor his failure of ultimate valor could be removed. They would remain his stigma of conscience.

The power of speech failed him. His voice cracked and retreated into silence. The landscape grew dim and swam before his eyes. He left—a wordless witness.

EPILOGUE
I

——⟨⟨⟨——

Paris

Joseph Skakun in France, late 1940s

THREE YEARS AFTER THE end of the war, in early spring of 1948, Father arrived in Paris from Frankfurt-am-Main, after sojourning in the displaced persons' camps. He walked along the grand boulevards and sauntered in the Jardin du Luxembourg, redolent with the scent of flowers. He sat amid sidewalk cafés listening to the light banter of men in fedoras and women in smartly cut clothes, imbibing the music of their laughter.

A newborn *flâneur*, Father roamed the city's civic treasures and came upon Antoine Bourdelle's statue "Adam Mickiewicz the Pilgrim" at Place de l'Alma, observing the poet's staff and his eyes cast skyward. The French historian Jules Michelet said at the College de France in 1847 that the young Mickiewicz's sympathy for the retreat of Napoleon's Grande Armée in the east—through Vilna, Lida, Novogrudek, and the Polish plain—made him "almost more French than France."

Paris was a city of perpetual mirth, where one could riot in any number of pleasures: *sheyn vi di velt*, beautiful as the world, as Yiddish immigrants could at last say, an expression that had no currency during the Nazi occupation. The French capital was at once cosmopolitan and provincial. Emerson in a twist on the Roman saying *nihil humanum alienum* had written, "The French say, 'I am a woman and a Parisienne and nothing foreign appears altogether human.' " Despite its vaunted insularity, Paris could not cloak the hidden calamity felt by its newest immigrants. It was in the City of Light that Father learned that there was no love of life without despair of life.

Within a few days of his arrival, he was sent to La Pepinière in Bailly on the Seine and Oise rivers to live in a chateau converted into a residence for displaced yeshiva and rabbinical students. Amid its solitary gardens, faded brocade, and shabby gentility, he returned to a lost way of life, to the rigors of Talmud and *mussar*. In the heart of Ile-de-France, he joined remnants of the great European Talmudic academies.

This was also the time of the independence of Israel and the struggle of a nation trying to be reborn. Four days after the Jewish state was created in storm in May of 1948, Jean-Paul Sartre wrote to Simone de Beauvoir: "Palestine. It's the kind of thing that makes one indignant as the war in Spain and, in addition, there's that sort of malediction against the Jews that seems unbearable. If you think for instance about a certain Polish Jew who miraculously escaped the camps and gas chambers and English solicitude, who settled in over there after a clandestine voyage, to find the armies of anti-Semitism all over again, the country invaded, and despair. And then the U.N., of course; it's outrageous."

In the frayed elegance of La Pepinière, Father thrilled to the rise of a Jewish state whose fate hung in the balance. Together with his fellow *mussar* students he sought to forge anew a fineness of moral perception, to trace again the soul's sovereign journey for meaning. Once more they opened the volumes of the Talmud with their dense yellowing pages and returned to the devotional literature of penance as if they could compel time to return to its source.

Mussar at La Pepinière, sharing nothing of the vulgar materialism of some Parisian thinkers for whom ethics was a form of materialism, an agriculture of the mind, a kind of mental husbandry to discipline unruly animal in-stincts, believed contrariwise in a shepherding of souls. Under the tutelage of the young and tragically short-lived Rabbi Mordecai Pogremeinsky, who lavishly disregarded his health, the *mussarniks* sought to master their evil impulses through the exercise of will, to avoid ensnarements of ego and the dangers of exaggerated humility. Too much modesty is half conceit, they were told. In the twilight air they listened to pensive lectures on the brevity of life and bathed once again in the bracing waters of expiation.

How strange and yet how apt that these *mussar* self-afflictions should resemble the secular anguish popular among Left Bank intellectuals in the late 1940s! At the Café Flore, Sartre had evolved a fashionable nihilism that considered man a useless passion, in a world where *tout passe, tout casse, tout lasse*—everything passes, everything perishes, everything pales. And in La Pepenière a vein of equally dark, albeit transcendent, pessimism prevailed, inflected, to be sure, in a far different accent.

The black-turtlenecked intellectuals in their various boulevard St.-Michel *caves* talked of the absurdity of life and of the multiple snares of bad faith and hypocrisy. And in the suburbs of Paris, *mussar*'s emphasis on the finitude of life and the diminution of the ego derived from similar human concerns. Small wonder that more than a few of Sartre's Jewish followers turned into Talmudists after his death in 1980.

How different this was from the world of the fascist fellow travelers across the border! German philosopher Martin Heidegger despised the postwar Parisian intellectuals and insisted loudly that if Sartre was an existentialist then he himself certainly could not be anything of the sort. A "Bruckner without music," Heidegger, prompt with long-winded neologisms, jettisoned mentors and students with equal facility. In an act of personal betrayal that still shadows his reputation on both sides of the Atlantic, he had banished his teacher Edmund Husserl, a Jew and phenomenologist, from the University of Freiburg and thus hastened his death—a small price to pay, he thought, for a revitalized, re-Hellenized Germany.

Sacrificing principle and loyalty to the terrors of idealism, Heidegger declared Hitler the man to return Germany to the "deep responsiveness of being," a responsiveness so profound in his own mind that it demanded the disappearance of the Jews. In a further instance of "overcivilized dehumanization," Heidegger saw nothing wrong in philosophically denouncing the triumph of the West's spiritless technology, while consciously overlooking the concentration camps closer to home. Indeed, his tragic foibles and character deficits are captured in Elias Canetti's aphorism: *"Es genug nicht zu denken; man muss auch atmet. Gefährlich die Denker, die nicht genug geatmet haben."* Thinking is not enough; man must also breathe. Dangerous the thinkers who have not breathed enough.

Despite the *mussar* yeshiva's effort to restore its students to the sacred world of their lost youth, it could not eliminate the persistent memory of war. Suspicion and distrust would often shake Father's religious faith: for, as the Polish Jewish aphorist Stanislaw Jerzy Lec wrote sagely, "Only the dead can be resurrected. It's more difficult with the living."

At La Pepinière, rabbinical learning could not easily bridge the chasm between postwar Bailly and prewar Baranowicze, the school of Father's youth. It could not leap over the gulf of history that "rolls her noise of skulls on the shore," in the words of the poet St.-John Perse. Each time Father opened a holy book, doubts assailed his mind. *Mussar* ethics presented a model of integrity, as the Waffen SS the very form of radical evil. Ambiguity and paradox would forever be his governing principles.

And yet, memory, which made faith difficult, also made it necessary. It was, after all, the ancient coastal city of Yavneh, an abode for scholars, that had clung to hope after the destruction of the temple in Jerusalem by codifying the holy books and establishing the centrality of the synagogue. Its teachers assured the continuity of a beleaguered tradition at a time when everything, but most especially the might of the Romans, sought to negate it. La Pepinière functioned as a kind of latter-day Yavneh, an island upholding a devastated reef of religious belief.

By 1945, the human image in Europe had been nearly destroyed. The children of Abraham, who had sought to elevate the life of the spirit and the world of conscience, had been its first and last victims, their lives and fate both a sign and a mission. The French Catholic writer Leon Bloy had already understood this paradox when he wrote at the twentieth century's start: "The history of the Jews obstructs the history of mankind as a dam obstructs a river, in order to raise its level." He could not have calculated the cost this truth would exact.

By the time he came to leave Paris, Father had learned that the past is a country from which one cannot emigrate.

EPILOGUE II

New York

Joseph Skakun after his arrival in
New York, 1959

L IKE THE SUN, HISTORY travels West. After the Second World War the English critic Cyril Connolly caught the Zeitgeist perfectly in writing that New York was "the supreme metropolis of the present. An unforgettable picture of what a city ought to be: continuously insolent and alive. If Paris is the perfect setting for a romance, New York is the perfect city to get over one, to get over anything. Here the lost *douceur de vivre* is forgotten and the intoxication of living takes place." But for all of Connolly's discernment, certain horrors defeated even New York's great amnesiac powers.

Nearly fifty years after Grandfather had landed as a stowaway in the port of New York, his son arrived to a new life on the same shores, to a city that was a riot of right angles and monumental verticality. Father's valises bulged with private possessions, but memory was the bulkiest of his consignments.

As if chance itself had assumed its own kind of symmetry, Father came to live precisely in the neighborhood his father had settled in at the start of the century. Then bucolic, today it is an urban American shtetl, teeming with Jewish life, Chassidic rather than Mitnagged (Lithuanian-style rationalism) in character and inflection. As if predestined, he landed on the doorstep of the American transplant of the *mussar* house of study he had once known in Poland.

For Father, Europe was the shipwreck, America the sanctuary. For

Grandfather it was something of the reverse. He had left the New World, given up on the dream. In 1910, he abandoned New York for the czar's cruel realm, only to be wounded on the bloody fields of Tannenberg at the outset of World War I.

Father, a half-century later, was to remain faithful to his adopted homeland. Yet he could not shake the weight of his past. Memory reverberated deep into the night. He never stopped living among the ruins of Novogrudek and tracing its unearthly echoes, embodying the principle described by the French moralist duc de La Rochefoucauld when he wrote, "The accent of one's birthplace lingers in the mind and in the heart as it does in one's speech."

The cadence of the past became part of the permanent rhythm of Father's life. He had been drafted into the SS but had never been sent into battle. And so the landscape of his conscience intrigued me as much as it consumed him. Both of us lived in the subjunctive, imagining what might have occurred had the end of the war come later. For many years we sifted through a grim inventory of possibilities: shuddering to think how he might have looked in a Waffen SS uniform, imagining its rough texture against his body and his forefinger fretting against its emblazoned swastika. We envisioned him tucking in the regulation shirt and gazing at himself in the mirror, knowing that an infernal machine had stapled this depraved insignia on his inmost self, that he had been branded by the iron of history. Then the walls around him would appear to weave, the ceiling to swoop. As he fixed the inglorious SS cap, his face would lose its outline, and he would want to hammer his fists against the wall, to shatter the indifference of the world, and to regain the lineaments of his lost childhood.

Father delved after the war for an explanatory key to the moral quandary of his putative collaboration with the enemy. He perused Maimonides' "Letter to the Jews of Yemen," which argued that if Jews are given the choice of embracing Islam or of being put to death, they are not obliged to be martyred. Thus apostasy was reluctantly permitted if it was the product of a considered life-saving strategy. It was pardonable if one reserved in one's soul a secret devotion to God. In fact, thousands of Spanish and Portuguese *conversos* publicly professed to be Catholics through the dreaded Holy Inquisition while at home they lived secretly as Jews, risking being burned at the stake.

Or, contrarily, Father might point to the Jewish martyrs who had opposed the Romans more than a thousand years before the Inquisition: namely, the hundreds of thousands burned and hung like felons across the Judean plain. Or the Jews of York who collectively ended their lives in Clifford's Tower rather than submit to the Catholic conversion foisted by an enraged mob of Crusaders. On the day they chose to die, March 17, 1190, they listened to the last sermon of Rabbi Yom-Tov of Joigny, who said, "God, whose decisions are inscrutable, desires that we should die for our holy religion. We must prefer a glorious death to a shameful life. Death is at hand, unless you prefer, for a short span of life, to be unfaithful to your faith. The life which our Creator has given us, we will render back to him with our hands." Which was the morally preferable: noble suicide, as exemplified by the Jews of York, or the outward repudiation of but inner adherence to core beliefs, as practiced by the *conversos* and sanctioned by Maimonides? As to so many questions of the age, there were no certain answers. Who in these circumstances could disentangle the skein of good and evil?

Father knew that donning the Waffen SS uniform would have been only the first rung of moral compromise. The assumption of the Nazi oath, the pledge of loyalty and allegiance to Adolf Hitler, would have deepened his moral shame.

I often wondered how Father would have endured the initiation ceremony. To swear fealty to the Waffen SS would force him to abjure all precepts and shatter his moral compass. But to have refused would have cast suspicion on him and invited torture and death. If only he could detach his inner life from his deeds!

Once mobilized, Father would have been trained by the Waffen SS to dig trenches, to lay mines, to blow up bridges and thereby slow the Allied liberation of the Continent. Combat training would require an erosion of self. SS recruits were welded into one steely unit, driven by common purpose and single desire: "sinewy bodies, sharped-edged faces, eyes petrified under the helmet of a thousand terrors," in Ernst Jünger's words—a confraternity of blood and loyalty. The sight of contorted bodies thickly dotting the ground would force Father into a complicitous world.

To be sure, he would have to engage the Soviets, whom secretly he had so desired to join. He would shoot at young Russians and Ukrainians from kolkhozes who had not yet tasted life before death was upon them. To defend himself against mortal suspicion from the eyes of the SS enforcers,

he might well have to kill those whom he most wished to join, to become
the reluctant author of their demise.

He might have purposely misfired, trying to cause as little harm as possible until he found a way to secretly cross the lines over to the Soviet side.
Shooting but not shooting—how long could he have kept up that charade
in hopes of saving himself? And even if he had gone over to the Russian
side, he might well have been considered a spy by their political commissars
and shot summarily.

And how would he react under fire? Would he survive the "lithe tigers
of the trenches and the forward march," in Jünger's phrase? Would he flee
at the first whistle of bullets or at the sight of trenches choked with the
dead and wounded? No matter his initial fear, the rain of Russian bullets
and the howl of theirs mortars carried the promise of life—that beautiful
cacophony of possible freedom. For it was safer to be on the battlefield than
in the SS barracks shadowed by discovery and inevitable betrayal.

But as he imagined the clamor of battle, an even greater horror emerged.
As a newly minted SS soldier, Father understood now, as he could never
have before, how easily he might have been sent to guard a concentration
camp as part of the Death's Head Units (SS-Totenkopfverbände) or lead
one of the hastily arranged death marches. Once the seed was sown, the
harvest must come. He would have witnessed the unearthly disquiet of the
crematoria, with their ever larger destructive capacities toward the end of
the war; he would have seen canisters of lethal Zyklon-B used in enlarged
death chambers to accommodate more bodies; and bone-crushing machines
cornering problems of final disposal.

There is a world of transgression for which there is no forgiveness, human
or divine; a realm of dark trespass before which one must fall silent. Here
was sin for which even penance was inadequate and the classic modes of
expiation useless. No atonement, no Solomonic courts, we were certain,
had been devised to absolve this kind of complicity. In such blasted places
the wrath of heaven and the fires of hell would pursue the perpetrator till
the end of history.

The Red Army had providentially liberated Father before the SS was
able to mobilize him. The Russians had arrived just in time to give him
moral harbor. Chronology was everything, or nearly so, the timing of events
redemptive. The collapse of Nazi Germany—too late for millions of
others—had saved him from actual collaboration. His mind echoed the

Yiddish market wives' saying: *"Men zol nit gepruft veren tsu vos men ken gevoint veren"*—Pray that you may never have to endure all that you can learn to bear.

Father's life had never come entirely under the jurisdiction of logic. After all, coddled by loving parents, he was the least likely of Novogrudek's Jews to have seen the end of the war alive. As an only child and a young Talmudist, his survival was the most improbable of gifts, a miraculous dispensation allowing him to reverse the arc of fate and transcend the narrowest confines, as if his life had extraterritorial rights. He had come forth from this hellish war to feel once again the holiness of the Sabbath.

Yet it was in the still solitude of the Sabbath that history came rushing in. The rabbis had taught that the seventh day had been designed to restore the broken unity of life, a gathering of the dispersion of the week under the aspect of eternity. But war's atrocity had brought disunion into the nature of things, a disarray that nothing could coax into coherence.

Far from being a foretaste of the world to come, the Sabbath had now become a bitter aftertaste of a world passed. The glow of its waxen candles hid a darker hue. For the generation after World War II, the very notion of the Sabbath as a day of heavenly rest insinuated new ironies: of a quiet God, but even more of a drowsing God, once all-seeing but now myopic, slumbering through history, hiding and finally absconding at the darkest hour. This was admittedly a darker exegesis than custom or even law permitted, but I persisted, not out of a schoolboy's relish for sacrilege, but out of a confused and nascent recognition that the parallels between earth and heaven were too stark to deny.

For all the Sabbath talk of this world and the next, so much in the end depended on Father's own choices and actions. Few other lives encompassed such haunting solitude. If, as Alfred North Whitehead has said, "religion is what we make of our aloneness," then Father is perhaps among the most religious of men.

ACKNOWLEDGMENTS

A book is an act of partnership between past and future, writer
and reader. It lays the ground where sorrow meets hope and
hope reaches for the possible. This memoir was born of a dialogue between two generations. To my father I owe the greatest
debt of gratitude for having laid bare a soul driven to its outermost limits and for having demonstrated daily that memory is
desire, a persistent purpose that cannot be denied. His life teaches
me what Czeslaw Milosz meant when he wrote, "It is possible
that there is no other memory than the memory of wounds."
My father is the source of this book—its heart and inspiration.

I am indebted as well to many individuals whose gestures of
kindness shown to me during the writing of this memoir were
invaluable: Alfred Kazin, my late teacher whose moral imagination, robust skepticism, and rapturous love of American literature were exemplary—his sage appreciation of "the mystery
of inquity" combined with the trajectory of my father's war
experiences taught me that evil and tragedy were central cate-
gories of the mind and key to interpreting life in our time; De-
vorah and Joseph Telushkin for their encouragement and moral
support, and for their love of Yiddish and admiration for the
world of "mussar"; Debbie Denenberg for her steadfastness and
acumen; Gary Shapiro for his wisdom, classically trained sensibility, and indefatigable energy; Robert Weil and Andrew Mil-
ler, both superb editors; my mother for her love of life and
fondness of the word; and to all the many others who have stood
by me during this journey into night.

About the Author

MICHAEL SKAKUN is a writer, translator, and memoirist, as well as a public affairs consultant. Born in Jaffa, Israel, he has lived nearly his entire life in the United States and studied with Alfred Kazin, the late literary critic and scholar of American literature. He served as editor and columnist for various metropolitan weeklies. As special consultant to the United States Holocaust Memorial Council, he prepared literary and educational materials for National Remembrance Week, observed in all fifty states and the American armed forces. Active as an events planner and coordinator in New York, he has helped organize a commemoration in honor of Sir Isaiah Berlin, a fiftieth-anniversary celebration of the Marshall Plan, and a host of lectures by civic and cultural figures.